Food Processing Management

About the Author

Dr. Samarendra Mahapatra was the former Professor and Head, Department of Agribusiness Management, OUAT, Bhubaneswar. He graduated in Agricultural Engineering from OUAT and holds a Post-Graduation in Management from Xavier Institute of Management, Bhubaneswar, as well as a Doctorate in Business Administration from Utkal University. After around two decades of corporate work experience in agri-input industry, he has switched over to academics. To his credit, he has authored eleven books and book chapters in various areas of Agribusiness and Marketing Management. He was nominated by ICAR as an Expert Member to develop the syllabus for Agribusiness Management. He has been nominated by various agricultural universities as a Member for Faculty Selection and also by Government of Odisha, Agriculture Department as an Expert Committee Member for various assignments. He has published technical papers in various journals and presented papers as a Key Note Speaker in various national and international conferences. He has received the Best Teacher Award in Agribusiness Management in an international conference organised jointly by Agri-Meet Foundation in collaboration with ICAR Institute and various State Agricultural Universities.

Food Processing Management

Samarendra Mahapatra

Former Professor and Head
Department of Agribusiness Management
Odisha University of Agriculture & Technology
Bhubaneswar, Odisha

Notion Press Media Pvt Ltd

No.50, Chettiyar Agaram Main Road,
Vanagaram, Chennai, Tamil Nadu 600095

ISBN
Paperback 979-8-89929-203-3
Hardcase 979-8-89929-204-0

Preface

Food processing management encompasses a broad spectrum of disciplines, including food science, engineering, supply chain management, quality assurance, and regulatory compliance. As such, this book aims to provide a holistic understanding of the field, drawing upon the expertise of seasoned professionals and cutting-edge research. Global food industry is undergoing rapid transformation; the significance of effective food processing management cannot be overstated. This book is designed as a comprehensive guide for navigating the complexities of food processing management, offering insights, strategies, and best practices for professionals. Throughout these pages, one will find a wealth of information on various aspects of food processing management, ranging from the fundamentals of food preservation techniques to the latest advancements in automation and technology.

In addition to covering core concepts and principles, this book also investigates into practical applications and real-world case studies, offering readers valuable insights into industry trends, challenges, and opportunities. From optimizing production processes to ensuring product safety and quality, the principles discussed herein are essential for anyone involved in the food processing industry. Moreover, this book is intended to serve as a dynamic resource that evolves alongside the ever-changing landscape of the food industry. As new technologies emerge, regulations evolve, and consumer preferences shift, it is crucial for food processing professionals to stay informed and adaptable. With this in mind, the content presented here will be periodically updated to reflect the latest developments in the field. Ultimately, the goal of this book is to empower readers with the knowledge, tools, and strategies needed to excel in the dynamic and challenging field of food processing management either seeking to enhance operational efficiency or ensure product quality and safety.

I extend my sincere gratitude to all the contributors who have generously shared their expertise and insights to make this book possible. It is my hope that this book will serve as a trusted resource and catalyst for innovation in the field of food processing management.

Author

Acknowledgement

I heartily acknowledge the contributions of my colleagues for updating the Food processing management area. I would also like to thank my students in various universities for the interactions I had with them as their course teacher, taking sessions continuously for about eighteen years. I am grateful to my corporate colleagues for the support and experience gained while working alongside them, prior to switching to academics. The inspiration and encouragement provided by senior academicians during the course of this project is praise-worthy. I am indebted to institutions like OUAT, IGNOU, BPUT and BJB Autonomous College for giving me an opportunity to be associated in academic assignments in Agribusiness Management. I thank the organisations like APEDA, Amul Diary, AAU, Agrighar, CFTRI, ICC, ISAE, NIFTEM, PHD Chamber of Commerce for organising conventions on Food Processing Sector to update information in the area. Besides this, I also thank the seasoned advice of reviewers for improving the chapters.

I am optimistic and value the suggestions, recommendations of the stakeholders in continuous improvement in updating the coverage of course contents. I am also grateful for the encouragement and support of my family members and friends in successfully completing the book project.

Bhubaneswar   **Samarendra Mahapatra**

Contents

1

Introduction

1. Introduction

Agro-processing refers to activities leading to value addition to the products of plant and animal origin. Several Asian economies such as Malaysia, Thailand and Philippines, which grew fast in the past, used agro-processing as a basis for growth. Agro-processing in India is significant due to its immense potential for job creation, minimal capital requirements, ample raw material availability, extensive opportunities for both forward and backward linkages, and substantial potential for foreign exchange earnings through exports. Studies have proved that capital labour ratio is much less in agro-industries as compared to non-agro industries. With the same level of capital being employed in non-agro industries, 4-5 times more employment generation can be made in agro-processing industries. The extent of value addition through agro-processing depends on the nature and extent of demand for processed items within the country as well as for exports. In India the per capita consumption of processed products based on agricultural output has been increasing for both edible goods like food grains, edible oils, sugar, tea, milk and non-edible goods like textiles, plywood paper etc. Agri-food processing in India is quite low in comparison to global standards. As per study carried out by Deloitte during 2020-21 the processing levels are 2.7% for vegetables, 4.5% for fruits, 21.1% for milk, 34.2% for meat and 15.4% for fishery and is increasing. The scope for value addition to agriculture through processing is tremendous. It ranged from cleaning and grading to milling, mixing and even chemical alteration. Commodities of value addition include fresh fruits, vegetables, cereals, pulses, spices, animal products etc. The technological requirements vary from primary processing to tertiary processing. The infrastructural network required for the development of processing technology is inadequate. Along with the development of processing technology, there is a great need to develop the agricultural production technology with processing technology so that the required processing efficiency can be achieved both, qualitatively as well as quantitatively.

World Food India in September, 2024 is the India's largest exhibition for food processing and allied sectors being organised by the Ministry of Food

Processing Industries, Government of India. Processing for prosperity is a global event to showcase, connect and collaborate.

With the objective of introducing the world to rich Indian food culture as well as promoting investments in the diverse food processing sector of the country, the Ministry of Food Processing Industries launched the first edition of World Food India in 2017.It celebrated 2023 as the International Year of Millets and to bring global food processing industry together, the Ministry is organising the third edition "World Food India 2023" from 3-5 November 2023 at Pragati Maidan, NewDelhi.

India as Food Basket of the World

Key Objectives are

- Exhibit: Innovation driven solutions to transform supply chain ecosystem of the food processing and allied sectors

- Explore: Opportunities to explore market access, sourcing, investments in technology, equipment, manufacturing, logistics and cold chain.

- Boost: Mutual interests of both domestic and foreign entrepreneurs by forging partnerships.

- Promote: Reduction of wastage, sustainable ecosystems, organic produce and indigenous processing techniques etc

Key highlights of World Food India 2023

World Food India 2023 brings together various stakeholders including food processing and manufacturing companies, food start-ups, exporters and importers of food products, government representatives, foreign missions in India, academic and research institutions, equipment manufacturers and solution providers, investors and venture capitalists, food packaging, cold storage and logistics providers, financial institutions, and media partners.

The Ministry of Food Processing focuses on

- Reducing postharvest losses of perishables

- Promoting value addition and generating farm jobs

- Enhancing processing and preservation capacities, and encouraging food processing clusters

- Identifying infrastructure gaps and supporting their creation

- Formalizing micro-food processing enterprises

Creating global champions in food manufacturing

- 14 numbers partner ministries/departments of Government of India & commodity Boards.
- Participation of 24 States and Union Territories.
- 16 number International delegations.
- 47 numbers sessions include Country, Thematic, state allied ministries & organisations.
- 6 number G2G meetings at Fiji, Mauritius, Greece, Lebanon, Australia and UAE.
- 27 MOUs worth USD 3.98 Billion.
- 1208 exhibitors
- 15 country pavilions,10 partner ministers 7 departments,25 states,6 commodity boards and 8 association partners present.
- 6 International Ministerial level meetings,112 G2B meetings,16283 B2B meetings.
- High-level industry round table interaction with union ministers.
- 7 ministries,5 partner states,7 focus states,22 Major Organisations.4 partners.

International Participation

- Partner country: Netherlands, Focus country: Japan and 15 exhibiting countries in WFI2023.
- Ministerial delegation from 9 countries, Bilateral meetings at ministerial level held at Greece, Labanon, Mauritius, UAE,Fiji and Australia.
- 16 Government Official delegation in countries like Netherland, Denmark, Seychelles, Saudi Arabia, Kuwait and Tajikistan etc.
- 715 international buyers from 90 countries and 16283 B2B meetings between exporters, importers, domestic and international buyers.218 domestic buyers participated in RBSM meetings.
- 91 CXO from over 70 leading companies

Domestic Participation

- 5 partner states of Bihar, Gujarat, Kerala, Punjab and Telengana
- 6 ministers of Odisha, Kerala, Jharakhand,,Andhra Pradesh, Gujarat and Meghalaya
- 7 focus states of Andhrapradesh, J&K,Jharkhand,MP,Meghalaya,Odisha and UP.

- 12 exhibiting states of Assam, Sikkim, HP, Westbengal, Maharastra, Haryana, Uttarakhand

Central Ministries and Departments

- Ministry of Agriculture & Farmer Welfare
- Ministry of Ayush
- Ministry of MSME
- Ministry of Environment, Forest and Climate change
- Ministry of Commerce & industry
- Department of Animal Husbandry & Dairying
- Department for promotion of Industry & Internal Trade
- Department of Fisheries

Commodity Boards

- APEDA
- Coconut Development Board
- Coffee Board of India
- MPEDA
- Spices Board of India
- Tea Board of India

CEO Round table & MOU Sign-A high level Industry Interaction

- Co-chaired by the Union Minister of Commerce & Industry, Consumer Affairs, Food and Public Distribution, and the Minister of Food Processing Industries.
- 8 Secretaries from allied ministries and Departments.
- 91 CXOs from 70 leading companies
- MOUs signed worth of USD 3.98 billion

Theme Pavillion, Sessions and food Street

- MOFPI Theme Pavilion-biggest highlight of WIFI 2023

  It was built with a cutting age modern look creating an immersive, interactive and informative walk-through from one end to another

Knowledge Sessions

47 conference sessions over 3 days of the event,

Food Street

Experential Food Street, uurated by celebrity Chef Ranveer Brar-offered an immersive experience of India's rich culinary heritage and 75 diveres regional cuisines.

World Food India 2024: Key Elements

- Exhibition, Sub segment specific Pavilions, Reverse Buyer Seller Meet, Sessions of thematic, country and states, Startup grand challenge, Food Street.
- New additions as Alco Bev sector, Pet-food, HoRoCa segment, Post-harvest machinery and FSSAI global food regulators summit

Focus Pillars

- Food Irradiation-ensuring safety and extending shelf life.
- Sustainable Packaging in Food Processing Industries.
- Plant based proteins-innovations and Impact
- Ensuring food safety for all from farm to fork.
- Minimum waste, Maximum value

Proposed Flow of Events

- Inaugural session
- Exhibition inauguration
- Plenary session
- Global CEO Roundtable Interaction
- Chef Competition and Food interaction
- Chef competition & food street

FPI 2024 day 2 & 3

- FSSAI-Global Food Regulators Summit
- Exhibition-Buyer & seller meet
- Parallel Sessions-Country, State,Allied Ministry & government Bodies, thematic
- Chef competition & Food Street

FPI 2024 day 4

- Exhibition
- Parallel sessions
- Chef competition & food street
- Awards to startups

Expected participents profile

- Food processing companies
- Food startups and Innovators
- Exporters and Importers of food products
- Ingredient manufacturers
- Government Representatives
- Foreign Missions in India
- Academies and Research Institutions
- Equipment Manufacturers
- Investers, Private Equity Firms, Venture Capitalists
- Food Packaging, Cold chain and logistics companies
- Financial Institutions
- Trade and Media Partners

Reverse Buyer Seller Meet: Exclusive opportunity to forge lasting business relationships and explore new horizons in the food industry as buyers invited on a single platform for forging partnerships.

- Enhance market access
- Interactions with potential partners
- Exposure to new products and innovations
- Insightful discussions on industry trends
- Creation of valuable B2B connections

Different Institutions benefitted are

- Tea Boaed
- MPEDA
- APEDA
- Spices Board
- Coffee Board

Startup Grand Challenge 2.0 - Launched on 21ˢᵗ June

- Valorization of residue/waste emerging from Agrifood value chains
- Novel Technologies for development of nutritious and palatable food products
- Improving water use efficiency through process modifications
- Cash reward to winning start-ups and incubation/acceleration support through NIFTEM

Planned Thematic Session

- Food Irradiation: Future of safe food
- Zero waste, Maximum value: Innovative approach to a circular economy
- Sustainable packaging Technologies in FPI: 5rs like Reuse, reduce, recycle, renew and redesign.
- Alternate proteins towards a better future.
- Revolutionizing food and Trade: Enhancing efficiency in food value chains through digital innovations.
- Global nutrition and health: focus on nutraceuticals, Ayush ahaar and Super foods
- Revolutionising the food processing machinery for an Atmanirbhar Bharat.
- Empowering talent and embracing global excellence: Transforming skills for going global.
- Food fermentation systems: Innovations and way forward.
- Sustainable food value chains: Leveraging indigenous technologies for climate resilience.
- Navigating success for startups; A master class.
- Local to Global: unlocking the potential of Indian Brands and Traditional foods

Food Street

- Creating cultural & live experience- representing India's richness and diversity of food.
- Showcasing and demonstration of various cultures through food.
- Dignitaries to discover and indulge with a stellar line-up of chefs, State & Country specific exhibitors, entertainment and artisan producers.
- Opportunities for fusion with global cuisines

Supportive Policy Environment

Business and Regulatory Reforms

- 100% FDI permitted in food processing. Retails trading including e-commerce.
- 40000+ compliances reduced
- National Single Window portal hosts applications for approvals from 31 central departments and 22 state governments.
- Agro-processing included in priority sector lending-loans upto INR 100 crore per borrower

Tax Reforms

- One of the lowest corporate tax globally @ 15% for new businesses
- Remission of duties and taxes incurred on exports from India
- 100% exemption of income tax on profits and gains for new food processing units for the initial five assessment years.

Other Reforms

- FSSAI transitioned from a product-by-product approval process to an ingredient and additive-based approval process.
- Credit Guarantee Fund Trust for Micro & small Enterprises (CGTMSE)

Advantage of India

One of the leading food producers globally.

- Possesses diverse agro-climatic conditions suitable for a wide range of crops.
- Boasts an extensive raw material reservoir for food processing enterprises.
- Benefits from a significant research and development talent pool.
- Abundant untapped potential in backend and frontend infrastructure, packaging, and marketing.
- Advancing support infrastructure development.
- Rapid urbanization, increasing literacy rates, evolving lifestyles, greater female participation in the workforce, and rising per capita income are driving rapid growth and opening new avenues in the food processing sector.
- Approximately 50% of Indian household expenditure is allocated to food items.
- Strategically positioned geographically with escalating demand for Indian produce in international markets

About Indian Agri-Horticulture Sector

According to research papers from the RBI on food inflation, Indian farmers receive only about one-third of the final selling price for fruits and vegetables, while a significant portion is taken by wholesalers and retailers. In contrast, farmers in the dairy sector earn around 70% of the final price, egg producers receive 75%, and poultry meat farmers and aggregators together capture 56%. However, for staple crops like tomatoes, onions, and potatoes (TOP), prices fluctuate due to seasonal factors like rainfall and temperature. Farmers receive

33% for tomatoes, 36% for onions, and 37% for potatoes of the consumer price.The RBI report notes that for fruits, farmers earn 31% for bananas, 35% for grapes, and 43% for mangoes in the domestic market. In the export market, the share of mango earnings increases, while that of grapes decreases, despite the overall higher price. To address price volatility in TOP crops, the report suggests establishing private mandis that leverage e-NAM, promoting farmer collectives, and relaunching futures trading. Other recommendations include increasing processing capacity, promoting solar-powered storage, and raising consumer awareness of processed TOP products. Improving productivity through better crop varieties and polyhouse tomato farming is also advised to stabilize supply and prices.The research emphasizes the importance of forecasting price spikes and stabilizing prices through short-term measures like adjusting trade policies to manage imports and exports based on supply and demand conditions. In the long term, improving productivity through innovation, better storage, and collective farming could increase farmers' earnings. Enhancing the efficiency of the marketing system, integrating digital platforms like e-NAM, and improving processing technologies are key to ensuring better price stability and transparency. For the dairy, poultry meat, and egg sectors, the report recommends creating feed banks to store and supply affordable fodder, utilizing barren lands for grass cultivation, promoting artificial insemination, and improving disease control to enhance livestock productivity. For fruits, it advocates improving the supply chain with better storage and transport, promoting diverse fruit varieties, expanding crop insurance, boosting processing and exports, adjusting import duties to match demand, and using digital tools to track supply and reduce price fluctuations

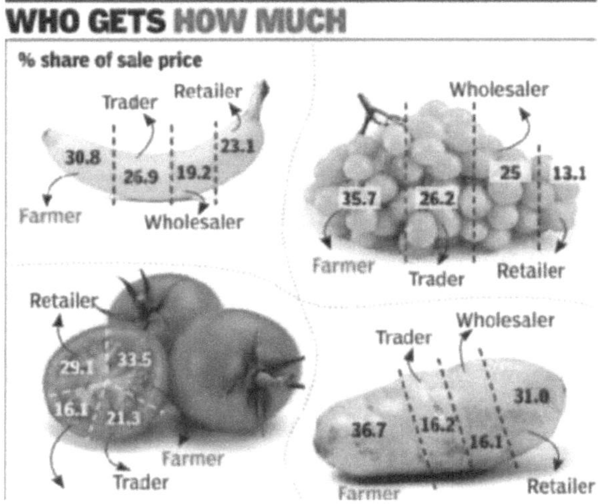

Average Annual Growth in Value of Output* (2014–15 to 2022–23)	Growth (%)
1. Fishing & Aquaculture	9.08
2. Livestock	5.76
(a) Milk	5.78
(b) Poultry meat	9.22
(c) Eggs	6.58
3. Crops	2.34
(a) Horticultural crops**	3.94
(b) Non-Horticultural crops	1.64
Foodgrains	2.63
Cereals	2.4
Pulses	4.67
Oilseeds	2.96
Sugarcane	4.33
Cotton	0.11
Jute	-2
Tea & Coffee	1.29
Tobacco	-3.31

Note *At 2011–12 prices; **includes Fruits & Vegetables and Condiments & Spices

Top Agricultural Growth States: 2014–15 to 2022–23*	# Agriculture	# Crops	# Livestock	# Fishing
Andhra Pradesh	7.97	3.65	8.41	18.45
Madhya Pradesh	6.9	5.96	12.6	15.31
Karnataka	6.32	4.53	11.49	11.74
Telangana	5.63	5.13	8.22	7.58
Tamil Nadu	5.39	2.72	9.73	3.65
Chhattiegarh	5.2	3.47	7.28	9.73
Odisha	5.11	4.45	5.16	11.79
Rajasthan	4.83	1.9	10.9	10.04
Jharkhand	4.73	3.59	6.18	11.88
Uttar Pradesh	4.64	4.44	5.17	7.98
Maharashtra	4.54	3.58	6.95	2.08
Bihar	4.3	1.83	8.28	7.84
Gujarat	4	2.44	5.59	5.75
ALL-INDIA	3.94	1.98	7.39	8.98

Note: *Average annual % growth in Gross Value Added at 2011–12 prices

Average Annual Growth Output & Top Agricultural Growth States

According to a study by NITI Aayog, India's agricultural growth over the past two decades has been driven more by livestock, horticulture, and fisheries than by crop production. The farm sector's annual growth rate, measured by gross value added (GVA), increased from 3.5% to 3.7% in the last decade. Cereal production rose from 185.2 million tonnes in 2004-05 to 303.6 million tonnes in 2022-23, while household cereal consumption remained stable at 153-156 million tonnes, creating a significant surplus. Milk production also increased from 92.5 million tonnes in 2004-05 to 230.6 million tonnes in 2022-23 without a corresponding increase in consumption, raising policy considerations. The performance of agriculture subsectors varies significantly. Crop production grew by only 2.3% per year between 2014-15 and 2022-23, while livestock and fisheries saw growth rates of 5.8% and 9.2%, respectively. Poultry meat, fishing and aquaculture, eggs, and milk experienced the highest growth, while non-horticultural field crops like cotton, jute, tobacco, and tea grew much slower. Thirteen states achieved an average agricultural growth of 4%, driven largely by livestock and fisheries, with crop growth exceeding 5% only in Madhya Pradesh and Telangana. This accelerated agricultural growth is attributed to diversification into horticulture, livestock, and fisheries, driven by rising demand for vegetables, fruits, milk, meat, eggs, and fish. This diversification has also led to a shift in household diets from calorie-rich foods to those rich in proteins and micronutrients. Technological advancements, such as hybrids in vegetables and maize, drip irrigation, and high-density tissue culture in bananas, have also contributed. However, NSSO's 2018-19 survey shows that only 53% of agricultural households derived income from livestock, and just 6.5% cultivated horticulture crops. Most households (44.2%) still relied on cereals, pulses, oilseeds, sugarcane, cotton, and other non-horticulture crops. Despite the benefits of diversification and new production technologies, these advancements have not fully reached field crops. Yields for oilseeds and pulses remain low, resulting in a significant portion of demand being met by imports. Cotton production has also stagnated, with no breakthroughs since GM Bt hybrids were introduced. The crop subsector's slow growth, despite government interventions like the MSP regime, highlights the need for technological improvements rather than reliance on output prices or subsidies to drive agricultural growth

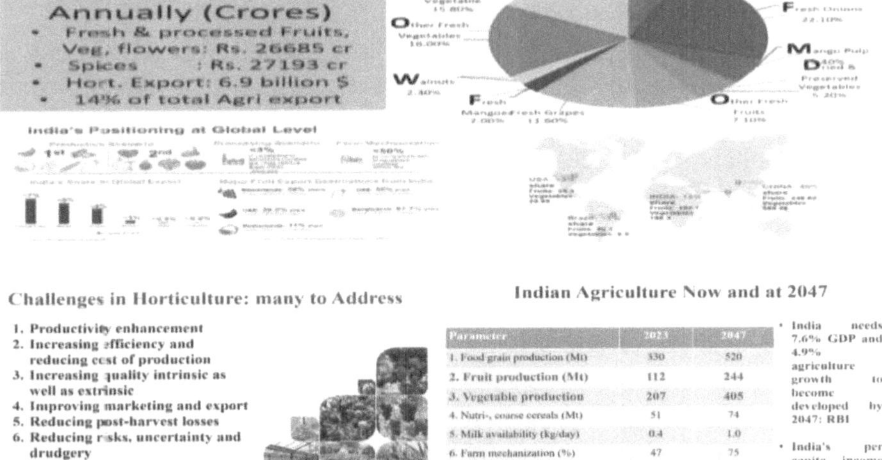

Challenges in Horticulture: many to Address

1. Productivity enhancement
2. Increasing efficiency and reducing cost of production
3. Increasing quality intrinsic as well as extrinsic
4. Improving marketing and export
5. Reducing post-harvest losses
6. Reducing risks, uncertainty and drudgery
7. Reducing GHG emission in agriculture
8. Adapting to changing climate
9. Income security to farmers

Indian Agriculture Now and at 2047

Parameter	2023	2047
1. Food grain production (Mt)	330	520
2. Fruit production (Mt)	112	244
3. Vegetable production	207	405
4. Nutri-, coarse cereals (Mt)	51	74
5. Milk availability (kg/day)	0.4	1.0
6. Farm mechanization (%)	47	75
7. Post-harvest losses (%)	15	10
8. Water use efficiency (%)	40	60
9. Nitrogen use efficiency (%)	35	50
10. Agri-export (% of world)	2.5	5.0

- India needs 7.6% GDP and 4.9% agriculture growth to become developed by 2047: RBI

- India's per capita income needs to surpass US$ 21,664, from current US$ 2,500: World Bank

Perspectives of Horticulture in Amrit Kaal(2023-2047)

- Sustainable,efficient and inclusive growth
- Climate resilient agriculture
- Digital and secondary agriculture
- Import substitution and esport promotion
- Participation of private sector

Strategic approach to shape the future of Indian agriculture:

- Technology Integration: Internet of things, Artificial Intelligence, Sensor utilisation, Automation to enhance efficiency, monitor crops and manage resources.
- Precision Management: Targeted use of inputs, Precise monitoring and Adaptive management techniques
- Climate Resilience: Varieties and production techniques to withstand changing climate conditions.
- Supply chain coordination: Efficient coordination among different stakeholders including input suppliers, farmers, processors and retailers is crucial for a seamless flow and timely delivery of horticultural products.
- Market Intelligence: Accurate market information and analysis, understanding consumer preferences, market trends and demand patterns, new market opportunities, potential export markets.
- Diversification and Innovation: Exploring novel crop varieties,value added products and innovative supply chain models in order to meet evolving consumer demands and create new market opportunities.
- Sustainable practices: Environmental sustainability and social responsibility, sustainable farming practices.
- Value addition and differentiation: Adding value through branding, packaging, processing and product differentiation strategies.
- Logistics and distribution: Efficient logistics and distribution systems for timely and cost effective delivery of horticultural products to consumers
- Policy Framework: Formulating supportive policy guidelines that encourage investments in research, infrastructure and human capital development fostering an enabling environment for the growth of the horticulture sector.

Digitisation can drive innovation and transformation in Horticulture

Five sectors in digitisation are-

- Precision horticulture: Application of sensors, Variable rate technology, drones, robotics, AI, protected cultivation, Vertical farming, Hydroponics.
- Climate smart horticulture: Weather monitoring, Crop management, Data management, Farm management.
- Supply chain management: Quality management, Improving transparency, Traceability and Efficiency.

- Financial inclusion: Promoting financial inclusion, Unified Payment Interface, Mobile banking, Microfinance.
- Use in Agriculture/horticulture education.

Above leads to increase productivity,reduce waste,increase export,improve food,nutrition and income security

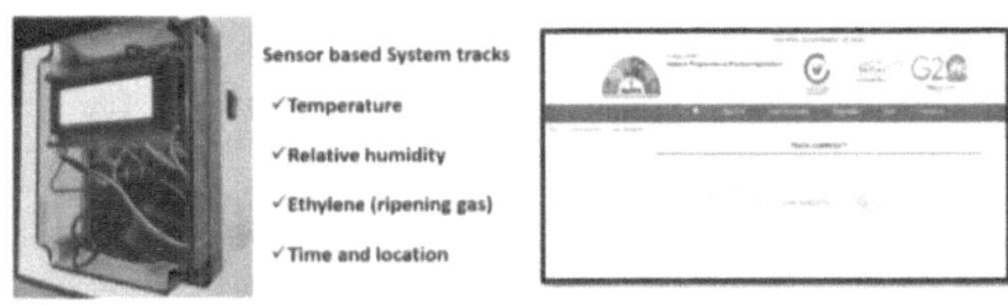

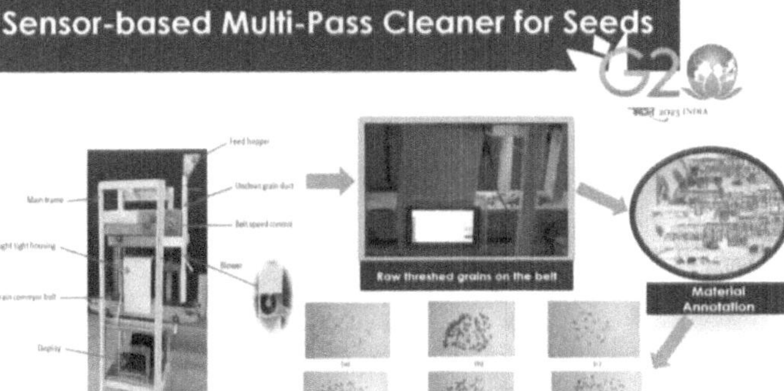

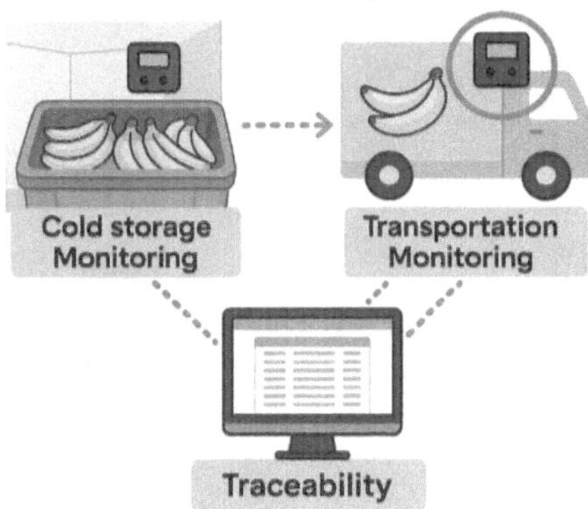

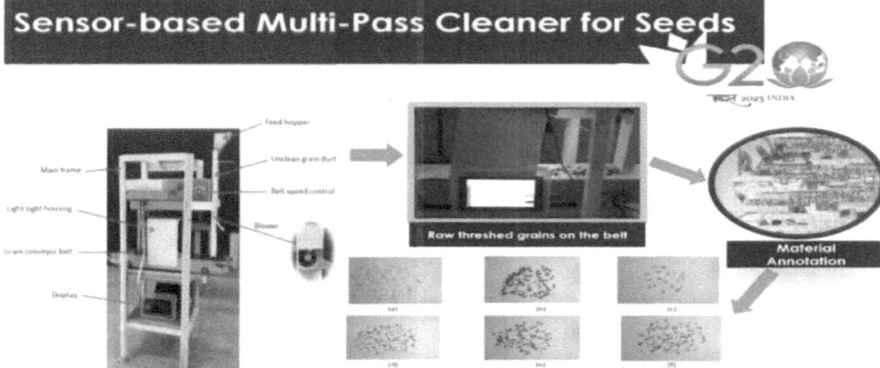

Marketing Fresh Fruits and Vegetables

- Agricultural marketing system – Link between farm and non-farm sectors
- Production stimulates forward linkages - regional production/marketing
- Market needs - demand driven than supply driven

- Farmer to be price setters than price followers
- Needs market information system – Horticulture led agricultural growth in India

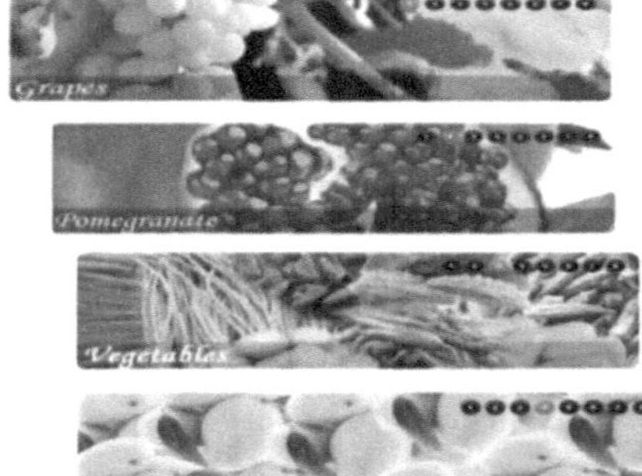

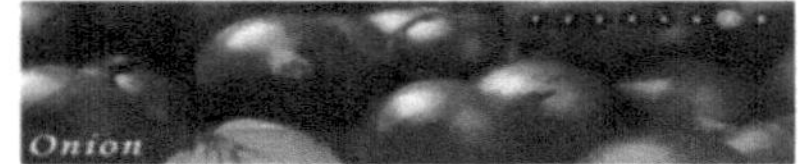

Goals to achieve
Agriculture Vision @ 2047

 **Food Security and Nutrition**

 **India as Global Powerhouse in Food**

 **Rural and Farmers Empowerment**

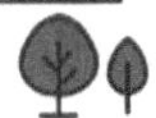 **Sustainable Natural Resources Ecosystem**

Food Security and Nutrition – Roadmap 2047

Now (Next 5 Years)	Next (5–15 Years)	Beyond (>15 Years)
• Private players Participation • E-commerce • Scientific & modern means of production • Agro ecological zone-based Planning, crop clusters, Improvi-productivity • Infrastructure-modern dry storage and integrated cold chains • Food basket diversification • Handling short gesta-tion & horticultural crops • Market incentives	• Precision farming, Regenerative Agriculture • Internet and applications usage • Intelligent irrigation • Variable input applicators-based irrigation system; nano fertilizers • Use of 100% indigenous materials • Systems biology approach to ocereme fodd quality and safety issues • Improve biotechnnolog-ical means of production	• Shift to Enhanced Hybridization • R&D – Now until 2047 • Development of degraded and other land use areas • Integration of conventional and molecular approaches • 2X Inland fisheries production • Autonomous and advanced Robots • Expect volume and productivity growth – Connected and Shared economy

Horticulture Vision for 2047

- Horticulture in more potential areas
- Input use in potential areas
- Potential crop in potential area

Forward looking holistic approach to address challenges and capitalise on opportunities

2. Indian Food Processing Sector at a Glance

It attracted USD 6.19 billion FDI equity inflow during April 2014 to March 2023.Average annual growth rate during the 5 year ending 2020-21is 8.38%.. Processed food exports during 2022-23 is USD 13.07 billion. It contributes to 8.04% GVA in manufacturing and 9.66% in Agriculture. It employs 12.2%of the total workforce in registered manufacturing sector.There is more than 300 food parks in India. In view of 2023 being established as International Year of Millets and to bring global food processing industry together, the Ministry of Food Processing Industries, Government of India organised the 2nd edition of International Mega Food Event "World Food India 2023" from 3rd-5th November 2023 at Pragati Maidan,New Delhi.The event was one of the biggest congregation of government department and dignitaries, global investors and business leaders of major global and domestic agri-food companies in the country.

The Indian food processing sector has grown rapidly with an average annual growth rate of 9 percent in the last five years. The sector facilitates strong linkages between industry and the agriculture sector through a wide range of activities, including farming, aggregation, processing, packaging, storage and distribution. The sector has also witnessed immense surge of opportunities in its champiansectors like frozen food, ready to eat/ready to cook products, millets/nutri-cereals etc. Recognising the potential of food processing sector in transforming India as the food basket of the world, the Ministry of food processing industries, Government of India has adopted measures to channelize investments in food processing sub-segments. This includes backward linkages, food processing equipment, processing related R&D, cold chain storage solutions, start-ups, logistics and retail chains encompassing the entire food processing value chain

Domestic and Export Opportunities in Food Processing

The food processing sector is one of India's largest industries in terms of production, growth, consumption, and export. This industry includes various segments such as fruits and vegetables, spices, meat and poultry, dairy products, alcoholic beverages, fisheries, plantation crops, grain processing, and other consumer goods like confectionery, chocolates, cocoa products, soy-based items, mineral water, and high-protein foods. Since the liberalization in August 1991, numerous project proposals have been initiated across different segments of the food and agro-processing industry. Additionally, the government has approved ventures for joint collaborations, foreign partnerships, industrial licenses, and 100% export-oriented units, leading to significant investments in the sector.

Key Opportunities

- Contract Farming
- Protected Cultivation
- Processing Industries (Primary, Secondary & Tertiary)
- Investments in pre and post-harvest infrastructure through PPP
- Mega Food Parks
- Food Safety Management Systems
- Export Opportunities

Conclusion

Food processing management is the strategic oversight and control of transforming raw agricultural products into consumable food items. It involves a complex interplay of various factors, including production planning, quality control, distribution, and marketing. This process is crucial in ensuring food safety, extending product shelf life, and meeting consumer demands.

Key Components of Food Processing Management

- Procurement and Supply Chain Management:
- Sourcing high-quality raw materials.
- Building strong relationships with suppliers.
- Efficient inventory management.
- Logistics and transportation optimization

Production Planning and Control

- Developing production schedules.
- Allocating resources effectively.
- Implementing quality control measures.
- Ensuring food safety standards.
- Utilizing advanced technologies (e.g., automation, ERP systems)

Quality Assurance and Control

- Establishing quality standards.
- Conducting regular inspections and testing.
- Implementing HACCP (Hazard Analysis and Critical Control Points).
- Ensuring compliance with food safety regulations

Packaging and Labeling

- Selecting appropriate packaging materials.
- Designing attractive and informative labels.
- Complying with labeling regulations.

Distribution and Logistics

- Managing transportation and warehousing.
- Building efficient distribution networks.
- Ensuring timely delivery

Marketing and Sales

- Understanding consumer preferences.
- Developing effective marketing strategies.
- Building strong brand identity.
- Managing sales channels

Challenges in Food Processing Management

- Food Safety Concerns: Maintaining stringent hygiene and safety standards.
- Regulatory Compliance: Adhering to complex food laws and regulations.
- Supply Chain Volatility: Managing fluctuations in raw material prices and availability.
- Consumer Demands: Meeting evolving consumer preferences for healthy, convenient, and sustainable products.
- Competition: Standing out in a highly competitive market

Importance of Food Processing Management

- Ensuring Food Safety: Protecting public health by preventing foodborne illnesses.
- Reducing Food Waste: Extending product shelf life and minimizing losses.
- Increasing Food Availability: Providing a wider range of food products throughout the year.
- Economic Growth: Creating employment opportunities and boosting the agricultural sector.
- Nutritional Security: Fortifying foods to address nutritional deficiencies

Future Trends in Food Processing Management

- Sustainability: Adopting eco-friendly practices and reducing environmental impact.
- Technology Integration: Leveraging AI, IoT, and automation for efficiency and precision.
- Consumer-Centric Approach: Tailoring products and services to meet individual preferences.
- Product Diversification: Expanding product lines to cater to different market segments

Food processing management is a multifaceted discipline that requires a holistic approach. By effectively managing various components, businesses can ensure the production of safe, high-quality food products that meet consumer expectations while contributing to the overall food system.

3. Food and Nutritional Security through Post Harvest Management

India has emerged as a global leader in food production, with an abundant supply of diverse crops, fruits, vegetables, livestock, and seafood. The Indian population now enjoys a greater variety of foods, available throughout the year, with improved nutrition and quality. However, issues such as starvation, malnutrition, and uneven food distribution persist across different regions. Despite the steady growth in population, a significant portion of the population still lives below the poverty line. In this context, food security has become a burning topic for the Indian sub-continent and the policy makers, researchers and all those who are concerned are worried how to make more food available for the people. Increase in the production to meet the growing demand is one solution. But these days the actual cultivable lands are rapidly decreasing due to industrialisation at many places. The degradation of soil is adding woes to the farmers. The developments in the laboratories to boost the agricultural production is not properly replicated in field due to several factors including climate changes. In above circumstances the food production is not increasing as per need. But there is another option to make more food available, that is through proper post-harvest management and value addition. Studies have found that post-harvest losses for grains and durables are to the tune of 10%,for semi-perishables 20-30% and for perishables more than 40%. Thus, if post-harvest losses can be minimized can help more food available by modern techniques. Most of the produce are sold raw form giving producer a low return on investment and labour. In many parts of the country, crops are sold at throw-away prices during the glut seasons. The traditional storage practices adopted for the food grains, fruits and vegetables add to the problem.

The processing methods and equipment adopted for different food materials are mostly unscientific and lack of proper technology. So whatever goes to the market also fetches a low price. Hence, great scope exists to reduce these losses to make more food available for consumption and add income to the farmers. It will also create scope for establishment of small and cottage industries creating employment opportunities. Looking to the production figures of different food materials in the country and the quantum of losses, cost economical food processing, preservation and value addition have a vital role which can contribute substantially to be a safe step to ensure food security. Primary food processing is a significant industry, including numerous rice mills, hullers, flour and pulse mills, and oil mills. The unorganized sector consists of thousands of bakeries, traditional food units, and vegetable pickle and spice processing units. Despite being the world's second-largest producer of fruits and vegetables, India processes only a small fraction (2-4%) of its produce. Renowned as the land of spices, India accounts for approximately 25-30% of global production. It also cultivates over 22 million tonnes of oilseeds, in addition to plantation products such as tea, coffee, cocoa, and cashew.

Meat and poultry are essential food products, with India ranking as the largest milk producer globally, of which about 15% undergoes processing through the organized sector. Tea serves as a significant foreign exchange earner, with India being the leading producer and exporter of black tea. The country boasts vast marine resources, with potential for processing various fish species along its extensive coastline of 8041km, 28,000km of rivers, and millions of hectares of reservoirs and brackish water bodies. Marine catches include prawns, shrimps, tuna, and cuttlefish.

Despite abundant food resources, the food processing industry remains in its infancy, with only a small portion (4% of fruits and vegetables and 15-20% of milk) undergoing processing. The government has prioritized the sector by offering numerous fiscal incentives and reliefs to encourage the commercialization and value addition of agricultural produce. This aims to minimize pre- and post-harvest losses, stimulate employment generation, and foster export growth. Scientific methods are available for post-harvest management and value addition of different types of food but still huge loss occurs. Wide gap between produced and processed fruits in the country with an appreciable portion retained at farmer's level due to poor transport and processing network. In fact low cost technologies for short term storage of fruits and vegetables in different forms have not been suitably transmitted to the small producers and end users. The food processing industry at present is able to utilize less than 4% of the total fruits and vegetables. The product profile of the food processing industry has remained static using only a few fruits like mango, pineapple and citrus. The production of new products besides being necessary for the survival and growth of the processing industry, can also meet the demand for new taste for domestic as well as the export market. Besides, the use of latest machines and equipment can simplify most of the operations and increase the throughput of the processing plants. Hence modernization of food processing industry and value chain management, as and where required, is essential in order to keep pace with the development as well as to be competitive in the international markets. This involves innovations in equipment, process and nutrious products of mass appeal.

The following strategies may be adopted for increased value addition and better post-harvest management.

- The grain milling, threshing, storage and other systems should be modernized to minimize the losses at each of these unit operations.

- A multidisciplinary approach has to be adopted to identify critical problems related to post harvest, processing and marketing aspects of food grains, fruits and vegetables and their products. A proper co-ordination among scientists, growers and industrialists at certain common strategies of food materials and their wastes is needed.

- The farmers should be assured of some minimum price for quality raw materials. Similarly supply of good quality raw material to the farmers ensure manufacture of high quality finished products.

- Establishment of procurement centers, which should include the provision of grading, sorting, washing, packing and pre-cooling facilities in centralized locations at production area causes an effective post-harvest care and handling.

- Refrigerated or insulated trucks and intermediate cooling storage and central godowns with small capacity cold storage at district level needs to be employed for collection and distribution of the commodities.

- Establishment of cooperative societies for proper marketing, distribution, processing, retail outlets at potential consuming areas, multi-raw material distribution and multi-product processing units are essential to process seasonally available fruits and vegetables.

- Ways need be evolved for effective use of grains, fruits, vegetables including their wastes keeping in view the production, processing industries, variety of product and consumption patterns especially in the changing economic and social scenario of the country.

4. Research, Development and Extension Needs

- Proper low cost technologies for preservation and value addition of food grains, fruits and vegetables, small and medium scale industrial processes and machinery should be developed keeping in view the farmer's needs. Popularisation of the above developed processes and machinery should be undertaken by demonstrations, field trials and multilocation evaluation.

- Research efforts to reduce qualitative and quantitative losses due to different post-harvest disorders such as chilling injury, spongy tissue etc. and to increase self-life under high ambient temperature conditions, which is the only feasible technology for Indian conditions.

- Area specific models for suitable package of practices to reduce losses during different post-harvest operations and value addition have to be developed.

- Development of storage/packaging techniques for individual commodities are to be carried out by using selective permeable package materials, corrugated fiber box etc. Packaging techniques for natural quality retention should be standardized with due consideration to cost and environment. The feasibility of their adoption with respect to individual commodity should be explored.

- The farmers' and small processors should be trained for use of preharvest treatments to regulate growth, delay maturity, reduce post-harvest diseases and disorders and to use small cost effective short term storage structures.

- The scientists should undertake research in frontier areas of post-harvest technology such as applications of bio-technology, cryogenic processing, system dynamics simulation and modeling, super critical fluid extraction to obtain high value oils, fabricated foods and feeds through extrusion technology, membrane technology and controlled/modified atmosphere storage etc.

- Suitable machineries in post-harvest and processing aspects such as commercial peelers, slicers etc. need to be developed.

- Transportation methods should be standardized, especially for local/rural transport.

- Emphasis should be made on utilization of food processing wastes and seed processing as the fruits and vegetable seeds involve high costs and form the base for successful production. Presently some methods are available for the use of food processing wastes, but the available technologies are under-utilized. Hence the scope should be widened to meet the need of farmers for on-farm use of wastes.

A thorough knowledge of the existing system is a prerequisite for establishing any programme of saving the food. Development of an accurate needs may require assistance of many specialists. Engineering expertise will be needed in areas of harvesting, threshing, drying, storage, milling and packaging. Biological capability, which may include knowledge of moulds, insects, rodents and birds is important at all level starting from harvesting to storage. Expertise in economies should enable cost analysis of production, processing, storage, marketing, pricing and transportation. Social science may be able to help recognize consumer's traditions and their preferences etc. vis-à-vis the Govt. policy. An interdisciplinary approach involving most if not all these disciplines is necessary to improve the design and management of the present system. Naturally the training needs of such a system would also be complex. Training programmes need to be developed for farmers, processors, storekeepers, procurement and marketing professional etc. giving the details under the existing Govt. regulations. Considerable importance is being given to the management aspects of different post-harvest operations and value addition being integral part of agricultural system needs to be developed on par with agriculture. A holistic approach is needed in R&D projects and execution for ensuring reduced losses and value addition for export and domestic consumption. Development and adoption of eco-friendly techniques for reducing the post-harvest losses and value addition have to be encouraged for catching up with the contemporary developments in socio-economic and technical sectors. Efforts are being made to develop action programmes through the help of agencies who have the knowhow in the methods of reducing post-harvest loses and production of quality food through advanced methods of post-harvest processing. However, postharvest technology system is an interdisciplinary system is to be recognized and emphasis has to be laid on integrated development of the system as a whole.

Value Addition through Entrepreneurship Development

Post-harvest management deals with the techniques used to safeguard and retain the quality and quantity of the perishable & non-perishable raw food commodities such as food grains, cereal, pulses, fruits and vegetables, meat, fish, poultry etc. till it reaches to the consumer either in the raw state or minimal processed food products such as flour, jams, juice, energy fruit drinks, energy bars, canned vegetables, processed meat, dal, cut vegetables, sausages etc. One of the vital and popular methods of post-harvest management is through value addition. According to the FAO's 2017-18 World Agriculture Statistics, India is the world's largest producer(25%) and Consumer(27%).

India is the cash crops like coffee and cotton. Furthermore, as of 2022-23, India was one of the top five largest producers of livestock and poultry meat, showcasing one of the fastest growth rates in this sector. Despite largest producer of fruit,vegetables,milk,Jute and pulses and second largest producer of rice,wheat,sugarcane,cotton and groundnut which are major global staples. Additionally, India is the second or third largest producer of several dry fruits, raw materials for agriculture-based textiles, root and tuber crops, pulses, farmed fish, eggs, coconut, sugarcane, and numerous vegetables. In 2024, India was among the top ten largest producers globally for agricultural commodities, including many being a major food producer the post-harvest losses in India is 10-25% in durables,semi-perishables and products like milk,meat,fish and egg degradation both in quality and quantity. In 2022 India lost about 5-13% for fruits & vegetables and 3-7% for other crops. Brief information regarding the post-harvest spoilage of various crops and food commodities is presented in Table below.

Losses in the various crops / Food commodities

Crop/Food commodities	Cumulative losses in%
Cereals	4-6.0
Pulses	15
Oil Seeds	3-7.0
F&V	5-13
Milk,fish,egg	10-25

Source: CIPHET, Ludhiana

Without proper preservation and storage measures, seasonal variations can lead to significant levels of wastage or shortages in food supply. Hence, post-harvest management and value addition is the call of the hour. But despite the call it's a sad fact for Indian post-harvest management system that it has been plagued by factors such as low public investment, may be due to inadequate information to investors regarding policies, benefits etc. poor infrastructure due to small number of entrepreneurs, inadequate credit availability and high levels of fragmentation etc. Effective post-harvest management system allows not only the minimization of post-harvest losses but also increases the value of the marketed agricultural products by transforming the agricultural raw materials into value added products in attractive packaging hence, making it more appealing to the consumers. Post-harvest management system offers the following benefits to the society.

Farmers: get higher yield, better revenues and reduced risk of product spoilage.

Consumers: have access to a greater new variety of products at cheaper rate,

Economy: gets benefitted with new business opportunities for the entrepreneurs and the work force to get employment.

Responding to the need of post-harvest management system and considering its benefits, Government of India is providing huge incentives and aid for budding entrepreneurs in post-harvest management/ food processing sector through its various schemes and policies of government keep changing time to time, entrepreneurs or interested person need to visit concern department or ministry for exact scheme/policies available at that time, few of it's policies and schemes are discussed in the preceding lines. The Government of India has exempted numerous food processing and post-harvest management enterprises from industrial licensing under the Industries (Development and Regulation) Act, 1951. For foreign investment, automatic approval is granted for up to 100% equity participation in most processed food ventures. Government policy initiatives include automatic approvals for foreign technology agreements, allowing the sale of 50% in the domestic tariff area for agro-based 100% Export Oriented Units (EOUs), and extending the zero-duty Export Promotion Capital Goods (EPCG) scheme to the food processing sector with a reduced threshold limit of Rs. One crore in the EXIM policy. Furthermore, the government has designated the food processing industry for priority lending by banks. Various schemes offer loans at very low interest rates, such as 4%, and grants-in-aid to selected cooperatives and NGOs for upgrading standards to international levels, supporting research and development, developing agricultural export zones, and establishing mega food parks. Under the scheme for technology upgradation, establishment, and modernization of food processing industries, financial assistance is provided as grants-in-aid for setting up new food processing units, and for technological upgrading and expanding existing units across the country. The Ministry offers financial assistance to entrepreneurs at 25% of the cost of plant and machinery and technical civil works, up to a maximum of Rs. 50 lakhs in general areas, or 33.33% up to a maximum of Rs. 75 lakhs in difficult terrains.

Entrepreneurs are the vital part of post-harvest management system and are considered as potential players of the system. Entrepreneurs can also be called as life line of the post-harvest management system. CIPHET, government institutions and other organisations very clearly highlights the problems of post-harvest losses of high quality fresh fruits and vegetables and low returns of produced goods, faced by the Indian farmers and consumers as the recent price hike of onions. These organisations consistently pays the emphasis over entrepreneurship development in the post-harvest management system as the solution to the problem as entrepreneurs can develop infrastructure like cold storage, pack house and refrigerator van at strategic locations and provide modern packaging and processing facilities for converting the produced fruits and vegetables into preservable and value added products, which in turn can fetch the reasonable price for the produced goods to the farmers, hence encouraging the agri practice in the area. At the same time it also provides employment to the unemployed youths of the rural area and it also brings huge benefits to the entrepreneur through the marketing of value added products. Rising to need of the hour, Central Institute of Post-Harvest Engineering and Technology(CIPHET), Ludhiana has come up with new Business Planning and Development Unit(BPD) under NAIP-ICAR, funded by World Bank to provide platform to rural and small entrepreneur to establish and operate processing plants and to act as knowledge hub for effective transfer, commercialization and entrepreneurship development through technologies of CIPHET. Some of the technology extrudes and biscuits fortified with B-Carotene, dried onion flakes and powder, flaxseed based nutritious energy bar, ginger powder, glow U: a face care system, groundnut based flavored beverage, curd and paneer, method of determining maturity of intact mango in tree and predicting maturity stage and eating quality of Indian mangoes using near infrared spectroscopy, process for stabilization of rice bran by ohmic heating system, osmotic dehydrated pineapple candy, pearl millet based extrudes, pasta and weaning mix, process for making beetroot shreds and powder, carrot shreds and powder, green chili puree and powder, process for preparation of alcoholic beverage with nutraceutical properties from kinnow peels, mix for ready to constitute makhana kheer, blended guava bar, ready to reconstitute mustard saag, sunflower kernel based confectionary products, tamato puree manufacturing and bottling technology, process for making porous bricks, anomal feed from food industry waste etc.

BPD unit of CIPHET will work on the following objectives:

- To identify and educate potential entrepreneurs about the commercial viability technologies developed by the institute.
- To develop entrepreneurial skill among potential processors and entrepreneurs through demonstration, training, planning, project profiling, commissioning and continuous support to the entrepreneurs for successful business of operational plant.
- To develop entrepreneurship through transfer and production of processing equipment and machineries.

BPD unit at CIPHET Ludhiana will showcase the processing technologies developed by CIPHET for easy adoption of technologies by entrepreneurs. Production of prototypes will help to overcome shortage of appropriate machineries for efficient processing of agricultural produce. The basic objective of BPD is to have efficient transfer and commercialization of technologies developed by the institute up to the level of entrepreneurship development. Not only this, but BPD unit at CIPHET will extend support from project formulation, technical support, erection, commissioning to a successful operational enterprise. BPD unit at CIPHET will fulfill it's objective via 3 strategic steps:

1. Entrepreneurship Development through Product Based Technologies: CIPHET has developed various food product based technologies viz, fruit leather, extruded products, groundnut and soy milk, curd and paneer, green chilli powder, onion and beetroot powder, ginger flakes and powder etc. All these technologies have been transferred to several entrepreneurs. These technologies have potential to process the produce at rural level to increase food value and shelf life and in turn processor gets better return and employment through processing at small and catchment level. Utilisation of processing by/co-products is also catching as emergent technology for value addition.

2. Entrepreneurship Development through Agro-processing Centre in Production Catchment; Agro-processing has emerged as leading rural industry. In order to reap the advantages of processing, concept has to reach production catchments. With this view several agro-processing models have been developed by various research organisations including CIPHET, Ludhiana. They can add value to each and every crop from harvest onwards. Threshing, cleaning, grading, bagging, minimal primary and secondary processing units can be established at production catchment itself for better employment and income opportunities at rural threshold. Adding to this CIPHET has developed mobile agro processing unit which can move to the production site/field easily. BPD unit at CIPHET will also provide agro processing center, rice mill, dhal mill etc. for incubate/ entrepreneurs at CIPHET Ludhiana. Rural entrepreneurs, farm women and unemployed youths can adopt these models for upliftment of their livelihood. This incubator has potential to generate employment and income opportunity at rural threshold.

3. Entrepreneurship Development through Processing Machineries: Rapid urbanization and change in life style has increased demand of ready-to-eat products. Also with the increase in agricultural production handling of surplus produce has emerged as major challenge. Processing of agricultural produce to increase shelf life is need of the hour. To handle large quantities there is urgent need of processing equipment. For small and medium scale processing quality machineries are major limitation.

CIPHET will develop entrepreneurs to produce proven agro-processing machineries developed within NARS system. Some of the popular machineries under this scheme are banana-comb cutter, pomegranate aril extractor, maize degermer for dry degerming of maize, low cost tray dryer, cryogenic spice grinding system etc.

With the aforesaid objectives and strategies BPD unit at CIPHET shall bear the following fruits:

- Increased number of processing units
- Reduction in post-harvest losses
- Increased availability of processing machineries.

Contribution of FPI to GDP has grown substantially, averaging an annual growth rate of around 7.3% during 2015-2022.The sector has contributed 10.54% of the gross value added in manufacturing and 11.57% of GVA in Agricultural sector during 2020-21. Food processing sector forms an important segment of GDP and employment.The sector constitutes around 9-11% of GDP in manufacturing and agriculture sector respectively.

5. An Overview of Indian Food Market

Primary Processed Food Market: The primary processed food products constitute the majority of the processed food sales in India. It is estimated that around 58% of the total processed food sales come through primary processed food items. Primary processed food comprises products such as packaged fruits and vegetables, unbranded edible oil, packaged milk, milled rice, flour, tea, sugar, coffee, pulses, and more. During the period 2008-22, it is expected to grow at a CAGR of around 8.1% which will make the market value to reach at around INR 6724 Billion by the end of 2022. The overall share of primary processed food in the processed food sales in India is expected to decline in years to come as the value added food is expected to gain foot hold in India.

The Great Grain Milling: Grain based processed food is the largest contributor towards the sales of processed food in India where around 90% of the grain based products falls under the primary processed food category. In 2011, over 31% of the total processed food sales were accounted through the grain based products only. The processed food grain market has clocked revenues is expected to cross INR 3532 Billion by 2022 due to increasing demand. The compounded annual growth rate during the period 2008-22 for processed food grains market's value is expected to be around 7.8%. The grain based products share in processed food market is projected to decline in days to come as demand for other processed food such as meat and poultry, bread and bakery is expected to rise.

Ripening Fruits and Vegetables Processing Market: India is the 2nd largest producer of fruits and vegetables and nearly accounts for around 11% and 9% of the global production respectively. But India has still not utilized it's potential fully due to which its fruits and vegetables trade is not quite significant. The level of fruits and vegetable processing in India is merely 2.2%. The huge difference between the production and level of processing of fruits and vegetables in India indicates the untapped opportunity that is present in India. The market value of fruits and vegetables processing in India was valued at USD 876.56million in 2024.Some of the major processed fruits and vegetables products in India are fruit pulp, juices, jams, chutneys, chips, pickles etc. The factors such as increasing acceptance of processed items, paucity of time, increasing middle class individuals, high export demand etc. are likely to drive the growth of processed fruits and vegetables market in India.

6. Modernisation of Cold Storages in India

The cold chain sector in India is emerging as a vital industry, especially considering the nation's leading position in milk, fruits, and vegetables production, as well as substantial output in marine, meat, and poultry products. Despite this, there remains significant potential for the expansion of cold chain infrastructure. Cold storage facilities serve as the cornerstone of the cold chain, with historical development starting in the early 20th century, primarily focusing on potato storage in regions like UP, West Bengal, Punjab, and Bihar. However, significant advancements occurred in the 1960s when Maharashtra pioneered the concept of multi-product, multi-chamber cold stores. Since then, the cold storage sector has undergone substantial transformation, with a renewed emphasis on food preservation and energy efficiency due to the energy-intensive nature of cold stores. Technological advancements have led to improvements in construction, insulation, refrigeration equipment, and control systems. Recognizing the importance of the cold chain, the government, through organizations like the National Horticulture Board (NHB), has been establishing standards for various aspects of the cold chain industry. Efforts are underway to develop environmentally friendly practices, such as the Green Cold Chain concept. This revolution in the cold chain sector encompasses advancements in cold storage infrastructure, utilization patterns, design, construction practices, and energy-saving techniques.

At the time of independence, cold storage facilities were limited, primarily situated in states like UP, Punjab, and West Bengal, primarily for bulk storage of potatoes. However, the introduction of multi-product cold storage was realized as early as the 1930s, with experimental units like the one in Pune's fruit research station. Subsequent decades saw the development of medium to large-scale cold storage units in various states, particularly focusing on bulk storage for potatoes. The concept of multipurpose cold storage units gained traction between 1965 and 1970, with facilities established in cities like Bangalore and Pune. Government initiatives, such as the Maharashtra Agricultural Marketing and Fisheries Corporation (MAFCO), further promoted multipurpose cold storage, food processing, freezing, and storage of frozen foods. Presently, multipurpose units cater to a wide range of food products, including fruits, vegetables, dry fruits, spices, milk products, confectionery, and various frozen foods.

Growth of Cold Storage Industry

The perishable food production is estimated as:

India's cold chain logistics market was estimated at US$9.75billion in 2023 and is expected to grow to US$ 12.85 billion by 2028 at a CAGR of 5.67%.

The Indian cold chain market size reached INR 2052.7 billion in 2023 expected to reach INR 5596.9 billion by 2032with a CAGR of 11.8%.As per a study by Mordor Intelligence India's cold chain is expected to reach $ 11.64billion in 2024 and grow to $ 18.19billion by 2029. The key reason for a steady growth is a rise in demand for perishable goods both domestically and internationally driven by e-commerce. Currently there are 8653 cold storages in India with a capacity of 394.17 lakh MT as on December 2023. India's cold chain logistics market was estimated to grow to US$12.85 billion by 2028 at a CAGR of 5.67% as on March 2024 Mordor Intelligence report. An efficient cold chain infrastructure involves movement of temperature sensitive goods from one place to another within the required time frame.

The food processing sector is witnessing steady growth, with processing capacity increasing from just 2% to 6% of fruits and vegetables production, reflecting a growth rate of 14 to 15%. The target for processing fruits and vegetables in the coming years is set at 20%, highlighting significant potential for expanding the cold chain sector in India.

Precooling of Fruits & Vegetables: The concept of pre-cooling of grapes was introduced in the '80s primarily in Maharashtra, which is the leading grape growing state in India. This helped the farmers to export grapes to Europe, Gulf countries etc. Later this technology was adopted for other fruits like mango, pomegranate, orange etc.

Controlled Atmosphere Storage

With the onset of 21st century, the need was realized to set up controlled atmosphere following the trends in Europe, America & other countries. A number of CA stores have already been established in the northern part of the country at locations which have proximity to apple growing regions. The capacities generally ranged between 1000MT to 12000MT. The project of 12000MT setup by CONCOR is the largest in the country so far. A few units of smaller capacities have also been established in west and south.

Ripening Units

In recent years, there has been significant interest in the scientific ripening and storage of food items such as bananas and mangoes, leading to the establishment of units in various regions. Particularly noteworthy progress in this area can be observed in the southern regions, Gujarat, and Maharashtra.

Distribution Centres

As the cold chain infrastructure expands across the country, food distribution centres are also emerging, with the inaugural unit established in the Navi Mumbai region. Several smaller centres have been initiated by the food retail sector, and further expansion is anticipated in the years ahead.

Cold Storage Classification

In contemporary practice, cold stores can be categorized as follows:

Bulk Cold Stores: Typically designed for the seasonal storage of single commodities like potatoes, chilies, and apples.

Multipurpose Cold Stores: Engineered for year-round storage of diverse commodities such as fruits, vegetables, dry fruits, spices, pulses, and milk products. These facilities are predominantly situated near consumption hubs.

Small Cold Stores with Precooling Facilities: Primarily for export-oriented fresh fruits and vegetables like grapes. Initially concentrated in Maharashtra, this trend is now spreading to states like Karnataka, Andhra Pradesh, and Gujarat.

Frozen Food Stores: These facilities are equipped with freezing and processing capabilities for fish, meat, poultry, dairy products, and processed fruits and vegetables. Although these units have contributed to the growth of the frozen foods sector in both domestic and export markets, the percentage of processed foods remains low, indicating substantial potential for further expansion.

Mini Units/Walk-in Cold Stores: Found in hotels, restaurants, malls, and supermarkets for storing perishable goods.

Controlled Atmosphere Stores: Tailored for specific fruits and vegetables such as apples, pears, and cherries to extend shelf life.

Ripening Chambers: Dedicated facilities primarily established for bananas and mangoes to facilitate controlled ripening.

Construction Practices Trend

While bulk cold stores typically feature a smaller number of large-sized chambers, multi-purpose units boast a larger number of smaller chambers, catering to the diverse needs of farmers, traders, and other customers. Common construction methods in the Indian cold storage industry include:

Conventional Buildings: These structures typically feature RCC frames, brick walls, and either truss-type sheet roofs or RCC slabs. Internal floors are made of RCC or steel frames, supported by wooden or steel grating.

Single-Floor Structures: Designed specifically for the mechanized loading and unloading of products.

Pre-Engineered Building Structures: These use cold chambers constructed from sandwich insulated panels. Recent trends favor single-floor designs with heights ranging from 5 to 12 meters or more, incorporating mechanized loading and unloading facilities as well as storage racks.

Recent Practices

Walls & Ceiling: Constructed with insulated panels

Roof: Sheet metal roofing on trusses

Internal Structures

a) **Steel structures with steel grille floors designed for conventional loading.**

b) **Racks designed for mechanized loading.**

Construction practices differ based on factors like unit size, location, and usage patterns. Small cold stores usually utilize sandwich panel construction, while medium and large cold stores may feature additional components such as loading and unloading areas, ante rooms, cold storage chambers, staircases, lifts, machine rooms, offices, and restrooms.

Thermal Insulation Trends

- Effective thermal insulation plays a critical role in the cold chain system, serving two primary functions:
- Minimizing heat flow from the surroundings into the storage space.
- Minimizing moisture flow from surrounding areas into cold chambers.

Selecting appropriate materials, thickness, vapor barriers, cladding, and application methods is crucial to ensure optimal thermal insulation performance. While refrigeration systems may operate intermittently based on load requirements, insulation maintains a continuous duty cycle, operating 24/7 throughout the storage period.

Insulation Materials

In the past, older units used inexpensive materials like rice husks for thermal insulation. While cost-effective, this material required substantial thickness and led to maintenance and hygiene issues, making it nearly obsolete today. In cold stores built after the 1970s, conventional insulation materials such as Expanded Polystyrene, fiberglass, Polyurethane Rigid Foam, and similar substances have been commonly used. More recently, extruded Polystyrene has been introduced as an insulation option. Previously, insulation involved securing it with bitumen as a vapor barrier, using wooden pegs and battens covered with chicken wire mesh and cement-sand plaster. Current practices, however, have shifted to using metallic runners to support sheet metal cladding, typically profiled precoated sheets, instead of wooden battens.

Sandwich Insulated Panel Structure

Insulated panels have transformed cold storage construction globally. While they have been utilized in developed countries for over forty years, they were introduced in India about 25 years ago. These panels come primarily in two types:

Expanded Polystyrene (EPS) Panels: These panels feature EPS bonded to sheet metal skins using a specialized adhesive.

Polyurethane Foam (PUF) Panels: These panels use Polyurethane foam as the insulation material, sandwiched between two metal skins. PUF panels provide superior structural strength and insulation value compared to EPS panels for the same thickness.

Insulated panels are versatile and used in various applications, including small walk-ins, large cold stores, processing plants, prefabricated houses, warehouses, clean rooms, and more. They are also employed in fabricating cold store doors, offering enhanced flexibility, faster construction, and improved thermal efficiency. The use of these panels eliminates the need for brick walls and RCC slabs, allowing for greater cold store volume within the same footprint. Panels come with various skin finishes, enhancing hygienic quality.

Trends in Refrigeration Systems

Previously, over 90% of cold storage units in the northern and eastern regions relied on outdated technology, including slow-speed ammonia refrigeration compressors without capacity control, atmospheric condensers, and bunker-type evaporator coils or floor-mounted air cooling units with ducting for air distribution. These systems were inefficient, leading to high energy consumption and wasted cold storage space.

Today, modern practices feature energy-efficient equipment designs, including reciprocating and screw compressors with capacity control, evaporative condensers with MS or SS coils, and ceiling-suspended finned air cooling units with MS or SS coils and aluminum fins. Fans with SS, aluminum, or FRP blades are now used, with FRP offering the advantage of requiring lower horsepower motors.

Refrigeration systems for cold storage can be classified into the following types:

Modular Units: Utilizing HFC/HCFC refrigerants.

Central Plants: Employing HFC/HCFC refrigerants with air-cooled or water-cooled machines.

Central Plants: Using ammonia refrigerants.

Vapour Absorption Systems: Utilizing ammonia-water combinations, which are suitable for rural areas due to the availability of alternative fuels like biogas and agrofuel.

Material Handling

Efficient product flow is crucial for the functioning of cold storage facilities. While manual loading and unloading are still prevalent in conventional cold stores, recent installations are incorporating electrical hoists/lifts and/or forklift trucks for product handling. These modern storage facilities often include rack structures for storing products in pallets or boxes, and arrangements for loading pallets into containers/reefer vans. Some modern cold store units also employ computer systems to control loading, unloading operations, and maintain stock records.

Energy Saving

Refrigeration is essential for cooling, precooling, freezing, and cold storage, making it a fundamental process in the cold chain. While refrigeration ensures quality and extended shelf life, it comes with significant costs, both initially and in terms of energy consumption. Rising energy rates and inadequate energy supply pose challenges for the cold storage sector. Consequently, there is a growing realization among owners and manufacturers of the need to adopt energy-saving methods. The "Green Building" movement has garnered attention globally, with the concept of a "Green Cold Chain" gaining traction, particularly in India.

7. Conclusion

Over the past 50 to 60 years, there have been major advancements in cold storage construction, thermal insulation, refrigeration technology, automation, and material handling. Modern cold stores now offer greater functionality and versatility compared to the past. Energy efficiency and the adoption of sustainable practices are becoming increasingly important for forward-thinking entrepreneurs and designers. Despite India's leadership in milk and fruits & vegetables production, the current cold storage capacity of approximately 25 million MT remains insufficient. There is significant potential for developing modern, energy-efficient storage facilities.

The National Horticultural Board has been instrumental in setting technical standards for cold chain projects, including cold storage for fresh horticultural products, multi-commodity storage, and controlled atmosphere storage. Recently, standards for ripening chambers and refrigerated transport have also been introduced for public review. These efforts represent the first initiative by any government agency in India to establish such standards for cold chain projects. Financial incentives for new projects and expansions are tied to compliance with modern, efficient technologies that meet these technical standards. A scientifically developed cold chain, capable of preserving the vast quantity and high quality of India's food products, has the potential to become a "Gold Chain" for the nation.

The food processing industry plays a vital role in our daily lives, transforming raw agricultural products into the food items we consume. Effective food processing management ensures this transformation happens efficiently, safely, and profitably.

Food processing management encompasses the planning, organizing, directing, and controlling of all activities involved in converting raw materials into edible products. It ensures food safety, quality, cost-effectiveness, and adherence to regulations.

Key Activities: Managers oversee various aspects, including

- Procurement: Selecting and acquiring high-quality raw materials.
- Processing Operations: Managing the various stages of processing, like cleaning, sorting, chopping, cooking, packaging, etc.
- Quality Control: Implementing procedures to ensure food safety and meet quality standards.
- Inventory Management: Maintaining appropriate stock levels of raw materials, packaging materials, and finished goods.
- Production Planning and Scheduling: Optimizing production processes for efficiency and meeting customer demand.
- Waste Management: Minimizing waste generation and implementing sustainable practices.

- Regulatory Compliance: Ensuring adherence to food safety regulations set by national and international bodies.
- Benefits: Effective food processing management offers numerous benefits for businesses and consumers:
- Enhanced Food Safety: Reduces the risk of foodborne illnesses through proper handling and processing techniques.
- Improved Food Quality: Consistent quality standards ensure consumers receive safe, delicious food.
- Increased Efficiency: Streamlined processes lead to cost reduction and higher profitability.
- Reduced Waste: Minimizes environmental impact and optimizes resource utilization.
- Greater Product Variety: Allows for innovation and development of new food products.
- Career Opportunities: The food processing management field offers a diverse range of career paths for qualified individuals. Some examples include:

Production Manager

Quality Control Manager

Food Safety Specialist

Research and Development Manager

Supply Chain Manager

By understanding the principles of food processing management, individuals can contribute to a safe, efficient, and innovative food supply chain that nourishes the world.

2

Indian Food Industry

1. Introduction

The Food Processing Industry serves as a crucial bridge between industry and agriculture, being one of the largest sectors in terms of production, consumption, exports, and growth potential. It involves enhancing the value of agricultural or horticultural produce through processes such as grading, sorting, and packaging to extend the shelf life of food products. Recognizing its importance, the government has accorded it high priority, offering various fiscal incentives and schemes to promote commercialization and value addition to agricultural produce, thereby reducing pre/post-harvest wastage, fostering employment, and boosting exports. The Indian food processing industry is seen as a burgeoning sector with vast untapped potential to enhance the agricultural economy, establish large-scale processed food manufacturing, develop food chain infrastructure, and create employment opportunities while increasing export revenues. The food processing sector provides employment opportunities to about 13 million people directly and about 35million people indirectly. Worldwide processed food sales total is about $2trillion and USA accounts for around 37.5% and other large markets include western Europe and Asia with China growing fastest.

According to recent estimates, the food processing industry holds the fifth position in the country in terms of size, contributing to over 6% of the GDP. It constitutes approximately 13% of the nation's exports, 6% of total industrial investment, and about 12-15% of the manufacturing GDP. The market size of food processing in India is estimated to reach US$ 1274 billion in 2027 from US$ 866 billion in 2022, backed by the rise in population, changing lifestyle and food habits due to rise in disposable income and urbanization. Food and Grocery market in India is the sixth largest in the world. As per a Deloitte study in 2020-21 processing levels in India are 4.55 for fruits, 2.75 for vegetables, 21.1% for milk, 34.2% for Meat and 15.4% for fishery. Food waste is another challenge and around 40% of perishable produce goes to waste. Food processing Industry's contribution to agricultural exports has since grown to 23% with India ranked 7th in the World in agricultural and processed food exports in

2022-23. The Indian food processing sector encompasses a diverse range of products, including fruits and vegetables, meat and poultry, dairy products, alcoholic beverages, fisheries, plantation crops, grain processing, and various consumer goods such as confectionery, chocolates, cocoa products, soy-based items, mineral water, and high-protein foods.

Fruits and Vegetables Processing in India

The Indian food processing industry is currently undergoing a technological revolution driven by changing consumer demands and increased consumption of fruits and vegetables. As an essential component of Indian cuisine, India stands as the world's second-largest producer of fruits and vegetables, often referred to as the "fruit basket of the world". The country boasts a diverse range of tropical fruits such as mangoes, guavas, papayas, and bananas, alongside vegetables like potatoes, green peas, tomatoes, cabbage, and cauliflower. Major fruit-producing states include Maharashtra, Andhra Pradesh, Gujarat, Karnataka, and Uttar Pradesh, while West Bengal, Uttar Pradesh, Bihar, Madhya Pradesh, and Gujarat lead in vegetable production. These states collectively contribute 40-50% to the nation's total fruit and vegetable output.

Despite this abundance, India ranks 111th out of 125 countries in the 2023 Global Hunger Index. A significant factor is the high wastage rate in the fruits and vegetables sector, ranging from 4.6% to 15.9%, primarily due to inadequate cold chain infrastructure and the lack of modern harvesting methods. Consumer preferences are shifting towards processed foods, and supermarket shelves are increasingly stocked with various processed fruits and vegetables. This trend has further propelled advancements in food processing technology, aiming to meet the evolving demands of consumers.

Importance of Fruits and Vegetables Processing in India

The primary objective of processing perishable commodities is to ensure a year-round supply for consumers while maintaining their nutritional value. Additionally, food processing aims to prevent microbial spoilage, extend shelf life, and provide wholesome, palatable food throughout the year. A significant benefit of increased food processing is the reduction of wastage in the food industry. Instead of discarding surplus fruits and vegetables, farmers can send the excess to food processing units. These units transform raw produce into pulps, juices, jams, pickles, squashes, dehydrated vegetables, canned foods, and more. This process not only extends the shelf life of these products but also ensures a continuous supply throughout the year.

Moreover, the production of processed foods enables producers to export these items to various countries, thereby boosting the Indian economy. By addressing both wastage and supply issues, the food processing industry plays a crucial role in enhancing the availability and economic value of fruits and vegetables in India.

Tropical Fruits

Traditional and Modern Methods of Processing Fruits and Vegetables

The practice of food processing has existed for decades, though it has evolved over time. Historically, food preservation was achieved by adding sugar syrup or salt. Common household preservation techniques included pickling, freezing, fermenting, sugaring, canning, and drying. These traditional methods effectively extended the shelf life of fruits and vegetables, albeit for limited periods, and also enhanced the bioavailability of micronutrients in plant-based diets. Modern food processing methods differ significantly from traditional ones. Traditional processing typically involved categorizing food into primary and secondary products. In contrast, modern techniques encompass advanced processes such as canning, pasteurization, sterilization, aseptic filling, freezing, and irradiation.

Today's processed fruits and vegetables undergo various sophisticated procedures, including thermal processing, aseptic processing, chemical preservation, irradiation, and advanced packaging and storage techniques. These methods significantly enhance the shelf life and safety of food products while meeting contemporary consumer demands.

Current Scenario of the Fruits and Vegetables Processing Industry

The food processing sector in India has emerged as a "Sunrise Sector" over the past few decades, owing to its technological advancements and significant contributions to the Indian economy. According to the National Horticulture Database (1st Advance Estimates) published by the National Horticulture Board for 2023-24, India currently produces 11.21 million metric tons of fruits and 209.39 million metric tons of vegetables.

India's food processing sector is one of the fastest-growing industries, with exports estimated at USD 2,248.96 million (INR 18,090.80 crores) for the fiscal year 2022-2023. This includes processed vegetables, such as pulses, valued at USD 1,511.14 million (INR 12,146.32 crores), and processed fruits and juices, reaching a value of USD 737.81 million (INR 5,944.49 crores).

Upcoming Technological Trends in the Fruits & Vegetables Processing Industry

Fruits and vegetables are rich in nutrients, offering significant health benefits. India's diverse agro-climatic conditions ensure a steady supply of fresh and seasonal produce. To maintain this supply year-round, the food processing industry is embracing new technological advancements. These innovations have moved beyond traditional methods of processing and preserving fruits and vegetables, enhancing their nutritional value and making consumption more efficient.

One of the latest technological upgrades in the industry is the Aseptic Processing and Packaging System, which is part of a broader trend of advancements in the processing and packaging of fruits and vegetables. These improvements are crucial for maintaining the quality and availability of these essential food items.

Aseptic Processing and Packaging System

Aseptic processing and packaging involve storing a sterile product in a pre-sterilized container within a sterile environment. This method, conducted in a continuous and closed system, produces products with superior quality and high nutritional retention. It is particularly used for processing and storing pulps, purees, and concentrates derived from fruits like mango, tomato, guava, papaya, and apple.

This system is gaining popularity due to its ability to extend the shelf life of fruits and vegetables, prevent contamination, and maintain hygiene compared to traditional canning methods. The advantages of aseptic processing and packaging include:

- **Extended Freshness and Shelf Life**: Products can remain fresh for up to 24 months without requiring refrigeration.
- **No Added Preservatives**: This method maintains optimal flavor, texture, and nutrient retention.
- **Cost and Energy Efficiency**: It eliminates the need for refrigeration, reducing costs, logistics, and energy associated with the cold chain.

Overall, the aseptic system is an effective and efficient method for processing and packaging fruits and vegetables, offering significant benefits over traditional canning.

Sterilization and Filling of Processed Fruits and Vegetables

Once fruits and vegetables are processed into pulps, purees, and concentrates, they are packed in aseptically sterilized containers. These packaging materials undergo a series of sterilization steps, including heating with dry or moist heat, chemical sterilization, and gamma radiation.

Aseptic fillers, which can be single-head or double-head depending on the sterilizer's capacity, are used for this process. Single and double-head aseptic bag-in-box fillers accommodate bags of 3 kg, 5 kg, 10 kg, and 20 kg. Additionally, bulk aseptic bags of 220 kg and 1,000 kg are pre-sterilized with gamma rays and used to fill products in a sterile environment.

Other Technologies

New technologies in fruit and vegetable processing include High-Pressure Processing (HPP), Pulsed Electric Field Processing (PEFP), and Microwave Thermal Assisted Sterilization (MTAS). These advancements further enhance the quality, safety, and shelf life of processed fruits and vegetables.

Fruit and Vegetable Processing Lines

Fruit processing involves converting fruits into products like jams, juices, jellies, and pulp. The fruit processing line includes four main variants: candy, jam, jelly, and marmalade. Similarly, the vegetable processing line features four variants: tomato, potato, leafy vegetables, and fresh-cut salads.

Fruit processing lines allow for the easy conversion of fruits into a variety of products, such as purees, nectars, cloudy and clear juices, diced fruits, essential oils, dehydrated and sugar-coated candies, and whole fruit jams. Vegetable processing lines are equally versatile. For instance, tomatoes can be processed into juice, paste, ketchup, and sauce, as well as diced and peeled forms. Leafy vegetables can be processed into portions without losing their nutritional components, ensuring the retention of their health benefits.

Converting a Single Fruit Plant to a Multi-Fruit Plant

In India, fruit and vegetable processing plants typically handle capacities ranging from 1,000 kg per hour to 20,000 kg per hour, with global figures reaching up to 60,000 kg per hour for a single line. By converting to a multi-fruit processing line, production and profitability can significantly increase.

A single processing line can only handle one type of seasonal fruit, rendering the line dormant once the season ends. However, a multi-processing line can process various suitable seasonal fruits, such as a mango line that can also handle guava, papaya, tomato, sapota, and other fruits. This adaptability allows the unit to operate year-round, enhancing productivity and profitability.

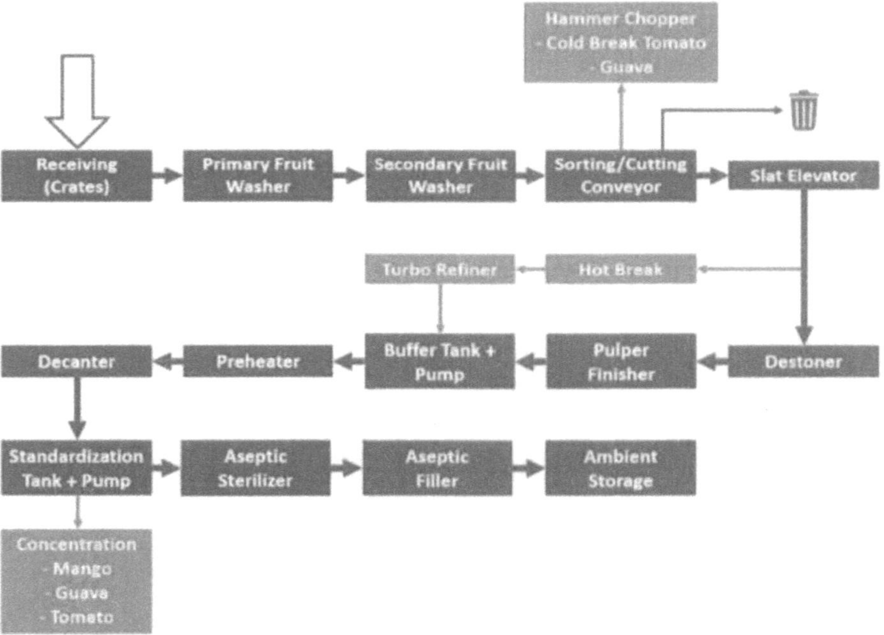

Multi Fruit Processing Line

India currently contributes 1% to the processed food industry, a figure expected to rise due to rapid technological advancements. These advancements promise increased production and supply of processed food while maintaining quality, nutritional properties, aroma, and shelf life.

Government Schemes Supporting the F & V Processing Sector

Fruits and vegetables play a crucial role in India's food processing industry and economy. Recognizing their importance, the Government of India, in collaboration with the Ministry of Food Processing Industries (MoFPI), has launched several schemes and subsidies to promote the production and export of processed fruits and vegetables.

Key components driving growth in the Indian Food Processing Technology Sector include:

- 100% Foreign Direct Investment (FDI) approval under the automatic route, enhancing investor confidence.
- Concessional customs duty rates on imported equipment for project imports.
- 150% income tax deduction on capital expenditure for setting up and operating cold chains or warehouses.
- 100% income tax exemption for new food processing, preservation, and packaging units for the first 5 years, and 25%-30% thereafter.
- Creation of a ₹20 billion fund with the National Bank for Agriculture and Rural Development (NABARD) to provide affordable credit to designated Food Parks and units.
- Priority Sector Lending (PSL) by banks covering loans to food and agro-based processing units and cold chains.
- Establishment of Mega Food Parks and Cold Chain Processing units to bolster infrastructure, with 24 Mega Food Parks operational to date.
- Facilitation of 100% FDI through approved routes for e-commerce trading of Indian-manufactured food products.

Government Initiatives for Farmers

Government initiatives such as Pradhan Mantri Kisan Sampada Yojana (PMKSY), Pradhan Mantri Formalization of Micro Food Processing Enterprises (PMFME) Scheme, and Production Linked Incentive Scheme for Food Processing (PLISFPI) support agricultural and food processing sectors.

Export and Economic Impact

In fiscal year 2022-23, India exported USD 1635.95 million (INR 13,185.30 crores) worth of fresh fruits and vegetables, according to APEDA. This export potential enhances India's economic growth and stimulates demand for advanced technology in the fruits and vegetables sector.

Conclusion

India's robust position as a major producer and exporter of processed and value-added food products, coupled with its conducive regulatory environment and expanding market, makes it an attractive destination for food processing technology investments. Innovations in technology and infrastructure, particularly in cold chain development, are crucial for reducing wastage and enhancing the shelf life of perishable food items, thus fostering a vibrant entrepreneurial ecosystem in the food processing industry.

Challenges faced by Food Processing Industry:

- Gaps in supply chain infrastructure (i.e. lack of primary processing, storage and distribution facilities.
- Inadequate link between production and processing
- Seasonality of operations and low capacity utilization
- Institutional gaps in supply chain viz., dependence on APMC markets etc.
- Inadequate focus on quality and safety standards
- Lack of product development and innovation

Accordingly, the focus should be to smoothen the supplychain by creating infrastructure, promoting exports, improving quality standards, expanding supply of formal credit, particularly to small and medium enterprises and broading skilled labor pool in the economy.

Enablers

Transportation of produce which can be more time efficient due to minimal disruptions. Build a better network of cold chain facilities and a national food grid consisting of cold chains and food parks for seamless transfer of minimal wastage from production to consumption. Indian Government has embarked on an ambitious 60 billion rupee project called Sampada ,a national scheme to develop an integrated supply cold chain for agricultural products. The food processing sector was opened to 100% FDI in 2016 under the automatic route.Further in 2017, 100% FDI under the Government route for retail trading, including through e-commerce is permitted in respect of food products manufactured and/or produced in India. Technology is a key enabler DHL Smar Trucking taps on data analytics to help its drivers determine the fastest route to reach its transport destination. With technology driven logistics equipped to make more informed decisions with higher levels of safety and regulatory compliance, faster transit times and real time visibility into the status of consignments.

Food Processing Segments

In India, the level of processing is the highest in the Dairy sector (35%) i.e. 13% in the organized and 22% in the unorganized sector, followed by meat processing sector (21%), Marine Fisheries (10.7%) and Poultry (6%) and fruits & Vegetables (2.2%). The Ministry of Food Processing, Government of India, has classified the Food Processing Industry into the following categories:

- Processing of Fruits & Vegetables
- Processing of Meat
- Processing of Dairy Products
- Fisheries Sector
- Grain Processing Sector
- Consumer Food Industries

Major Players

- AMUL
- Agro Tech foods
- Britania Industries ltd.
- Cadbury India Ltd.
- Conagra Foods
- Dabur India Ltd.
- Gits Food Products Pvt. Ltd.
- Godrej Industries Limited
- Hindustan lever Limited
- ITC limited
- Milkfood
- MTR Foods Limited
- Nestle India Pvt. Ltd.
- Nissin Foods
- Parle Products Pvt. Ltd.
- Perfetti India Ltd.
- Pepsico India holdings
- Unilever
- Venky's
- Walmart

Segmentation of Indian Food Processing Sector in 2020-21

The food processing industry in india is still in its early stages, contributing less than 10% to the total food output. According to a Deloitte study on level of food proessing in India,processing levels are as given below:

Vegetables	-2.7%
Fruits	-4.5%
Fishery	-15.4%
Milk	-21.1%
Meat	-34.2%

The key sub-segments of the food processing industry in India are fruits, vegetables, Poultry & meat processing, Fisheries, food retail and dairy industry etc. Four major segments of the food industry are production, processing, distribution and marketing.

Inspite of having comparative advantage in terms of raw material/agro production, and growing demand for processed food, the level of food processing is not significant as compared to other countries like USA (65%), Philippines (78%) and China (23%) mainly due to lack of pre & post harvest infrastructure facilities, weak supply chain involving large number of intermediaries, significant post harvest losses, poor logistics and high cost of raw material.

2. Food Processing Structure and Policy

In the Indian food processing industry, unorganized players (42%) and small-scale players (33%) dominate over organized players (25%). This sector comprises approximately 516 flour mills, 568 fish processing units, 5293 fruits & vegetable processing units, 171 meat processing units, and numerous dairy processing units at state and district levels. According to data from the Food Safety and Standards Authority of India under the Ministry of Health and Family Welfare, the installed capacity of fruits & vegetables processing units (FPO licensed units) increased from 26.38 lakh tonnes as of January 1, 2008, to 30.89 lakh tonnes as of January 1, 2009. FPO, regulator of fruit and vegetable sector and hence the mark is necessary to start a fruit processing unit/industry in India. Hence all food processors must have FPO license issued by the Ministry of Food Processing Industry to carry out their operations and abide by the guidelines to continue food business.

Among the total processed fruits & vegetables, the breakdown is as follows: pulp and juice (27%), jams and jellies (10%), pickles (12%), ready-to-serve beverages (13%), syrups (8%), squashes (4%), tomato products (4%), canned vegetables (4%), and other products (18%). The fruits and vegetable processing industry in India is highly decentralized, with many units operating at the cottage/home scale and small-scale sector, with capacities of up to 250 tonnes per annum. However, large Indian and multinational companies have capacities ranging up to 30 tonnes per hour. Key processed items include fruit pulps and juices, fruit-based ready-to-serve beverages, canned fruits and vegetables, jams, squashes, pickles, chutneys, and dehydrated vegetables. Additionally, the industry has expanded into manufacturing products such as frozen pulps and vegetables, freeze-dried fruits and vegetables, fruit juice concentrates, vegetable curries in resealable pouches, canned mushrooms, and mushroom products.

Structure of Indian Food Processing Industry

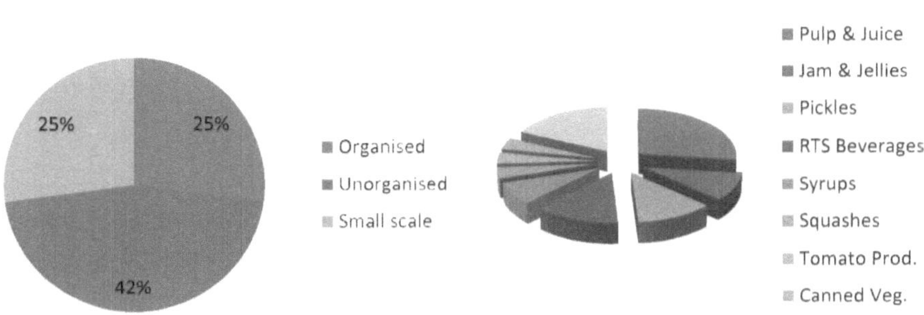

Key Growth Drivers

Growing awareness and demand for health and nutrition-oriented foods.

- Increase in the number of nuclear families and the working population.
- Rising disposable income and evolving lifestyles.
- Emergence of functional foods, both fresh and processed.
- Expansion of organized retail and penetration of private label products.
- Shifting demographics and emphasis on branding.

The primary states in India where food processing thrives include Andhra Pradesh (contributing to 13.4% of India's food processing industry, specializing in fruits, vegetables, and grains), Gujarat (12.7%, known for edible oils and dairy), Maharashtra (14%, focusing on fruit, vegetables, grains, and beverages), and Uttar Pradesh (12%, encompassing various product categories).

Statewise Share of Food Processing Industries

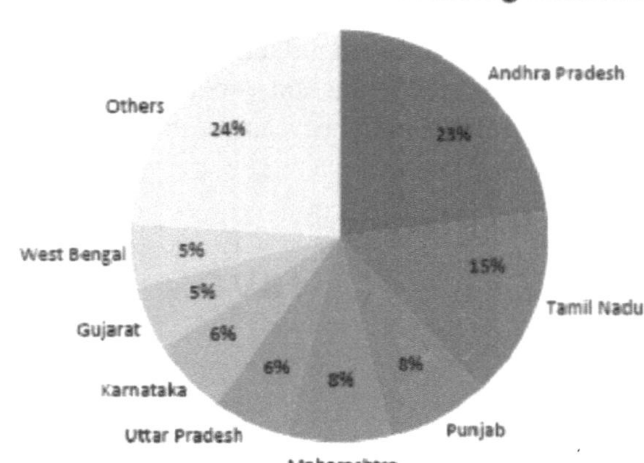

Source: fruits and vegetables Maps of India 2021

In recent years, there has been notable growth in the ready-to-serve beverages sector. However, domestic consumption of value-added fruits and vegetables has remained comparatively low in comparison to primary processed foods and fresh produce. This discrepancy is largely attributed to several factors, including high taxes and duties, particularly on packaging materials, underutilized production capacity, limited adoption of cost-effective technologies, high financing costs, infrastructural limitations, and insufficient linkages between farmers and processors, resulting in dependence on intermediaries.

Since 1991, India's food processing industry has attracted approximately US$1 billion in Foreign Direct Investment (FDI). The food processing sector allows 100% FDI under the automatic route and has recorded a cumulative FDI equity inflow of US$ 12.59 billion between April 2000-March 2024 constituting around 1.855 of the total FDI equity inflow in all sectors placing it in top 15 sectors.

As outlined in the national policy on food processing, the objective is to enhance the level of food processing from 10% in 2010 to 25% by 2025. Key source countries for FDI in India's food processing sector include Switzerland, USA, Germany, and Mauritius.

The food processing industry encompasses a wide range of activities including the processing,preservation,packaging and distribution of food products.The Indian food processing sector contributes to almost 65 of GDP,13% of Indian exports and 6% of overall industrial investment in the country.The parliament of India enacted the National Food Security Act in 2013 to provide subsidized food grains to around two thirds of India's population. The food industry in

India is yet to fully develop looking at the potential food processing industry can grow greater than 20% per year.

Processed Food Exports percentage in Agrifood Export;

2019-20	19.1
2020-21	22.1
2021-22	22.6
2022-23	25.6

During the period 2022-23 india's agricultural exports reached USD 53.1billion with APEDA contributing a significant 51% of India's agri-exports.India is a major player in the global agricultural market and maintained its position as world's eighth largest exporter of agriculture products in a year for its diverse range of fresh exports.The top 7 agricultural products exported from India include Non-Basmati Rice,Basmati Rice,Spices,Tea,Pulses,fruits , Vegetables and sugar.

Despite the global significance of the retail sector contributing around US$7 trillion, with over 72% of food sales occurring through supermarkets or retail stores, India's retail sector is undergoing a transformative phase. One of the main challenges hindering the competitiveness of the Indian food processing industry is the cost and quality of marketing channels. However, India presents a vast untapped opportunity in retail and is poised for a significant retail revolution.

Branding Potential in Packaged Foods

Food Item	Mkt Size in 2010	Million $ 2030	%age growth 2010	Per annum 2030	Branded prod. %age of TOT
Milk	7767	32900	08	31	73
Cheese	144	1958	14	NA	NA
Butter	254	1340	09	06	19
Veg. & edible Oil	3931	10331	04	32	59
Sweet & Savoury snacks	1286	16399	13	42	66
Atta	574	8158	13	04	44
Processed poultry	398	8340	17	06	49
Fruits & Beverages	720	12204	15	NA	NA
Biscuits	2753	13145	08	NA	NA

The recent CII-McKinsey report titled "India as an Agriculture and High-Value Food Powerhouse by 2030" highlights the significant potential of the packaged food segment, projecting a 9% annual growth rate. By 2030, this segment is expected to evolve into a Rs 6 lakh crore industry, with dominant categories including milk, sweet and savory snacks, processed poultry, among others. The report underscores the importance of branding, suggesting that emphasizing branding efforts could potentially increase packaged food revenues by up to 30%, thereby propelling growth in the country's processed food sector.According to the CII-McKinsey report, the packaged milk category is forecasted to experience substantial growth, surging from $7.76 billion to $32.9 billion by 2030, at an annual growth rate of 8%. By 2030, it is anticipated that about 73% of the milk sold will be branded, a significant increase from the current 31% market share.

Sweets and savory snacks will be second largest category at an estimated $16.39billion by 2030 from $1.28 billion in 2010, clocking a 13%growth annually. Processed poultry products will clock the fastest growth of 17% per a year to $8.34 billion by 2030 against $398 million in 2010. Similarly, biscuits will be around 8% growth to touch $13.14 billion in 2030 followed by fruit beverages at $ 12.20 billion and vegetable and edible oils at $10.33 billion. Packaged atta (wheat flour) is expected to grow 13% to $8.15billion from $574 million in 2010.

Food Processing –Policy environment

Food Vision Report 2030: Vision for food system transformation in India

It incorporates multiple perspectives from many stakeholders and linkages amongst various areas. Technological developments has changed the food industry forever to make food available.

The mission is to establish value addition with infrastructural facilities like sorting, grading, packaging and processing horticulture including organic produce, marine, dairy, poultry etc.the objective is to improve food safety, improve nutritional value extend the shelflife by eliminating micro-organisms of food products, preventing contamination of food, facilitating food storage and transportation. in 2025 india's food processing market is expected to grow at a compound annual growth rate of 15.2%.The future of India's Indian food processing industry seems to be promising with technological advancement,rising demand for convenience foods and increasing focus on sustainable and healthier food products. The national vision 2030 reflects a common focus on fostering national unity, stability and progress.

The Objectives are:
1. Infrastructure Development
2. National Mission on Food Processing

   i) Enhancing Technology in Food Processing Industries:

   ii) Cold Chain Infrastructure, Value Addition, and Preservation Facilities for Non-Horticultural Products:

   iii) Developing Human Resources:

   iv) Promotional Activities Scheme:

3. Establishing or Upgrading Quality Control, Food Testing Laboratories, Research and Development, and Promotional Initiatives:

4. Strengthening of Institutions

3. Conclusion

The Indian food processing industry has experienced significant growth and transformation in recent years, fueled by factors such as abundant raw material availability, rising disposable incomes, evolving market trends, changing consumer preferences, and regulatory shifts. These ongoing trends, including shifting demographics, population growth, and rapid urbanization, are expected to continue in the future, thereby driving demand for value-added products and bolstering the food processing industry in India. The Government of India's prioritization of the food processing industry is anticipated to result in supportive policies aimed at fostering investment in this sector and attracting more Foreign Direct Investment (FDI).

India possesses vast natural resources, a growing technical knowledge base, and a substantial research and development infrastructure, providing it with significant comparative advantages over other nations in the food processing industry. Consequently, the food processing sector in India presents an appealing investment opportunity, offering promising growth prospects and potential for investors.

Indian Agriculture Strength in 2024

Items	Rank	Share
Tea	II	18.0%
Milk	I	25.0%
Cattle Pop.	I	35.94%
Sugar Cane	II	22.0 %
Fruits	II	10.0%
Vegetables	II	10.6%
Paddy	II	26.0%
Wheat	II	12.5%

FPI Units in MSME Sector

Sl	Principal Characteristics	Unit	Regd. Units	Un-Regd. Units
1	Working Enterprises	Lakh	2.23	22.89
2	Employment	Lakh	14.68	48.31
3	Orgi. Value of Plant & Mach	Rs Crore	13261	14431
4	Market Value of Fixed Assets	Rs Crore	60196	31106
5	Gross Output	Rs Crore	137287	51561
6	Gross Input	Rs Crore	94628	30264
7	Gross Value Added	Rs Crore	42659	21297

Global Organic Food Market, By Value in USD Billion, 2008-17

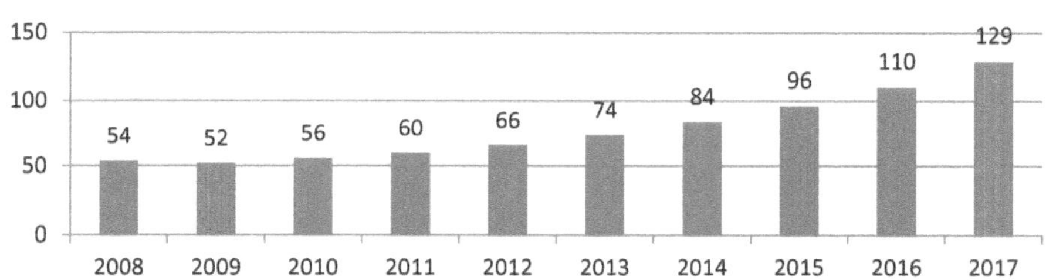

International Grain Price in USD/Ton

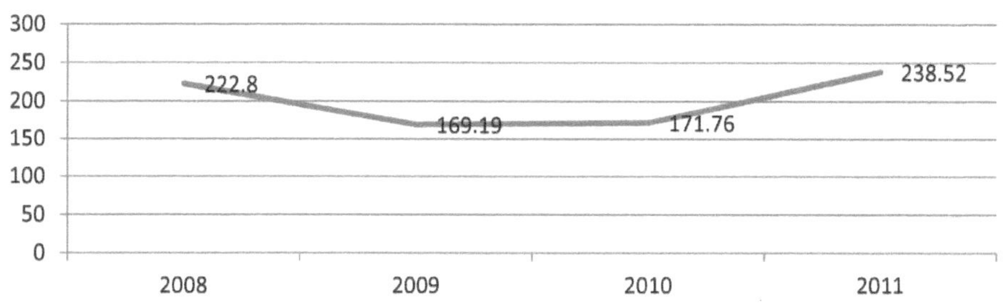

Source: FAO

List of Major Food Grain Processing Companies

Company Name	Sale Turnover in INR Lakh (Apr11-Mar12)	Food Grain Share in Total Turnover
LT Food Ltd	14217644 (2011-12)	Rice (94%)
REI Agro Ltd	422548 (2011-12)	Rice (88%)
KRBL Ltd	164042 (2011-12)	Rice (94%)
Usher Agro Ltd	56255 (2010-11)	Rice (80%) Wheat (16%)

Food and food products constitutes the largest portion of the Indian consumer's spending-about 39% share of wallet in urban India and 52% in rural India. A population of close to 1.2 billion growing by about 1.5% annually is expected to keep the food Industry on the fast growth, rising income levels, rapid urbanization and increasing working population is expected to fuel this growth going forward. The share of expenditure on food in rural has fallen from 52.9% in 2011-12 to 46.38% in 2022-23,while the share of expenditure on food in Urban India has fallen from 42.62 in 2011-12 to 39.17% in 2022-23.The size of the Indian food market is estimated to be more than USD 190 billion and is expected to grow to USD 300 billion by 2015.More importantly; this growth is bound to be accompanied by dramatic changes in the food plate composition of the nation.

Trends in monthly per-capita expenditure on food in India

Average estimated MPCE in 2022-23

Rural India-Rs 3773 and 46% of rural HH expenditure on food items

Urban india-Rs 6459 and 395 of urban HH expenditure on food items

I. Food consumption Trends in India

Food consumption information collected and analysed about the quantity,types and patterns of food consumed by individuals. It includes food intake, dietry preferences, nutritional content, portion sizes, meal frequencies and eating habits etc.

Nationwide food consumption survey is carried out to measure the food and nutrient content of diet and money value of food consumed.In rural India, food expenditure dropped from 53% to 46% whereas in urban India ,it dreased from 43% to 39%. On svery Rs 100 that a rural HH spends Rs 46 is spent on food which has fallen from Rs 59.40 in 1999-2000 to 53.11 in 2004-05, grew again to 56.98 in 2009-10, fell to Rs 52.90 in 2011-12 and further to Rs 46.38 in 2022-23. Food Consumption score (FCS) is a composite score based on dietary diversity, food frequency and the relative nutritional importance of different food groups. Healthy eating index (HEI) uses food index scores range from 0 to 100.

NSSO consumption expenditure survey indicates a substantial increase in consumption expenditure over the past decade. Rural monthly consumption per person increased by 164% from 2011-12 to 2022-23, while urban monthly consumption per person grew by 146%.

Per capita monthly Household consumption expenditure more than doubled during 2011-12 to 2-22-23.

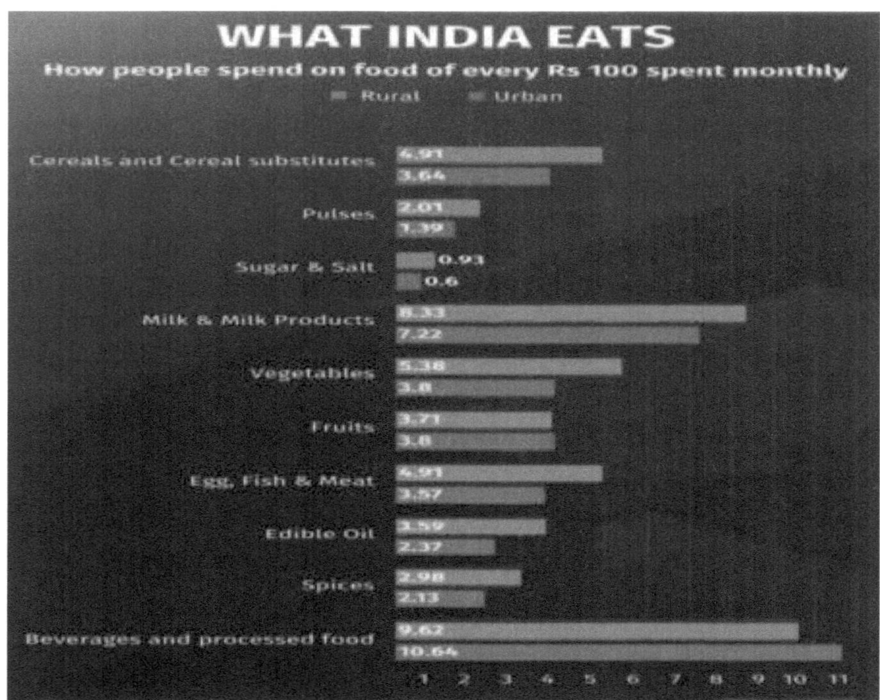

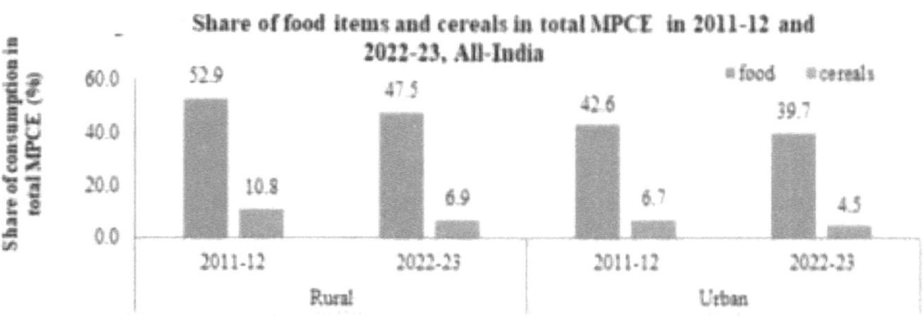

Sector	Average MPCE (Rs.) over different period				
	1999-'00 NSS (55th round)	2004-05 NSS (61st round)	2009-10 NSS (66th round)	2011-12 NSS (68th round)	2022-23
Rural	486	579	1,054	1,430	3,773
Urban	855	1,105	1,984	2,630	6,459
Difference as % of Rural MPCE	75.9	90.8	88.2	83.9	71.2

WHAT URBAN INDIA EATS

Composition of food consumption expenditure (%)

	1999-00	2004-05	2011-12	2022-23
Cereals	25.78	23.77	15.63	9.29
Pulses	6.14	5.28	4.79	3.55
Milk	18.06	18.61	16.45	18.43
Vegetables	10.67	10.47	10.86	9.7
Fruits	5.04	5.28	8.02	9.73
Egg, fish, meat	6.51	6.37	8.56	9.11
Edible oil	6.53	8.12	6.24	6.05
Spices	4.31	3.63	5.68	5.44
Sugar & salt	3.75	3.88	2.7	1.53
Beverages, etc*	13.21	14.59	21.07	27.16

Food spending

Share of cereals and food in average monthly per capita consumption expenditure decreased in both rural and urban areas

Period	RURAL		URBAN	
	% share of cereals	% share of food	% share of cereals	% share of food
1999-00	22.23	59.4	12.39	48.06
2004-05	17.45	53.11	9.63	40.51
2009-10	13.77	56.98	8.16	44.39
2011-12	10.75	52.9	6.66	42.62
2022-23	4.91	46.38	3.64	39.17

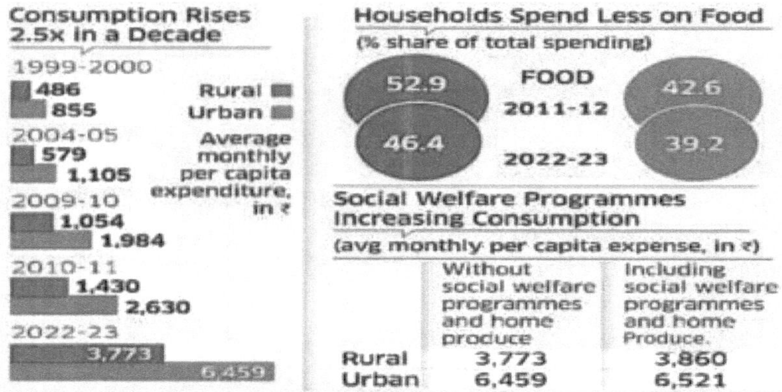

	Without social welfare programmes and home produce	Including social welfare programmes and home Produce.
Rural	3,773	3,860
Urban	6,459	6,521

II. Supply Strengths Auger Food Production

In addition to the strong demand trends for high value food products, the country has inherent supply strengths for key agricultural commodities. Diverse agro-climatic zones, varying soil types and a vast irrigated area have contributed towards making India one of the largest producers of food commodities in the world. India is presently among the largest producers of milk, meat, foodgrains, fruits and vegetables and several other food products in the world.

III. Outlook Positive for Processed Food

Consistent growth in demand for high value food products combined with strongly complementing supply strengths has helped in the creation of a positive outlook for the processed food segment. These coupled with forward looking government sponsored schemes and initiatives aimed to draw private sector participation have created the much needed vibrancy in the food processing sector. In this knowledge report, the current scenario of the Indian processed food industry is highlighted and opportunities & challenges are reviewed that unfold in this fast growing sector. The key action steps are identified that need to be taken to unleash the true potential of the processed food industry.

2. The Indian Processed Food Industry: A Snapshot

India is the second largest producer of food in the world. While food production is significant, the food processing industry is still nascent-which is reflected in the fact that the processing levels for perishable produce such as milk and fruits & vegetables are extremely low. Despite low processing levels, Indian food processing sector is important to the national economy due to its high employment generation propensity especially in the rural areas of the country. For instance, the direct employment generation in the food processing sector was estimated to be about 14 million while indirect employment was estimated at 30million in 2005-06. It is estimated that a one percent growth in this sector has the potential to generate an additional direct employment for 5 lakh people while generating indirect employment for 15lakh individuals. Recognising the important of the food processing sector the government has accorded the industry a high priority status and has taken up a number of initiatives to boost the sector. This coupled with increased private participation, FDI, increasing domestic demand for high value food products and improved governmental focus on rural infrastructure development has taken food processing industry into a fast growth trajectory.

a) Industry Size

Industry estimates suggest that the current value of the food processing sector stands at approximately USD 70 billion, contributing over 35% to the total food market. With a notable growth rate of around 14% in recent times, this sector is anticipated to maintain its momentum in the foreseeable future. The food processing vision 2030 of ICAR articulates the strategies to overcome the challenges and tap the opportunities by harnessing the power of science and undertaking partnership with different stakeholders in food supply chain at the national and international level.

b) Industry Structure

Food Processing covers a large spectrum of products from a large number of sub-sectors comprising agriculture, horticulture, plantation, animal husbandry and fisheries. Some key sectors include fruits and vegetable products, milk and milk products, beverages (both alcoholic & non-alcoholic), poultry and meat products, marine and aqua products, edible oil and grain and cereal products. Most of these sectors have shown a strong growth rates in the recent past. For instance, poultry has grown at a CAGR of 10 to 15% in the recent past while the processed fruits and vegetables category is growing at about 11%.

Processing levels across key perishable segments

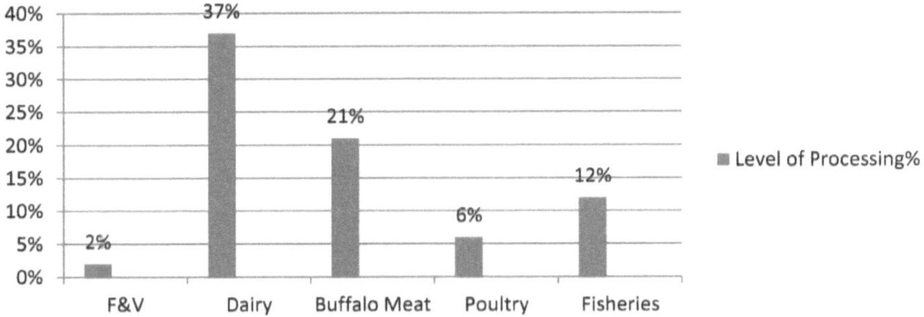

Source: MOFPI annual reports

Though the industry is growing rapidly it is still nascent and in its early stages of life cycle. This is reflected in the fact that the processing levels and value addition across key perishable segments are extremely low. For instance, in the case of fruits and vegetables just about 2.2% of the production is processed compared to 30% in Thailand and close to 80% in Phillipines and Malaysia. Likewise the level of processing in the Dairy sector is about 37% compared to above 60 to 70% in developed countries. Given that the post harvest wastage levels are to the tune of 25to30% in perishable food products, processing provides the right avenue to reduce these losses and create greater value to farmers.

Contribution of organized sector to levels of processing:

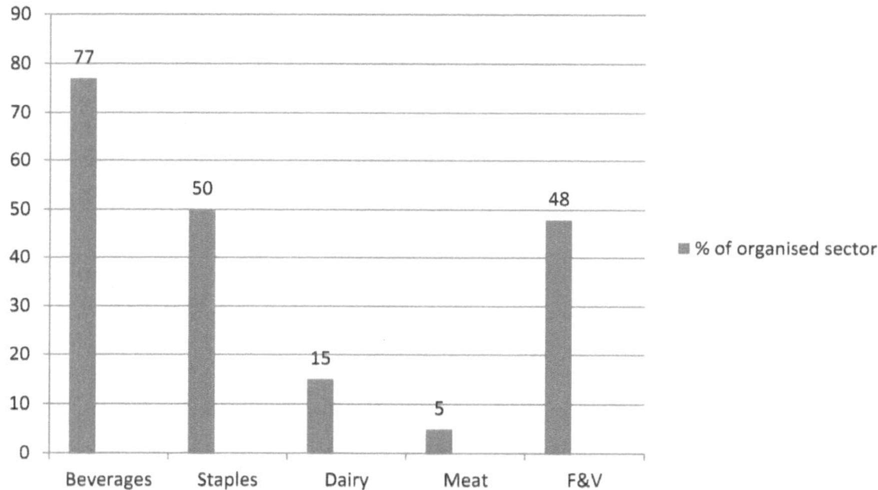

While the penetration of organized players into food processing segment is high in certain segments such as beverages and high value staples,the industry continues to be dominated by small and unorganized players. However, the industry has been witnessing keen interest for investment by reputed global as well as domestic players such as ITC, Pepsi, Coke, Dabur and Godrej among others.

c) Key Segments of the Industry - An Overview

MOFPI has classified the food processing industry into six segments as depicted. An overview of these segments and their sub-segments is discussed herewith.

Segments of the food processing industry

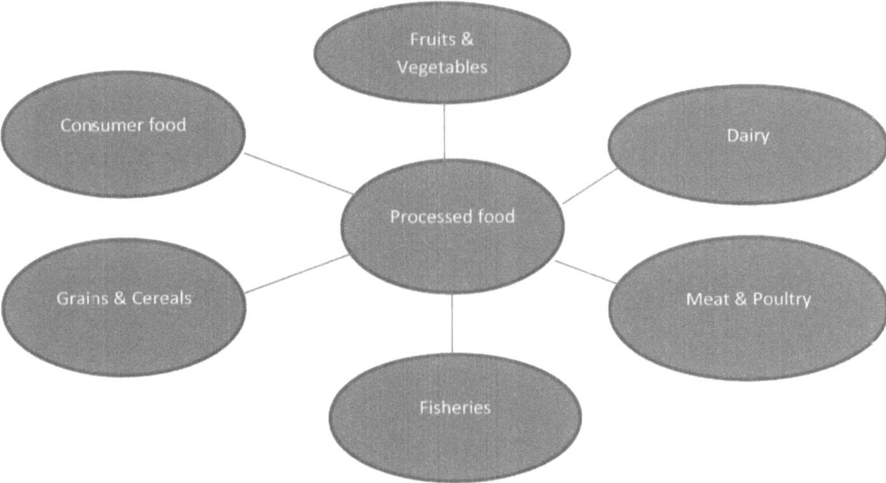

Source: MOFPI

I. Fruits & Vegetables: Fruits and vegetables overwhelmingly dominate the Indian horticulture sector, covering approximately 65% of the total area under horticultural crops and contributing over 90% to the total horticultural production. As per National Horticulture Board during 2023-24, India produced 112.62 million metric tonnes of fruits and 204.96 million metric tonnes of vegetables.India is 2nd largest producer of fruits and vegetables in World of 256 Million Metric ton in 2022.

State	Number of Registered Units	Output (USD Bn)
Maharashtra	182	0.3
West Bengal	30	0.2
Uttarakhand	32	0.2
Andhra Pradesh	143	0.2
Gujarat	85	0.1

Source: Annual Survey of Industries

Indicative Processing Opportunities

Commodity	Major producing states	Processing Opportunity
Green Peas	UP/Uttarakhand, M.P, Jharkhand, H.P, Punjab	Frozen (IQF), canning, pulp, puree, paste, sauces, snacks, dressings, flakes, dices, dehydration, pickles, juices, slices, chips, jams, jelly, RTS drinks
Tomato	M.P. A.P, Karnataka, Odisha, Gujarat	
Potato	U.P, West Bengal, M.P Bihar, Gujarat	
Onion (white onion)	Maharashtra, Karnataka, M.P, Gujarat	
Mango	A P, U.P, Karnataka, Bihar, Gujarat, Telangana	
Pineapples	Kerela, West Bengal, Assam, Karnataka, Tripura, Bihar	
Grapes	Maharashtra, Karnataka, Tamil Nadu, A P, Telangana, Mizoram	
Banana	A.P, Karnataka, Gujarat, Tamil Nadu, Maharashtra	
Citrus fruits	A P, Telangana, Maharashtra, M P, Punjab	
Pomegranate	Maharashtra, Karnataka, Gujarat, A P, Telangana	

Source: MOFPI

National Horticulture Board

Despite being the second-largest producer of fruits and vegetables globally, India processes just over 2% of its annual production—a stark contrast to countries like Malaysia, where the processing rate stands at approximately 83%.

Level of F&V Processing in India vis-à-vis other countries

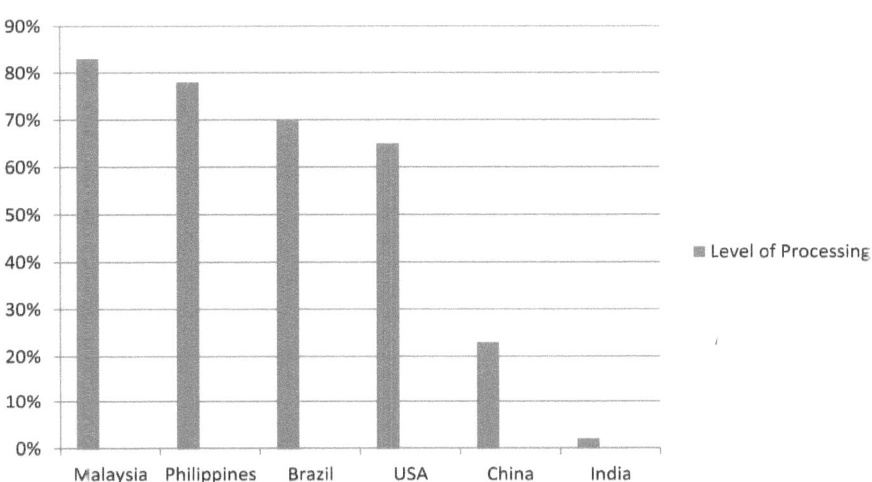

Planning Commission, MOFPI

Though the organized sector contributes substantially towards processing of fruits and vegetables, most of the processing units are managed by small and medium enterprises. While more than 5000 industries are registered under the Fruit Products Order (FPO), 1955, industry estimates indicate that the share of organized sector in processing is about 48% with 85% of the units in small and medium sector. Individual capacities of most of the processing units range from 250 MT/annum for very small scale industries to 30MT/hour for bigger manufacturers. However, MOFPI is bullish about the growth of this segment and has projected that F&V with a production of 112.62 million MT of fruits and 204.96 million MT of vegetables as per NHB during 2023-24.

Prominent categories of processed fruits and vegetables

Category	Sub-Category
Non-Alcoholic beverages	Juices, Nectars & Drinks
Alcoholic beverages	Wine from grapes, Apple & other fruits
Concentrates	Fruit concentrate, pulps, bars, paste
Jams, Jellies& Marmalade	
Pickles & Chutneys	
Canned & Frozen fruits& Vegetables	
Ketchups & Sauces	
Dried & Dehydrated fruits and vegetables	
Ready to eat	Chips & Wafers

Processed fruits and vegetables contribute to about 49% of the total export of fruits and vegetable category. Export of processed fruits and vegetables including pulses were valued at $ 1,72 billion during 2021-22 with $ 1.1 billion from processed vegetables and $ 610.69 million from processed fruits clearly indicating the potential that this segment holds for global trade.From april to December 2022 processed fruits and vegetables export grew by 30.36% compared to the same period in 2021. The top five fruits exported in processed form were mango, tamarind, pineapple, citrus and guava while the top five vegetables exported in processed form were cucumber, dehydrated onion flake/powder, dried beans, frozen potatoes and tapioca starch and substitutes. Top seven Indian fruits with high global demand are Pomegranates, Mangos, Apples, Oranges, Watermelon, Bananas, Grapes etc.

Key constraints for growth are

- High inefficiency in procurement: Fragmented supply base , lack of information regarding crop availability, extremely high intermediation in supplychain, difficulty in controlling quality and high seasonality are critical factors that have been hindering the efficiency of procurement.

- Demand lacking critical mass: due to high price difference between fresh and processed products.

- Fragmented industry resulting in poor economy in scale.

- Inadequate adherence to quality standards for raw materials and limited adoption of traceability and certification impede exports.

- The absence of an integrated regulatory framework: Various laws fall under the purview of different ministries and departments, resulting in a multitude of food safety regulations and enforcement agencies working concurrently.

- Poor infrastructure: lack of adequate cold chain facility.

II. Dairy Processing

India holds the title of being the largest milk producer globally. Over the last five decades, milk production has seen a Compound Annual Growth Rate (CAGR) of 3.5%, reaching 110 million metric tonnes in 2008-09. The National Dairy Development Board (NDDB) envisions boosting milk production to 180 million tonnes by 2020-21. According to estimates by the Central Statistics Office (CSO), milk contributes to 68% of the total value of output from the livestock sector. Notably, in terms of output value, milk has emerged as the foremost agricultural commodity in India.

Milk Production in India

Per Capita Availability of Milk by States/UTs (gms/day)

State	09-10	10-11	11-12	12-13	13-14	14-15	15-16	16-17	17-18	18-19	19-20	20-21	21-22	22-23
All India	**273**	**281**	**290**	**299**	**307**	**319**	**333**	**351**	**370**	**390**	**406**	**427**	**446**	**459**
Andhra Pradesh	342	364	391	409	413	522	579	649	728	794	799	768	799	799
Arunachal Pradesh	59	63	44	49	93	88	95	99	100	101	110	79	82	81
Assam	69	71	70	69	69	70	70	71	71	71	73	75	77	78
Bihar	175	184	175	188	195	193	202	209	218	228	240	260	273	274
Chhattisgarh	110	117	120	127	130	126	128	136	144	151	159	164	172	180
Goa	96	93	113	92	98	122	99	93	99	102	109	106	111	112
Gujarat	418	435	445	476	506	506	522	538	563	593	615	631	656	670
Haryana	662	679	720	767	800	813	847	896	965	1040	1118	1063	1081	1098
Himachal Pradesh	397	446	447	460	461	456	494	509	529	552	573	588	599	596
Jammu & Kashmir	379	378	352	316	302	413	476	494	507	520	507	534	557	572
Jharkhand	130	136	145	146	146	137	141	145	152	162	170	176	187	195
Karnataka	226	237	244	262	272	266	273	280	302	332	375	452	483	523
Kerala	201	210	223	216	203	218	211	200	203	200	198	197	196	198
Madhya Pradesh	278	287	308	327	349	387	428	467	504	538	568	591	616	644
Maharashtra	190	197	206	213	219	225	236	240	254	264	269	305	315	329
Manipur	88	88	80	80	80	76	72	72	74	76	79	62	65	62
Meghalaya	83	83	74	83	84	74	74	74	74	74	74	75	75	77
Mizoram	29	31	35	36	40	50	52	57	59	60	54	58	55	55
Nagaland	96	93	108	94	95	102	102	104	96	93	78	71	76	61

Odisha	112	113	112	114	122	121	121	125	129	142	144	143	144	148
Punjab	944	937	945	961	980	992	1020	1061	1105	1165	1221	1219	1271	1283
Rajasthan	509	538	539	555	572	645	691	769	817	850	904	1075	1150	1138
Sikkim	200	194	202	186	200	217	286	231	247	254	345	302	350	347
Tamil Nadu	278	278	265	280	280	265	267	277	283	304	316	353	362	369
Telangana						321	336	352	371	401	410	422	422	423
Tripura	77	80	83	88	95	102	108	113	122	128	136	140	146	153
Uttar Pradesh	283	289	310	312	318	329	339	352	363	377	387	377	402	426
Uttarakhand	387	383	384	403	418	404	421	426	433	441	447	437	446	442
West Bengal	133	137	140	145	145	147	146	149	154	160	165	173	179	194
A&N Islands	137	142	187	131	84	110	108	113	118	126	130	101	115	117
Chandigarh	95	87	117	103	101	109	105	88	101	106	113	120	129	126
Ladakh												138	271	280
Dadra & Nagar Haveli	86	83	89	101	98	57	34	28	27	7	8	4	4	4
Daman & Diu	15	14	11	13	10	8								
Delhi	72	72	82	41	39	43	42	41	40	-	-	-	-	64
Lakshadweep	84	71	85	82	219	174	135	132	149	150	152	154	17	16
Puducherry	96	94	99	113	111	97	96	94	93	92	90	88	87	85

Source : Basic Animal Husbandry Statistics, MoFAHD, DAHD, GoI

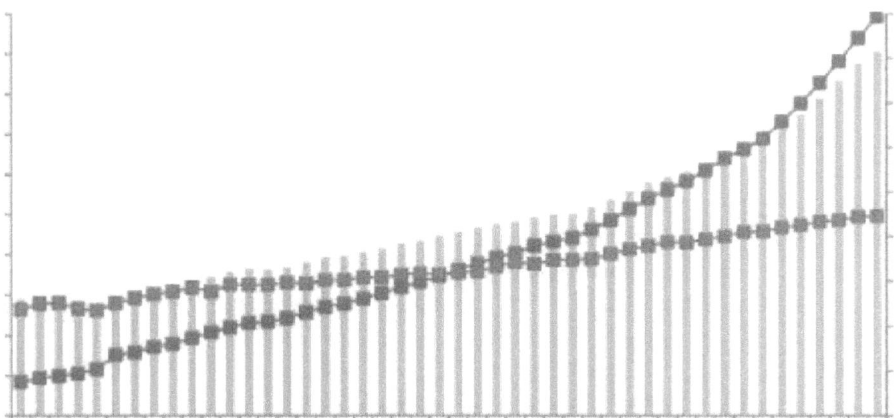

Milk production in India and the USA and per capita availability in India from 1950-51 to 2019-20 (*Source:* FAOSTAT 2019 and DoAHD&F 2019)

On the processing front, out of the total milk produced in India, about 35% is utilized for further processing. Milk is processed for the manufacture of pasteurized milk, traditional as well as western dairy products. Currently, approximately 46% of the total milk is consumed as liquid milk, while 47% is utilized in traditional dairy products, with the remaining 7% being consumed as western dairy products.

Dairy products in India

Traditional milk products

Paneer, Butter, Ghee, Khoa, Cream, Butter milk, Fresh milk

Value added milk products

Processed cheese, Infant foods, UHT milk, Flavored milk, Ice cream, Dairy whitener, Condensed milk

Roughly 15% of India's milk production undergoes processing within the organized sector. The dairy industry is projected to experience a growth rate exceeding 5% annually. A result of delicensing of dairy industry under MMPO, private sector has shown great deal of enthusiasm in setting up of new processing plants. Increased organized private sector participation in dairy production and processing is likely to occur due to the following reasons:

- Potential for high profitability of the dairy products business
- Presence of small scale & cottage industries with inconsistent quality products and hygiene standards and unable to cater to market needs.

Entry of organized players can help enhance product shelf life without compromising on food safety and hygiene.

- Lack of scale which opens up huge opportunities for integrated dairy processing facilities.

Though India has significant production strengths in dairy, less than 0.5% of total dairy products are exported. However, India's comparative advantages such as low farm gate prices and proximity to milk deficit markets can be leveraged to enhance participation in global dairy trade. The opportunity is further influenced by the new WTO regulations that require the US to grant increased market access for butter, cheese, skim milk powder, while export subsidies for butter will need to be reduced. Similarly, the EU will have to reduce its subsidized exports of cheese and meet production deficit through imports. Exhibit below shows the major export destinations of processed dairy products in 2008-09. Within the export basket, whey is an attractive option for the growing importance in high end food and non-food applications globally. Trade in other intermediate food products such as cheese powder,casein and lactose is rising for international market potential.

Export destinations of dairy products

India's export of dairy products was 63738.47 MT to the world for worth of Rs 2260.94 crore (272.64 USD Millions during the year 2023-24.major destinations are to UAE, Saudi Arab, USA, UK, Netherlands, China, Germany, Italy Singapore, Bangladesh and Bhutan. India is the largest producer and ranks first position in the world contributing 25% of global milk production.

Source: APEDA

Key constraints in Dairy processing segment include

- Low milk productivity and dispersed nature of production leading to serious challenges in aggregation. In 2021-22, the average daily milk production per animal in India varies by species.

  Exotic cows-11.36 kg per day, Crossbred cows-8.32 kg per day, Indigenous cows-4.07 kg per day and non-descript cows-2.83 kg per day.

- Absence of adequate quality controls: In Indian Food Laws, application of HACCP in a food plant is not mandatory so far. Out of over 650 MMPO registered dairy plants,around 90 have HACCP/ISO certification and more dairy plants are going to implement this. The industry needs more serious efforts to strengthen the international food safety and quality standards and is required to implement codex recommended approaches and practices in an effective manner.

- Lack of adequate temperature controlled storage and transport infrastructure leading to contamination.

- Lower scale of operations on account of lack of ability to invest in procurement infrastructure, quality control, controlled temperature transportation and market development.

- The production of traditional dairy products is confined to the unorganized sector characterized by lack of modern technologies for large scale production, lack of appropriate packing systems and labeling and lack of quality control & mechanism.

- Despite the potential for processing, the capacity utilization of dairy plants is about 60% assuming 300 working days in a year. The reasons for low capacity utilization include lack of availability of raw materials (Milk) in the lean season and limited diversification of the product mix.

- High level taxations and duties on dairy equipments and machinery amount to almost 35 to 40% of the basic prices leading to increase in the final price of the product and lesser utilization of the quality equipments and machinery at farm levels and processing levels.

II. Meat and Poultry

In 2022-23 India produced 9.77 million tonnes of meat,which is an increase of 5.62% from the previous year.India is the world's eighth largest producer of meat and the largest producer of buffalo meat and second largest producer of goat meat.The current processing levels in poultry are 6%,while for meat it stands at 21%.

The meat category includes buffalo meat,sheep & goat meat and pork. India has the largest livestock population in the world and accounting for more than half the buffalo population and 1/6th of the goat population in the world. The country produces 485 million tonnes of livestock. FAO estimates indicate that the slaughter rate for sheep and goat is 31% and 39% respectively while that of buffalos is 10%. Indian consumers predominantly favor fresh meat sourced from wet markets. Only a minimal portion of the production undergoes further processing into value-added products, primarily intended for export. Key players such as Allana's, Hind Agro, and Al Kabeer largely operate within the buffalo meat export segment. Despite the presence of 3600 slaughterhouses, 9 modern abattoirs, and 171 licensed meat processing units under the Meat Products Order, a significant portion of the produce is distributed through the unorganized sector, with less than one percent being converted into value-added products. However,changing consumer lifestyles has meant increased willingness to explore ready-to-eat and semi-processed meat products, thus creating greater opportunities within the segment. The meat segment as a whole is estimated to be growing at about 10% annually. However, growth of the beef segment is slower at about 4.5% due due to cultural restrictions on consumption.

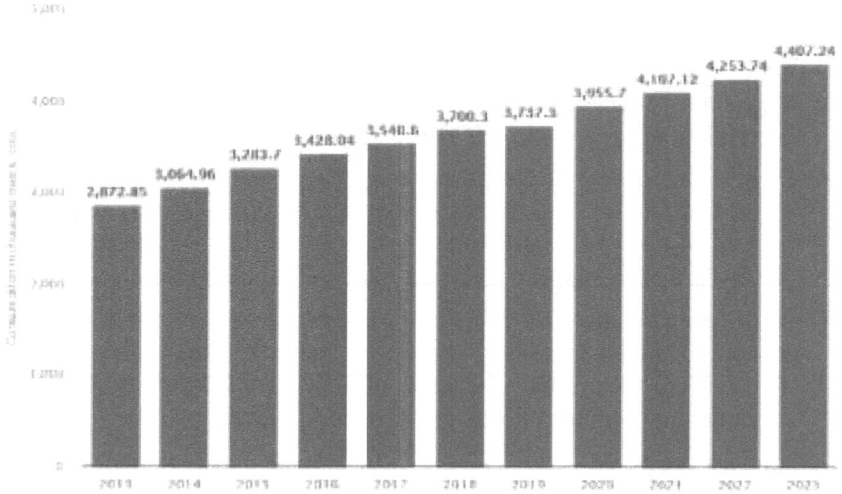

Poultry

The poultry sector in India has emerged as one of the fastest growing in the agriculture domain in recent years. This sector has been growing consistently in the last couple of years .

Trends in production and consumption of broiler meat in India

The domestic poultry segment is characterized by the prevalence of small and unorganized players with only a few organized players selling branded, processed products(Eg. Godrej Real Good Chiken, Venky'schiken). Indian poultry exports are negligible and are mainly confined to eggs and egg powder. Exports are made mainly to Middle East and Germany until the recent entry into Japanese markets. The falling competitiveness of the poultry industry in Thailand(due to increasing labour cost) has provided an opportunity for India to enter into the highly attractive Japanese market.

The main constraint for growth of processed meat and poultry segment include:

- Nascent demand for processed and packaged products due to price sensitivity and consumer preference for the product in fresh form.
- Low scale of operations and fragmented and dispersed rearing of livestock.

- Infrastructure constraints such as lack of modern abattoirs and processing, packaging and distribution systems.

- High feed and labour costs in the poultry segment (which account for almost 60-70% and 20% respectively of the total production cost) despite the low labour cost, competitiveness of the Indian poultry industry has been adversely affected due to the high feed costs.

III. Fisheries

In fiscal year 2023, India has witnessed a tremendous growth by showcasing a production of around 18 million metric tons of fish,which was an increase from the previous year's 16.25 million metric tons.India's inland fish production has also been increasing rapidly,from 97.20 lakh tonnes in 2018-19 to 131.13 lakh tonnes in 2022-23,which is a 34.9% increase.India is the third largest fish producing country ,contributing 8% to the global fish production. The fish production in 2021-22 is 16.24 million tonnes comprising of marine fish production of 4.12 million tonnes from and 12.12 million tonnes from aquaculture.In 2023 Andhra Pradesh was the top producer of inland fish in India,with a production of 4.5 million metric tons.West Bengal came in second with about 2 million metric tons and India's total inland fish production was over 13 million metric tons.Gujarat was the top producer of marine fish in 2023,with a production of 730000 metric tons.India's total fish production was over 4 million metric tons.

Kerala leads in daily consumption of fish daily,followed by Goa at 36.2%, West Bengal at 21.90%, Manipur at 19.70%, Assam at 13.10% and Tripura at 11.50%

Major Export Destination

MPEDA as an apex body is responsible for registration of infrastructural facilities for sea food export trade besides collection and dissemination of trade information and promotion of Indian marine products in overseas market.

As for overseas markets, the USA continued to be the major importer of Indian seafood in value terms,with an import worth US$ 2549.1 million accounting for a share of 34.53% in terms of US$ value. Exports to the US increased by 7.46% and 1.42% in quantity and value terms,however they decline by 3.15% in US$ terms. Frozen shrimp continued to be the principal ietm exported to the US with a share of 91.90% in US term. Export of black tiger shrimp to US increased by 35.37% in quantity terms and 32.35% in value in US terms.

China (excluding Hongkong and Taiwan) emerhed as the 2nd largest seafood export destination country for India in terms of US$ with an import volume of 451363 MT worth US$ 1384.89 million accounting for 25.33% share in Quantity and 18.76% in US$ terms.Exports to China grew by 12.80% in quantity.

Japan is the third largest importer with a share of 6.06% in quantity and US$ Value terms,frozen shrimp continued to be the major item of exports to Japan, with a share of 33.26% in quantity, 65.94% Indian rupee and 65.98% in US$ value.

Vietnam holds the 4th largest market position importing 132086 MT worth US$ 391.41 million.Frozen shrimp dominates the import with a share of 55.43% in US earnings and 30.11 in quantity followed by dried items.

Thailand is the fifth largest market with a US$ share of 3.82% and a third place position by volume (7.77% share) with 138457 MT worth US$ 281.97million. Frozen fish remained the significant item exported to Thailand accounting for a share of 44.37% in US$ earnings and 63.91% in quantity.

Canada ranks as the 6th largest market in US$ share of 2.70% and 10th position by volume (1.40% share) terms with 24956 MT worth US$ 199.13million. Frozen shrimp dominates the exports to Canada with a share of 93.365 in US$ earnings and 89.48% in quantity terms.

Spain is the 7th largest market in US$(2.65% share) and 6th largest by volume (2.24% share) with an export volume of 39849MT worth US$195.95 million.

Belgium ranks 8th among seafood export destinations for India with US$ shae of 2.42% followed by UAE 2.15% share and Italy 2.14% share.

The top 10 markets contribute 79.89% by US$ terms.

Source: MPEDA

Some key constraints for growth of this segment include:

- Demand for processed fish products in the domestic market is low and yet to attain critical mass.

- The fishing sector in India remains essentially traditional and technologically underdeveloped.

- Deep sea fish has not been able to make a mark in the fishing sector. This is primarily on account of technological gaps such as-

  - Lack of sufficient expertise in long lining.

  - Inadequate processing infrastructure.

  - Lack of knowledge in on-board handling of tuna in order to prepare the fish grade products.

  - Trade barriers imposed by the US that has dramatically impacted fish exports.

V. Grains and Cereals

The grain processing sector comprises of milling of cereals, pulses and oilseeds. India is self-sustaining in grain production with annual production touching 3156.16lakh tonnes during 2021-22. India holds the position of being the world's second-largest producer of wheat and rice. Additionally, the country cultivates various other food grains, including cereals like maize, barley, jowar, bajra, and ragi, as well as pulses such as gram and lentils.

While processing of grains occupies a lion's share in the food processing sector accounting for 40% of the industry size, more than 96% of this segment is accounted for by primary processing and focused on three sub-categories-rice, wheat and dal (lentil). About 65% of rice production is milled in modern rice mills. Wheat milling is dominated by the unorganized sector with about 3 lakh small units operating in this sector while there are just about 820 large flour mills. Dal milling is the third largest in the grain processing industry and has about 11000 mechanised mills in the organized segment. Oilseed processing constitutes another significant sector, primarily concentrated within the cottage industry. As per approximations, India houses around 250,000 traditional animal-operated oil expellers (ghanis and kolus), 50,000 mechanical oil expellers, 15,500 oil mills, 725 solvent extraction plants, 300 oil refineries, and over 175 hydrogenated vegetable oil plants. According to industry estimates, the size of the Indian edible market is about 15 billion liters of which just about 10% is packaged and branded clearly reflecting the huge opportunity for organized players to enter this segment. The export of food grains is largely controlled by the government keeping in view the food security needs of the country. Food grain exports from India have largely been on account of rice. Total cereals production in India for the year 2023-24 is 304.36 million tonnes.Major export destinations during 2023-24 is for Saudi Arabia, Iran, Iraq, Benin, UAE and Vietnam.

VI. Consumer Goods

This segment comprises of packaged foods including ready to eat food such as bakery products, chocolates, chips and namkeen, ready to cook food such as noodles, soups and pasta, soft drinks and alcoholic beverages. Trend of some key categories in this segment are detailed herewith.

A. The Indian bakery market is estimated to have reached 919billion in fiscal 2022 from 603 billion in fiscal 2018 with a CAGR of 11%.As per 2023 the bakery industry in India is valued at a staggering INR 30000 crores with an annual growth rate of 12%.The per capita consumption of bread in India is only around 1.5 to 1.75 kg in various zones.According to a report by market research firm IMARC,the bakery Industry is expected to grow at a 10.8% to reach \$21.2 billion by 2028 from \$11.3 billion in 2022. Changing consumer lifestyle is influencing the demand for ready to eat and bakery products.The major players in bakeyry industry in India are Britania Industries Ltd, ITC Ltd, Parle Products Ltd, Surya Food and Agro Ltd etc. The Global bakery market is anticipated to rise at a considerable rate during the forecast period between 2024-2031. Indian bakery market size reached US\$ 12.6 billion in 2023 and is poised to grow at a CAGR of over 10% in foreseeable future.

B. Non-Alcoholic Beverages

i) **Tea:** India is the world's second largest tea producer and the black tea, producing 1350 million kilograms of tea in 2023.The country is also the world's largest consumer of black tea, accounting for about 18% of global consumption. The northen region of India is the largest tea producer accounting for about 83% of annual tea production in 2022. The states of Assam and West Bengal in north east contribute the majority of tea production. The remaining 17% of India's tea is produced in the southern region of Tamilnadu, Kerala and Karnataka being the top three producers.India's tea production has increased by 39% from 981 million kg in 2008 to 1336 million kg in 2022. But the average all India auction price for tea declined by Rs 14.81 per kg from April 2023 to March 2024 with declining margin.

ii) **Coffee** production for the year 2024 was estimated to be 374000 metric tons, which is a significant increase from previous years. The southern states of Karnataka is the largest coffee producer in India. In 2023-24 Karnataka produced over 1667000 60 kg bags of Arabica coffee and 4530000 60 kg bags of Robusta coffee. USDA predicts about India's coffee production for 2024-25 crop year, which begins in October may be lower than expected due to a projected drop in in Arabica production but Robusta production is expected to remain same. The extreme weather conditions could threaten world's coffee growing areas .India is among the top 10 coffee producing countries with about 3% of global output in 2020.

COFFEE STATISTICS

Statistics on Coffee

Production
Holdings
Exports
Consumption

Production in Major States/Districts Of India*(in MTs)*

State/District	Post Blossom Estimate 2023-2024			Final Estimate 2022-2023		
	Arabica	Robusta	Total	Arabica	Robusta	Total
Karnataka						
Chikkamagaluru	41,900	51,150	**93,050**	37,150	45,300	**82,450**
Kodagu	21,060	109,225	**130,285**	19,120	109,600	**128,720**
Hassan	19,000	24,550	**43,550**	15,750	21,100	**36,850**
Sub total	**81,960**	**184,925**	**266,885**	**72,020**	**176,000**	**248,020**
Kerala						
Wayanad	0	61,050	**61,050**	0	60,800	**60,800**
Travancore	975	8,050	**9,025**	875	8,000	**8,875**
Nelliampathies	1,100	1,650	**2,750**	1,100	1,650	**2,750**
Sub total	**2,075**	**70,750**	**72,825**	**1,975**	**70,450**	**72,425**
Tamil Nadu						
Pulneys	6,825	465	**7,290**	7,350	480	**7,830**
Nilgiris	1,350	4,375	**5,725**	1,175	4,420	**5,595**
Shevroys (Salem)	4,000	0	**4,000**	3,900	25	**3,925**
Anamalais (Coimbatore)	870	550	**1,420**	825	525	**1,350**
Sub total	**13,045**	**5,390**	**18,435**	**13,250**	**5,450**	**18,700**
Non Traditional Areas						
Andhra Pradesh	15,340	40	**15,380**	12,225	40	**12,265**
Orissa	500	0	**500**	465	0	**465**
Sub Total	**15,840**	**40**	**15,880**	**12,690**	**40**	**12,730**
North Eastern Region	80	95	**175**	65	60	**125**
Grand Total (India)	**113,000**	**261,200**	**374,200**	**100,000**	**252,000**	**352,000**

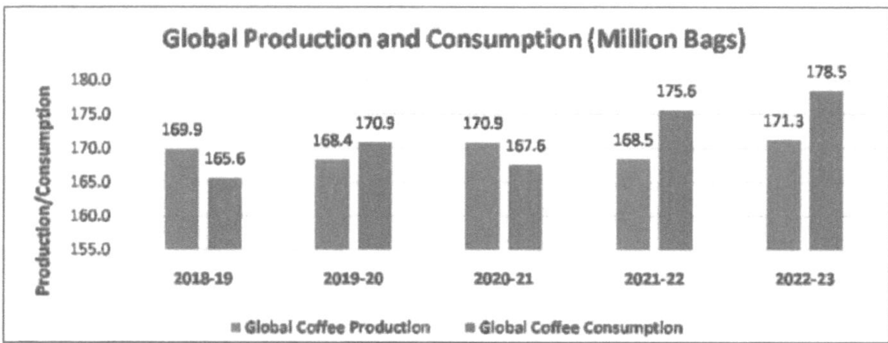

iii) **Soft drinks:** The carbonated beverage market segment was valued at INR 474.96 Bn in FY 2023 and is expected to reach a value of 601.85Bn by 2028. The Indian consumer has traditionally had a high preference for aerated drinks with a preference for cola, oranged lemon flavor. However with increased health consciousness, consumers are now turning to other options such as fruits juices and drinks. According to industry estimates, the fruit beverages industry in India now stands at about INR 11 billion and the market is growing at the rate of close to 30%. Tremendous scope exists for investments in packaged health drinks, fresh fruit drinks, juices, smoothies, energy drinks and ethnic Indian drinks.

C. Alcoholic Beverages

Social aversion to alcohol consumptions in the Indian society is fast changing. Mushrooming pubs and bars reflect the changing mindset of the urban consumer. Growing affluence, increased overseas travel and media exposure has also led the change in consumer attitudes towards alcohol. The key segments in the alcoholic beverages industry are Country liquor, Indian Made Foreign Liquor, Beer and Wine. With respect to alcohol consumption in india ,WHO report reveals that more than 31% Indians are current drinkers.

Liquor Industry segment in India

India alcoholic beverage market is estimated to reach USD 76.5 billion by 2032 with a CAGR of 7.74%.Recent years have seen a significant expansion and change in the Indian alcoholic beverages sector, primarily due to changing customer preferences and regulatory environments.

WHO report that captures the global scenario on alcohol and substance abuse,notes that over 31% Indians are current drinkers. Estimated market size of $52.4billion in 2021 about 2% of the country's GDP,the industry is significant. Beer wine and spirits experienced positive growth over the 2017 to 2022 period driven by offsales and with on sales category declining over the same period.The Indian market is shifting towards premium products and is opening up new market opportunities.

India alcohol industry Overview

Attributes	Key Insights
Estimated Industry size in 2024	US$ 54740 million
Projected alcohol industry revenue	US$ 112338.9 million
Expected value CAGR in 2034	7.2%

The Indian alcohol beverages industry is expected for margin improvement and sales in fiscal year 2025, as per ICRA credit rating organization.ICRA projects a revenue growth of of 8-19% for its sample set of domestic alcohol beverages.Total revenue of liquor generated during 2023-24 is 1734.54 crore during 2022-23 as per the figures provided by the Excise Department.In 2023 the size of alcoholic beverage market was about 55 billion US$ in India and is likely to increase at a CAGR of 7% to 73 billion dollars in 2027. The economic value of alcohol Industry in India amounts to US$ 47.1billion in 2024.Alcohol consumption rank of India is 3 in 2019.

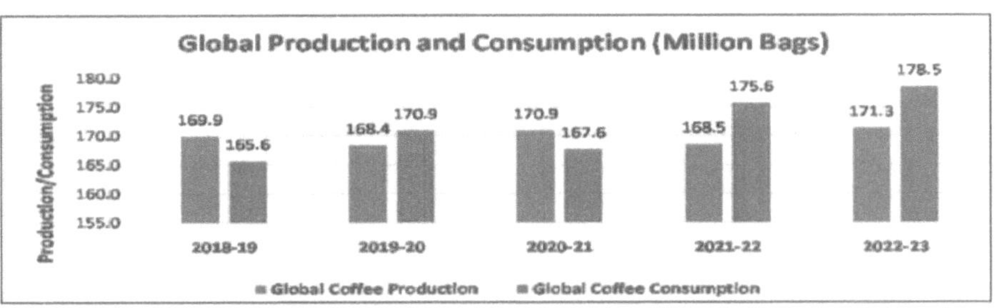

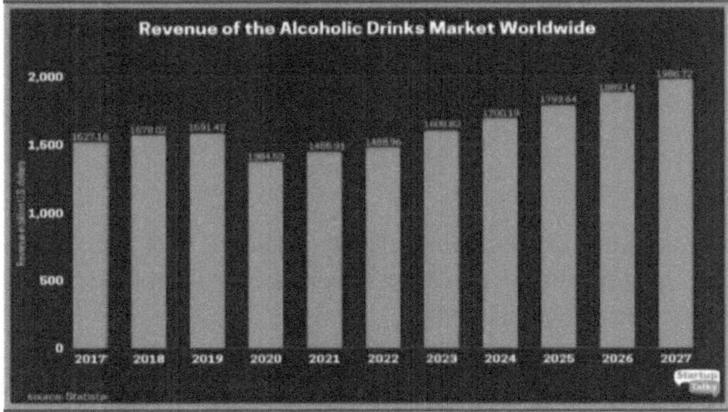

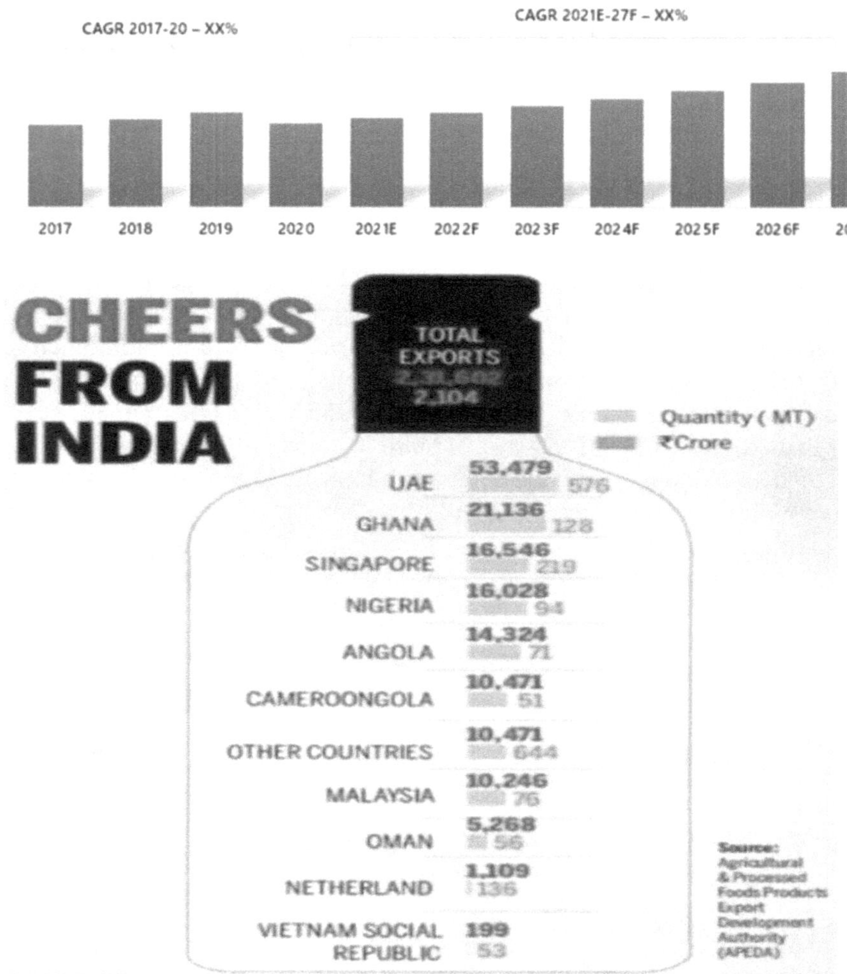

3. Key Growth Drivers

The growth rate across various segments clearly indicate that the Indian processing sector is transforming. This may be primarily attributed to the strong macro-economic fundamentals and

the changing socio-economic scenario of the country which are in turn leading to a demand led change in the food industry structure. These factors combined with diverse supply strengths, strong governmental focus on the sector and increased private investment are driving what was once traditional, small scale sector into a modern industry aimed at catering to the evolving tastes and needs of discerning consumers. Some key growth drivers are elucidated herewith.

Key Growth Drivers for Food Processing Industry

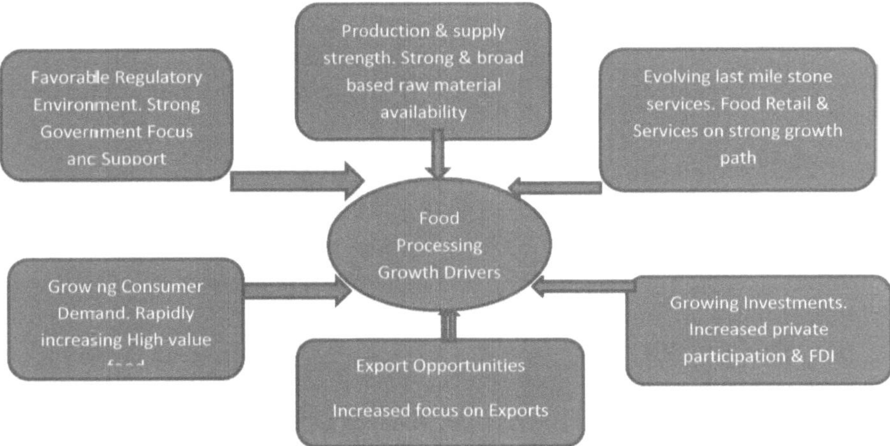

Source: Yes Bank

I. Growing Consumer Demand

A population of 1.2 billion people growing at about 1.5% a year in itself is a major driver for the food market. However, strong macroeconomic fundamentals of India during the recent past have had a dramatic impact on the demographic and socio-economic environment resulting in higher demand for high value food products including processed food.

A population of about 1.2 billion growing at about 1.5 %	→	They will eat/consume more
Rapid urbanization-expected to reach 36% by 2025	→	Increasing discern for quality and variety
Large and growing working population resulting higher disposable income.	→	Focus on convenience and choice increased pattern of eating out.
Changing lifestyle -Nuclear families, working women	→	Focus on convenience-ready to cook, ready to eat food and health food
Emergence of a global consumer due to increased exposure to western culture and media	→	New buying habits oriented more towards hygiene, health and style

Source: Yes Bank

II. Production and Supply Strength

India possesses strategic advantages that augur well for intense and diverse agricultural activity. Blessed with diverse ecosystems, seven agro-climatic zones, fifteen soil types, and twenty major river systems, India possesses the capacity to fulfill the raw material needs of various processing sectors. As the largest global producer of milk, second largest producer of food grains, fruits, and vegetables, and third largest producer of fish, India guarantees a steady supply of raw materials to the food processing industry. Additionally, the country's comparatively low-cost workforce presents an opportunity to establish large-scale, cost-effective production facilities.

III. Changing Face of Last Mile Food Services

The two key last mile food service sectors are retail and eat-out segment. Both these sectors have shown tremendous growth in the recent past. The retail sector in specific is rapidly transforming due to the emergence of multiple retail formats, entry of leading corporates in retail(Such as Reliance Retail, Bharti WalMart, Aditya Birla Group among others) and the emergence of retail in the two cities. The emergence of organized retailing has resulted in increased availability and thereby increased visibility and choice to the consumers thus auguring the growth in demand for processed food. Further the emergence of fast food joints has a significant effect on the food processing. While US brands such as McDonald's, Pizza Hut and Kentucky Fried Chiken have become household names domestic fast food outlets such as Nirulas, Haldirams and CCD are quickly expanding their pan India presence resulting in growing demand for processed food items.

IV. Favorable regulatory environment & Government support schemes

It has provided a positive impetus to the food processing industry. To realize India's vast potential in the food processing sector, a separate Ministry of Food Processing Industries was created. MOFPI aims to engage modern technology, create surplus for for exports, stimulate demand for processed food, act as a catalyst for bringing in greater investments into this sector and is responsible for promoting and regulating the sector. Moreover, the liberalized policy regime, coupled with incentives tailored for the food processing sector, creates a highly favorable environment for investment within the industry.

V. Growing investment for the private sector

Considering the sector's immense growth potential, several major corporations have ventured into the market to capitalize on this opportunity. The FDI in food processing sector stood at Rs 7194.13 crore in 2022-23 increase from 5290 .27 crore in 2021-22 as per MOFPI.

VI. Growing Exports of processed food

The vibrancy in the processed food industry is accentuated by the opportunities that are opening up in exports. Given the tropical nature and diverse agro-climatic conditions, the country has become a strong contender to compete in the international market for processed products of crops such as mango, garlic, marine products and spices among others. Further, ethnic processed food products of Indian origin such as pickles and branded ready to eat food products such as ITC's kitchen of India, Bikenerwala, MTR foods and others are finding increasing acceptance and shelf space in the international market.

4. Government Support Schemes and Incentives

PMFME (PM Formalisation of Micro food processing Enterprises) scheme at a glance:

Formalizing Micro-Enterprises:

The Pradhan Mantri Formalisation of Micro Food Processing Enterprises (PMFME) scheme, launched under the Aatmanirbhar Bharat Abhiyan initiative, supports the creation and improvement of small food processing businesses. This aims to make them more competitive and recognized, benefiting up to 2 lakh enterprises. The program also promotes the "One District One Product" approach to support growth and strengthen the entire food production chain.

Production Incentives: The government offers Production Linked Incentive Schemes (PLIs) to encourage increased production across various sectors, potentially including food processing. These schemes provide financial rewards to companies that meet specific production targets.

PM Kisan SAMPADA Yojana: This comprehensive program aims to modernize and strengthen India's food processing sector. It includes initiatives like:

- Building cold storage facilities to reduce spoilage
- Expanding food processing and preservation capabilities
- Enhancing food safety and quality standards

"Operation Greens" to improve distribution and price stability of perishable produce:

- Training and development programs for the workforce
- Establishing large food parks to consolidate resources
- Creating stronger connections between farmers and consumers (backward and forward linkages)

Key Features of PMFME

- Provides support to individual and group units (FPOs, Cooperatives, SHGs, Federations, Government agencies) with comprehensive assistance including training, capacity building, marketing, branding, and formalization.
- Facilitates enhanced access to credit and integration into organized supply chains.
- Assists in transitioning micro-enterprises into the formal sector, increasing access to common services, and supports product standardization, brand building, and marketing efforts.

Overall Achievements

- Credit Linked Subsidy: 46,116 loans sanctioned to micro food processing enterprises.
- Capacity Building: 46,759 beneficiaries trained.
- Seed Capital: Provided seed capital support of Rs 388.41 crores to 1,23,816 SHG members across rural and urban areas.
- Incubation Centers: Approved 76 incubation centers across 25 states/UTs; two centers are operational.
- Marketing and Branding: Launched 13 different brands from 11 states/UTs.

Production Linked Incentive Scheme

Approved on March 31, 2021, for implementation from FY 2021-22 to 2026-27, with a total outlay of Rs 10,000 crores.

Goals

- Cultivate Global Leaders: Empower Indian food manufacturers to become major players in the international market.
- Champion Indian Brands: Foster recognition and appreciation for Indian food brands worldwide.
- Expand Job Market: Generate more employment opportunities beyond traditional farming roles.
- Empower Farmers: Ensure farmers receive fair compensation for their produce, leading to increased income.

Targeted Food Segments

- Ready-to-Eat (RTE) & Ready-to-Cook (RTC) Meals: This includes options like millet-based products, processed fruits and vegetables, and marine products.

- Innovative Organic Products: Support small and medium businesses (SMEs) in developing and promoting innovative organic offerings, including eggs, poultry meat, and egg products.
- Global Branding & Marketing: Provide assistance for branding and marketing these food products internationally to establish a strong Indian presence in the global food market.

Pradhan Mantri Kissan Sampad Yojana-

It is an umbrella scheme approved in may 2017 was implemented during 14th FC cycle with a total outlay of Rs 6000 crore. Restructured PMKSY has since been approved with a total outlay of 4600 crore for implementation during 15th FC cycle.

Objectives

- To create modern infrastructure for food processing from farm gate to retail outlet.
- To create robust supply chain infrastructure.

   Integrated cold chain and value addition infrastructure=

It provides integrated cold chain and preservation infrastructure from farm gate to consumers. Maximum grant per project is 10crore. FPOs/SHGs/Govt, and private sector etc are eligible organisations.

Financial assistance:

- Storage infrastructure (cold storage etc) @ 35% for general & 50% difficult areas
- Value addition/processing infrastructure(pack house,frozen processing units,dairy etc @ 50% / 75%
- Iradiation facilities @5 0% / 75%

Creation/expansion of food processing & preservation capacities unit scheme.

- To provide food processing/preservation units for increasing level of processing ,value addition and reduction in wastage.
- Grant @ 35%/50% in general and difficult area of the project cost.
- Maximum grant of 5 crore per project
- FPOs/SHGs/Govt./private sector etc.

Infrastructure for agro processing clusters (mini food park)

- Assistance for creating common facilities and enabling infrastructure closer to production areas.
- Envisages a cluster of minimum 5 processing units with an investment of Rs 25crore.

- Grant @ 35% / 50% in general/difficult areas of the project
- Maximum grant of 10 crore per project
- Minimum 10 acres of land is required either by purchase or lease of 50 years.
- FPOs/SHGs/Govt./Private sector etc.

Food safety and Quality assurance infrastructure

- Facilitate industry to comply with domestic/international standards
- To make available modern commercial testing facilities for industry
- Grant @ 50% / 70% of equipment in general/difficult areas for private projects and 100% for public sector.
- So far 175 labs approved, 119 completed and 56 under implementation.

  Technical Institutions under MOFPI

- Two food technology institutes under the ministry
1. NIFTEM – National Institute of Food Technology,Entrepreneurship and Management at Kundli,Haryana and Thanjavur,Tamilnadu.
- Offer academic courses in B.Tech,M.Tech,MBA and PhD programs.
- Impart training on skill development & entrepreneurship
- Conduct R&D on food processing
- NIFTEM Act 2021 has been passed on 26.07.2021 and notified on 30.07.2021 and came into effect on 01.10.2021.

Detail information at-https://pmfme.mofpi.gov/pmfme/

Ministry of Food Processing Industries in partnership with State/UT Governments has launched to address the challenges faced by micro enterprises and to tap the potential of groups and cooperatives in supporting the upgradation and formalization of enterprises.

- Two lakh informal micro processing units to be upgraded in 5years
- Scheme period 2020-21 to 2024-25
- Centrally sponsored scheme with central 60% and State 40% contribution
- Scheme outlay of 10,000 crores
- Beneficiaries include FPOs /Producer cooperatives,SHGs and individual micro enterprises

Objectives

- Increased access to creditby existing micro food processing entrepreneurs, FPOs, SHGs and Cooperatives.

- Integration with an organized suppy chain by strengthening ,branding and marketing
- Support for transition of existing two lakh enterprises into the formal framework
- Increased access to common services like common processing facility ,laboratories, storage,packaging,marketing and incubation services.
- Strengthening of Institutions ,research and training in food processing sector.
- Increased access to professional and technical support for the enterprises.

Support for Common Infrastructure

- Provided to FPOs, SHGs, Cooperatives,any Government agency or private enterprises
- Available for other units and public to utilize on hiring basis for substantial part of capacity
- Eligibility would be decided based on benefit to farmers and industry at large,viability gap,absence of private investment,criticality to value chain.
- Credit linked grant would be available @35% and maximum limit of grant in such cases would be as prescribed.
- Premises for storage of agriculture produce,sorting,grading,warehouse and cold storage at the farm gate.
- Common processing facility for processing of produce
- Incubation center: should involve one or more product links which could be utilized by units on hire basis besides used for training run on commercial basis.

Branding and Marketing Support

- Graphic designing of packaging
- Advertisement and agencies for planning & executing marketing
- Warehouse/storage rental
- Market study
- Training relating to sales and marketing
- Quality control to ensure product quality meets required standards
- Marketing tieup with regional and national retail chains and state level institutions

- Developing a common brand and packaging including standardization to participate in common packaging
- Eligibility criteria for branding and marketing proposal

Identification of Beneficiaries: Micro-enterprise

- Potential micro beneficiaries data from the DICs
- Potential beneficiaries data of the State Rural Livelihood Mission. DRPs could consult District Mission Management Unit and Block Mission Management Unit and Community Organisations for obtaining the data of potential beneficiaries .
- Data from the Tribal Welfare Department
- Training data from the Rural Self Employment Training Institutes,Rural development & self-employment training institutes.
- Potential beneficiaries data from the Ministry of MSME
- Potential beneficiaries data from FSSAI shared by the MOFPI to all State Nodal Agencies
- Data from State level Technical Institute

Common Infrastructure

- Data of FPC and Cooperatives from NABARD, NCDC, SFAC
- Coordination with cluster based business organization sponsored by NABARD, NCDC, SFAC
- Data from District Cooperative Office
- Coordination with TRIFED
- Exploring the opportunities with the Van Dhan Vikas Kendra
- SNA will provide districtwise planning and business opportunities for common infrastructure.
- Seed Capital,Training and Incubation facility

List of Items not covered under PMFME Scheme

- Trading and selling of unprocessed cereals/millets/spices etc.
- Unprocessed or loose milk (Selling of milk/curd)
- Trading and selling of fruits and vegetables
- Trading and selling of unprocessed minor forest product
- Bee keeping/loose selling of honey
- Loose selling, trading and repacking of oil
- Trading and selling of groundnut and araconut
- Animal rearing activity

- Trading and selling of fresh fish/meat/chiken
- Repacking of manufactured product
- Canteen, grocery, hotel, tiffin services, restaurants or any other food services enterprises

Development of agriculture sector has been a key focus area for the Government of India. In this direction, the government has taken many initiatives to boost growth in agriculture in general and food processing in particular. The keen focus of central government to improve the level of food processing in the country is reflected in the initiative taken by Government in the last five union budgets.

Union budget announcements for growth of Food Processing Industry

Year Budget Key Initiatives

2023-24 2,912 - PM Formalisation of Micro Food Processing Enterprises (PMFME) - Mega Food Parks Scheme

Focus-Upgrading informal micro units, infrastructure development

2024-25 3,290 - Increased allocation for PMFME scheme - Funding for PLI (Production Linked Incentive) scheme for food processing

Focus-Micro unit growth, boosting exports and attracting investments

Notes

Budget allocation figures are in crore INR (1 crore = 10 million).

These are estimated figures based on recent trends and news reports. Actual figures may vary.

The table highlights potential future initiatives based on industry needs and government priorities.

The Union Budget of India has consistently emphasized the growth and development of the food processing industry, recognizing its crucial role in enhancing agricultural productivity, reducing waste, and creating employment. Here's an overview of the key budget announcements over different years:

1. Union Budget 2014-15

Mega Food Parks: The government allocated ₹200 crore for the development of Mega Food Parks across the country. This initiative aimed to provide infrastructure for food processing units and reduce wastage.

Food Processing Infrastructure: Emphasis was placed on building infrastructure for the food processing sector, including cold chains, which received increased funding to strengthen the entire value chain.

2. Union Budget 2016-17

100% FDI in Marketing of Food Products: The budget allowed 100% Foreign Direct Investment (FDI) through the approval route for marketing food products produced and manufactured in India. This was aimed at attracting foreign investment in the sector.

Boost to Agro-Processing Clusters: The government announced the promotion of agro-processing clusters to ensure better marketing and processing of agricultural produce.

3. Union Budget 2018-19

Operation Greens: A significant announcement was the allocation of ₹500 crore for 'Operation Greens,' modeled on the lines of 'Operation Flood,' to address the challenge of price volatility of perishable commodities like tomatoes, onions, and potatoes.

Support for Food Processing Enterprises: The government announced the doubling of the allocation for the Ministry of Food Processing Industries to ₹1,400 crore, highlighting its commitment to the sector's growth.

4. Union Budget 2020-21

Kisan Rail and Krishi Udan: The introduction of Kisan Rail by Indian Railways and Krishi Udan by the Ministry of Civil Aviation aimed to improve the logistics of transporting perishable goods, thus benefiting the food processing sector.

Promotion of Organic and Horticulture Produce: The budget allocated funds for the promotion of organic farming and horticulture, which are critical components of the food processing industry.

5. Union Budget 2021-22

Production-Linked Incentive (PLI) Scheme: The government announced the extension of the PLI scheme to the food processing sector with an outlay of ₹10,900 crore. This scheme aimed to encourage domestic manufacturing and boost exports in the sector.

Boost to Infrastructure: The budget focused on strengthening agri-infrastructure, including the development of food processing zones, which would help in the better integration of the supply chain.

6. Union Budget 2023-24

Support for Start-ups in Food Processing: The government proposed setting up an Agriculture Accelerator Fund to encourage agri-tech start-ups. This initiative aimed to promote innovation and entrepreneurship in the food processing industry.

Millets Focus: The budget recognized the potential of millets and proposed enhancing its processing and marketing, including branding them as 'Shree Anna' to promote their consumption and export.

7. Union Budget 2024-25

Agri-Tech Focus: The government continued its emphasis on integrating technology with agriculture, allocating funds for the digitization of the food processing sector to improve efficiency and transparency.

Sustainable Practices: The budget emphasized sustainable practices in food processing, including funding for research and development in eco-friendly packaging and waste reduction techniques.

These budgetary announcements reflect the government's long-term vision to enhance the food processing industry's capacity, reduce wastage, boost exports, and generate employment. The consistent focus on infrastructure, technology, and foreign investment demonstrates a strategic approach to making India a global hub for food processing.

Some key interventions and support schemes put forth by MOFPI for the development of food processing industry are:

I. Schemes for Infrastructure Development: MoFPI has brought about much needed focus on infrastructure development to facilitate better linkage between farmers and processors. Following are key initiatives taken up by the government in this domain.

Mega Food Park Scheme: Development of food parks is being promoted by MOFPI in the PPP mode through the **Mega food park** scheme under which each park is envisaged to attract an investment of about INR 1 to 2.5 billion. Each of the Mega Food Parks will have a Central Processing Centre(CPC) where food processing units would be established supported by common infrastructure. Mega Food Parks are proposed to be set up in high potential zones where requisite volumes of agricultural raw material(fruits & vegetables etc.) are available. With a view to connect the CPC to the farmers, farm level facilities in the form of collection centers and primary processing centers and need based infrastructure are envisaged to be developed. The scheme has been implemented in 6 states including AP, TN, WB, Assam, Uttarakhand and Jharakhand, in the first phase of implementation while in the second phase it is getting implemented in Punjab, UP, Karnataka and Maharastra. The scheme proposes government capital grant support of up to 50% of the project cost, excluding the land component, in general areas, and 75% in difficult areas, with a maximum limit of INR 500 million per park.

Integrated Cold Chain Infrastructure

Integrated cold chain infrastructure plays a crucial role in India's agricultural sector, particularly in minimizing post-harvest losses, preserving the quality of perishable commodities, and ensuring that high-value agricultural produce reaches markets efficiently. To strengthen this sector, the Indian government has provided substantial budgetary support through various schemes and initiatives.

Budget Support and Government Schemes

Pradhan Mantri Kisan Sampada Yojana (PMKSY)

Launched in 2017, the PMKSY is one of the primary initiatives under which the government has allocated funds to develop cold chain infrastructure. This scheme focuses on the development of modern infrastructure, including integrated cold chains and preservation facilities, to reduce wastage and increase farmers' income. The budgetary allocation for PMKSY has been periodically increased, reflecting the government's commitment to enhancing cold chain facilities across the country.

Agricultural Infrastructure Fund (AIF)

The AIF, launched in 2020, provides medium to long-term debt financing for investment in viable projects for post-harvest management infrastructure and community farming assets, including cold chains. The budget allocation under AIF also supports the development of cold storage, refrigerated transportation, and other essential components of the cold chain.

National Cold Chain Grid

The government is working on establishing a National Cold Chain Grid, aiming to integrate cold storage facilities from production centers to consumption centers. This initiative seeks to ensure a seamless supply chain for perishable goods across the country. Budget support for this grid involves investments in modernizing existing facilities and setting up new infrastructure, with an emphasis on public-private partnerships (PPP).

Subsidies and Incentives

The government offers various subsidies and incentives to encourage private sector participation in building cold chain infrastructure. This includes capital investment subsidies under schemes like the Mission for Integrated Development of Horticulture (MIDH) and tax incentives for companies investing in cold chain projects. These financial supports are crucial for offsetting the high costs associated with establishing and maintaining cold chain facilities.

Focus on Technology and Innovation

Recognizing the role of technology in cold chain management, the government has allocated funds for research and development in innovative cold storage solutions. This includes the promotion of solar-powered cold storages, which can be particularly beneficial in rural areas with limited access to electricity. Budget allocations in this area are geared towards creating sustainable and cost-effective cold chain solutions.

Impact of Budgetary Support

The budgetary support for integrated cold chain infrastructure has had a significant impact on the agricultural sector in India. It has led to the creation of a more robust supply chain, reducing post-harvest losses and ensuring that farmers get better prices for their produce. Additionally, improved cold chain infrastructure has facilitated the export of high-value agricultural products, contributing to increased foreign exchange earnings.

The government's continued focus on cold chain infrastructure through sustained budgetary support is essential for achieving the goals of doubling farmers' income and ensuring food security. By building a strong cold chain network, India can better manage its agricultural produce, reduce wastage, and improve the overall efficiency of its food supply chain.

Modernisation of Abattoirs: With a view to develop better forward linkages for meat products, the government has provided for financial assistance to local government bodies for setting up modern abattoirs. The scheme is planned to have flexibility for facilitating involvement of private investors through competitive bidding. The government plans to modernize 110 abattoirs and set up 50 new abattoirs in the XIth five year plan.

Incentives are also available for value added centers (includes infrastructural facilities including processing/multiline processing/collection centers for agriculture products like horticulture,marine,dairy,meat and poultry) and irradiation facilities.

II. Schemes for Technology up-gradation and modernization

These schemes encompass the establishment, expansion, and modernization of food processing units across various segments, including fruits & vegetables, milk products, meat, poultry, fishery, oilseeds, and other agri-horticultural sectors, aimed at value addition and shelf life enhancement. Key initiatives supporting technology upgradation and modernization include:

Government assistance provided in the form of grants, amounting to 25% and 33.33% of the plant & machinery and technical civil work costs, respectively, with a maximum cap of INR 5 million and 7.5 million in general areas and difficult areas. These schemes also offer increased assistance rates for difficult areas such as J&K, HP, Uttaranchal, Sikkim, and the NE States.

Apart from the 11th plan schemes, the ministry has also initiated specific plans for the development of difficult areas like the North Eastern region. Some of these projects are:

- Special Economic Zone Policy: To augment infrastructure facilities for export production by treating such zones as deemed foreign territory for tariff and trade operations.

- Technology Mission for Integrated Development of Horticulture in Eastern and Himalayan states. To augment integrated development of horticulture in the specified regions by providing higher levels of assistance(up to 50% and max.of INR 40 million for setting up and INR 10 million for up gradation of processing facilities available)

- Special component plan and Tribal Sub-Plan: Under this scheme MOFPI is providing assistance to projects in the food processing sector under its plan schemes, which benefit the tribal communities in the predominantly tribal states of North region, Jharkhand,MP, Rajastan and Chhatisgarh among others.

III. Schemes for Backward and Forward Integration

Government is taking various measures and initiatives to enhance backward and forward linkages between farmers,processors and the market.

To enhance backward linkages and encourage private participation, the government has proposed amendments to the APMC Act to allow private entities (processors, retailers, etc.) to participate as buyers and procure directly from farmers. Additionally, the Terminal Market Scheme, implemented by the National Horticulture Mission, aims to strengthen connections between farmers and end markets.

With a view to support forward linkages and specially for promoting exports government is providing various incentives through institutions like APEDA. These initiatives include:

- Providing relevant R&D support to enhance the quality of products.

- Financial assistance to exporters and producers to install quality systems to meet the international quality norms.

- Assistance for sale and market development of the products in the export market and dissemination of information about international market requirements etc.

IV. Schemes for Quality Assurance, Quality control, R&D and Promotional Activities

These schemes focus on improving the food testing and quality control infrastructure, improving the food safety and hygiene standards in the country, bringing in focused and integrated R&D efforts for the food processing value chain and supporting promotional activities for development of markets for processed food. Following are key initiatives under this scheme:

- Setting up or up gradation of quality control and food testing labs: Under the 11ᵗʰplan,increased level of financial assistance has been proposed for private sector to participate in establishing/upgrading the proposed eighty four food testing laboratories in various parts of the country and develop a mechanism for networking of these laboratories. This scheme offers agencies and private sector organizations a grant-in-aid covering 50% of the cost of laboratory equipment and 25% of the cost of technical civil works for housing the equipment, furniture, and fixtures associated with the equipment in general areas. In difficult areas, funding extends to 70% of the cost of lab equipment and 33% of technical civil works.

- Funds are also allocated for the implementation of total quality management systems, which encompass the adoption of quality assurance systems such as HACCP/ISO 22000, ISO 14000, and other quality and safety management systems.

- Promoting holistic research and development for food processing: In the XIth plan,while financial assistance in the form of 100% subsidy for equipment and consumables cost has been proposed for government organisations and universities, financial assistance for R&D activities has been proposed for private institutions in the form of 50% subsidy for equipment cost incurred for R&D activities. However, this grant is proposed to be provided for the Ministry sponsored projects to the reputed organisations only.

- Under the promotional activities component: MOFPI plans to provide assistance for participating in market activities and conducting feasibility studies.

- V. Schemes for HRD and Institution Building:

Thus schemes focuses on strengthening institutions for HRD for food processing sector. The various initiatives in this direction include:

- Setting up of food processing training centers in rural areas.
- Setting up of National Meat and Poultry Board and Grape Processing Board.

- Constitution of Fish Processing Development Council.
- Establishment of National Institution of Food Technology, Entrepreneurship and Management (NIFTEM)
- Strengthening of State Nodal Agencies

Clearly, the government is taking tremendous efforts for the holistic development of the food processing sector of the country. This opens up immense opportunities for PPP in this domain.

5. Key Challenges and Constraints

While the demand side opportunities are bright and policy makers are strongly supporting the growth and development of the food processing industry, entrepreneurs face some critical challenges while operating in this sector. It explains the key challenges that entrepreneurs in the food processing industry face across the food value chain.

I. Low productivity and availabity of processing varieties.

Low productivity and the availability of processing varieties are significant challenges in India's agricultural and food processing sectors. These issues have direct implications on the efficiency and competitiveness of the agricultural value chain, affecting everything from farm incomes to the quality of processed products available in the market.

Low Productivity in Agriculture

Factors Contributing to Low Productivity

Traditional Farming Practices: A significant portion of India's agriculture still relies on traditional farming methods, which are less efficient compared to modern, technology-driven practices. This results in lower yields per hectare.

Fragmented Land Holdings: The average farm size in India is small and fragmented, which limits economies of scale and leads to inefficiencies in resource use, including water, fertilizers, and seeds.

Inadequate Irrigation: Despite improvements in irrigation infrastructure, a considerable area of agricultural land remains rain-fed, making it vulnerable to fluctuations in monsoon patterns and leading to inconsistent productivity.

Limited Access to Quality Inputs: Small and marginal farmers often have limited access to high-quality seeds, fertilizers, and other inputs, which adversely affects crop productivity.

Soil Degradation: Overuse of chemical fertilizers, monoculture practices, and inadequate crop rotation have led to soil degradation, further reducing the productivity of agricultural land.

Impact on Processing Varieties

Limited Availability of Processing-Specific Varieties: Many farmers grow varieties of crops that are primarily suited for fresh consumption rather than processing. This is due to a lack of awareness, inadequate access to seeds for processing varieties, and the absence of a robust market for such varieties.

Quality and Consistency Issues: The low productivity of crops often translates to variability in quality, which poses challenges for food processors who require consistent quality for efficient production.

Availability of Processing Varieties
Processing Varieties Defined

Tailored Characteristics: Processing varieties are specific cultivars of crops bred for traits that are desirable in food processing, such as higher starch content in potatoes for chips, thicker skins in tomatoes for canning, or higher oil content in oilseeds.

Limited Cultivation: The cultivation of these processing varieties is limited due to several factors, including lack of awareness among farmers, inadequate market linkages, and the dominance of fresh-market varieties.

Challenges in Promoting Processing Varieties

Lack of Market Demand Signals: Farmers often do not grow processing varieties because there is no assured market or premium price for such varieties. The lack of strong contracts or demand from processors discourages farmers from shifting to these crops.

Supply Chain Constraints: Even when processing varieties are grown, the absence of an integrated supply chain that connects farmers with processors leads to inefficiencies. Poor post-harvest infrastructure further exacerbates these issues, as processing varieties often require specific handling and storage conditions.

Research and Development Gaps: There is a need for more research into developing processing-specific varieties that are suited to Indian agro-climatic conditions. The current focus of agricultural research in India has been more on increasing yield rather than developing specialized varieties for processing.

Impact on the Food Processing Industry

Inconsistent Raw Material Supply: The food processing industry relies on a consistent supply of high-quality raw materials. The low availability of processing varieties means that processors often have to use suboptimal raw materials, leading to lower efficiency and higher production costs.

Reduced Competitiveness: The lack of processing varieties affects the competitiveness of India's food processing sector in the global market. Products may lack the desired quality or consistency, making it harder to compete with processed foods from countries where specialized varieties are more readily available.

Limited Value Addition: The inability to source high-quality processing varieties limits the extent of value addition that can be achieved within the country. This affects the profitability of both farmers and processors and hinders the growth of the sector.

Addressing the Challenges

To overcome these challenges, several steps can be taken:

Promotion of Processing Varieties: The government and private sector should collaborate to promote the cultivation of processing-specific varieties through awareness campaigns, better access to seeds, and assured buy-back arrangements.

Strengthening Research: Investment in agricultural research should focus more on developing processing varieties that are suited to local conditions and meet the needs of the processing industry.

Improving Market Linkages: Developing strong market linkages between farmers and processors, supported by contract farming and better post-harvest infrastructure, can help in ensuring a steady supply of quality raw materials.

Encouraging Farmer Collectives: Organizing farmers into cooperatives or producer organizations can help in achieving economies of scale, thereby making the cultivation of processing varieties more viable and profitable.

II. Inefficient Procurement and Aggregation of Raw Material

Agriculture in India is characterized by highly fragmented land holdings. Consequently, the marketed surplus per farmer is extremely low. Further,agricultural trade is characterized by a long supply chain with multiple market intermediary participation. Fragmented and dispersed nature of production coupled with a long supplychain results in higher aggregation and procurement costs. Though different methods of aggregation are followed to enhance scale and make transportation cost efficient,the major challenges faced by processors,today are the lack of predictability of supply and the lack of homogeneity in quality.

III. Inadequate Post Harvest Infrastructure

Annually, an estimated USD 12.9 billion worth of harvested food is squandered in the country due to deficient post-harvest infrastructure, including cold chains, transportation, and storage facilities. Urgent measures are needed to enhance efficiencies in handling agricultural produce after harvest, especially perishable items, by establishing a basic level of infrastructure to maintain quality. Unfortunately, warehouses, cold storages, refrigerated transportation, modernized abattoirs, and other essential post-harvest facilities are severely lacking. Private investors are hesitant to invest in such infrastructure due to the financial challenges associated with standalone projects in rural areas. For example, operating costs for Indian cold storage units exceed Rs 240 per cubic meter per year, compared to less than Rs 120 in Western countries. Energy expenses alone constitute approximately 28% of total costs for Indian cold storages, whereas they account for only 10% in the West. These factors render the establishment of cold storages economically unfeasible.

IV. Low Scale Operation

Economies of scale are among the most critical success factors for efficient processing. Most of the food processing units in India are small scale. Their inability to scale up has often resulted in inefficiencies in operations and most players today find it difficult not only to invest in critical areas of efficiency such as state of art technology and manufacturing equipment, trained manpower, certification systems, marketing & promotion. They also find it difficult to put in place an appropriate sourcing system for ensuring quality and regularity of supply. Their ability to diversify into different product categories in accordance to seasonality and changes in demand trend is also diminished. Retention of competitive advantage for small players has therefore become a huge challenge.

V. Inadequate Credit Availability

One of the major hurdles for growth of processing industry is the low availability of finances and credit across the food value chain. Though there has been intense focus by both the central and state governments to extend credit to farmers and small scale processing units, financial institutions are generally not comfortable in extending credit primarily due to the high risk involved in lending to this sector. Lack of an efficient organized credit provision leads the farmer towards money lenders, mostly input suppliers or the trading middlemen. Likewise, small scale food processers face tremendous challenges in raising funds especially when they are not in a position to offer collateral security.

VI. Lack of Integration and clarity in food laws

Currently processors need to comply with numerous laws which are administered by a number of different Ministries and departments. The enforcement of food laws in India falls under the jurisdiction of State Governments and Union Territories, as health and agriculture are state subjects. Consequently, there is a multitude of food legislations and enforcement agencies, leading to challenges such as conflicting approaches, lack of coordination, and administrative delays. For example, manufacturers of packaged food products must adhere to quality standards and label declarations outlined in various legislations such as the Prevention of Food Adulteration (PFA) Act, the Standards of Weights & Measures (Packaged Commodities) Rules, and the Fruit Products Order. However, these laws often present contradictions and inconsistencies in specifications. To address these issues, the Government of India passed the Food Safety and Standards Act (FSSA) in August 2006. This legislation aims to establish a new authority, the Food Safety and Standards Authority, which will streamline food regulation by merging eight separate Acts and establishing an independent risk assessment body. This initiative represents a positive step towards integrating and harmonizing various food laws in the country.

VII. Low adoption of Quality and safety standards

The primary obstacle hindering export growth is the disparity in quality standards between the goods produced in India and the specifications demanded by importing nations.. The key requirement is a change in attitude of all stake holders from the existing practice of "marketing what is produced" to "produce what is marketable". There is a lack of adoption of practices such as traceability and certification-which if followed could substantially increase the trust in the products thus increasing turn over.

VIII. Inadequate availability of trained manpower

As the processing industry grows rapidly the expertise required across the value chain are changing dramatically. This has resulted in a vacuum in availability of trained manpower in specialized areas of operation and implementation that are unique to the industry.

IX. Mismatch in Research orientation and Industry requirements

The aim of public research in agriculture has primarily been to increase production. However, research lacks the orientation to meet specific trait requirements of processors such as process ability and shelf life. Further, the interface between public research and industry is extremely low resulting poor exchange of information. Hence on the one hand while the public research system has limited knowledge of the problems faced by the industry, the private sector has limited exposure to the wide pool of research findings and invention.

X. Low Domestic Market Size for High Value Processed Food

Lack of sufficient aggregate domestic demand is the single most critical factor that is restricting expansion and scale of high value processed products in India. The consumer is highly price sensitive and given the option, would prefer fresh and home made products to processed food if the cost differential is too high. Entrepreneurs need to be aware that the market is extremely diverse and consumer tastes and preferences dramatically change across regions and socio-cultural and economic strata-thus requiring a range of innovative products and brands that cater to different tastes and wallets.

Opportunities for Investment

The rapidly increasing demand for high value processed food in the country coupled with the strong and diverse agro-climatic conditions that exist in the country provides immense opportunities for investment. Some key opportunities for investment across the agri-value chain are discussed herewith.

I. **Opportunities to address the domestic demand-supply gap:** Increasing population coupled with factors such as rapid urbanization and increasing disposable income in India has opened up huge gap between demand and supply of many high value food products. There is huge potential to invest in the development of large scale integrated production, processing, storage& distribution facilities especially for fruits &vegetables, dairy, poultry, fish and other livestock products in the country.

II. **Opportunities to address the Global Market:** India possesses strategic advantages that augur well for intense and diverse agricultural activity and has the potential to emerge as a key global sourcing hub for processed food products. Despite notable strengths on the supply side, including being the largest producer of milk globally, the second-largest producer of food grains, fruits, and vegetables, and the third-largest producer of fish, India also boasts significant comparative advantages. These include its proximity to major consumption markets like the Gulf and Middle East countries, as well as access to cost-effective and highly skilled human resources. Further, the Government is providing a number of incentives and tax sops to promote export of processed food. These factors open up huge opportunities for entrepreneurs looking to set up export oriented processing units.

III. **Opportunities to invest in building efficiencies across the value chain:** Presently, the lack of proper infrastructure and inefficiencies and redundancies across the supply chain is hampering entrepreneurs to harness the true potential of the food processing sector. While on the production front, the farm holdings are small and highly fragmented and farm productivity is low and the post-harvest side of the supply chain is adversely impacted by factors such as lack of scale, lack of post-harvest quality standards and inadequate post harvest infrastructure. These challenges open up huge opportunities to build efficiencies across the supply chain. Some key investment opportunities are discussed herewith.

a) **Introduction of new planting material, animal breeds and farm technologies** There is huge scope to unlock the true potential of agricultural productivity in India by addressing basic issues such as making available high yielding planting material and breeding material. In addition, investment in advanced farm technologies such as drip irrigation systems, farm machinery and specialty plant and animal health protection chemicals also holds immense potential. Further there is immense potential to introduce new breeding stock and planting material that have the propensity and traits required to produce raw material tailor made for processing.

b) **Innovative Procurement and Aggregation Models:** Severe challenges in aggregation of agricultural produce throws up immense opportunities for entrepreneurs to develop innovative and efficient models for aggregation. The objective of developing such models is to assure quality, quantity and timely supply. A good example is the ITC e-choupal model. Other examples of such models include contact farming, contract farming, Bhagidari and corporate farming.

Procurement and aggregation model

Aggrega-tion model	Description	Pros	Cons	Examples
Contact Farming	Procurement agencies develop relationship with farmer by extending agronomical support to enhance productivity. Farmer has the option of selling the produce anywhere.	Farmer has a basic forward linkage with company for produce disposal. Procurement agency can plan purchases.	Varied farmer base results in heterogeneous quality. No supply assurance to procurement agency.	Safal Namdhari Reliance fresh

Bhagodari	Corporate ties up farmer produce to end user. Corporate gets assured returns and passes balance benefit to farmer.	Better bargaining power for produce. High realization in the market gives farmer better returns. Assured quality and low risk in business for corporate.	Fixed but low margins for corporate.	Mahindra in grapes.
Contract Farming	Farmers get into contract with processors or exporters. Off-take of produce is ensured.	Risk of returns covered. Better extension service and input provision increases yield. End users have control on quality and supply.	Farmers may not stick to contract and may sell in open markets when price is high there. Contract law cannot be enforced.	Global green in gherkins ITC & Pepsi Co in potato Mahindra in seed potato
Corporate Farming	Private companies are allowed to grow large farms of produce.	Homogeneity in quality, traceability, control on supply	High labour cost. Capital intensive, corporate overhead cost too high to be absorbed.	Bharti Field Fresh(baby corn) Reliance (mango)

Programs like contract farming expedite the transfer of technology, increase capital investment, and provide guaranteed markets for agricultural produce. However, trust and confidence of partners involved in the agreement is a pre-degree for contract farming to be successful.

c) **Infrastructure development** The poor state of agri-infrastructure from the 'farm gate to the food plate' has prevented large scale private sector investments in the agri-sector till no Yet, both central and state governments have offered a range of incentives, including capital subsidies and tax exemptions, to encourage investments in these sectors.w. They are also encouraging many participative models for post harvest infrastructure development. Key infrastructure projects promoted by the government and which have immense scope for private investment include Mega Food Parks, Terminal Markets and Cold Chain Development, Potential for investment in these areas is detailed herewith.

- **Integrated Agro-Food Parks**

Recognising the investment potential that consolidated agri-infrastructure development holds, Companies such as IFFCO have initiated the process of development of integrated Agro-parks. A typical Agropark has production functions such as green-houses, integrated dairy farms, poultry farms and aquaculture units integrated with processing functions such as cereal and pulse milling, fruit and vegetables processing and meat processing. These functions are ecologically designed in such a manner that there is mutually beneficial exchange of by-products and waste. To augment the efficiencies of production and processing within the park, world class common infrastructure are planned to be developed providing for not only basic amenities(such as roads,in-house power and water supply and waste management) but also specialized common post-harvest infrastructure such as trading platforms, cold storages, ripening chambers and common cold chain logistics solutions. These parks are forward and backward linked through Rural Transformation Centers(RTCs) at farmer level and Consolidation Centers or distribution centers at consumption centers. Integrated Agro-park is a demand driven model with strong backward and forward linkages that create a sustainable and intelligent agri-value chain networks.

Mega Food Parks: This scheme being implemented by MOFPI has tremendous potential for investors interested in utilizing the support provided for clustering of processing industry so as to facilitate scale and common use of infrastructure. Under this scheme, a consortium of minimum three members can apply for development of Mega Food Parks. As per the eligibility criteria one of the members needs to be from the Food Processing industry while other two could be from any other industry.

- **Terminal Markets:** Another option for entrepreneurs to leverage in the agri-infrastructure space is the government's push to develop Modern Terminal Markets. MTMs are trading platforms that are intended to develop the right infrastructure close to the area of production such that farmers have the opportunity for a transparent price discovery platform close to production centers MTM, or Multiple Trading Models, offers farmers various options for selling their produce while also addressing crucial infrastructure requirements for both sellers and buyers.. The MTM scheme has been conceptualized and introduced by the National Horticulture Mission under the Ministry of Agriculture. While each MTM is primarily designed to strength the handling, storage and market linkage of perishable commodities (such as fruits, vegetables, flowers, aromatics, herbs, meat, poultry etc.) it also allows handling of non-perishable commodities to a limited extent. MTM scheme is envisaged to promote PPP in Agriculture sector. The entire designing, development, operations and maintenance of the MTM is expected to be undertaken by suitable private players. The selection of the private players for each MTM would be done through a two stage competitive bidding process. Each state in India be eligible to undertake the development of MTM at suitable locations. Currently, various states have identified more than 20 locations for the development of MTMs. In the current guideline formulated by the NHM, each MTM would entail a subsidy amount of upto INR 500 million. Any private player in the Food and Agribusiness domain or infra structure development is eligible to bid for the MTM scheme. Preference is given to foreign players and players having prior experience of handling perishable commodities or development of Agri infrastructure. MTM scheme is under advanced stages of implementation in states such as Maharastra, Orissa, Bihar, TN, Andrapradesh, Chandigarh and Nagaland. Other states are at advanced stage of initiation of the scheme.

- **Cold chain Logistics Development** Given the increasing demand for good quality perishable produce by consumers in both domestic and export markets, the maintenance of cold chain from grower to the consumer is of crucial relevance and is turning out to be an attractive area of investment. Though the development of cold chain logistics faces critical challenges such as diverse requirement for different agricultural produce, lack of standardized pricing for provision of cold chain facility and lack of critical scale for organized player participation, the pull from demand for quality is quickly overtaking the obstacles of development. The opportunity for investment in this space is further strengthened by the fact that the Government of India has launched a number of schemes and concessions to boost growth of cold chains industry. For instance, the cold chain & strategic distribution center scheme envisaged in the XIth plan focuses on setting up of centers with infrastructure facilities such as material handling equipment,refrideration,blast freezing, cold storages and other ancillary equipment so as to handle a wide range of perishable or processed food products. These centers are expected to form the last point for export of processed foods and also provide the much needed forward linkage to the supermarkets and malls in the metropolises.

The fragmented and unorganized nature of cold chain logistics in India provides huge scope for investment in organized logistic service provision especially when entrepreneurs develop innovative solutions- such as multi-purpose cold chain service provision and container pooling systems-that effectively address the constraint of lack of scale.

d) **Introduction of Modern Technology:** Given the food processing industry is dominated by SME and unorganized sector, most of the technologies used is out dated and inefficient. There is high potential for introduction of modern technologies across value chain components including farm level technologies such as micro-irrigation and technologies involved in developing integrated large scale dairy farms, integrated abattoirs-cum- meat processing units, post harvest technology for preservation, packaging technologies bulk and cold storage among others.

e) **Standardisation of Quality and Safety Systems:** Food safety is now becoming a global concern due to consumer discern regarding the quality of food that to be consumed. Globalisation and the removal of tariff and non-tariff barriers have brought in international competition to the domestic markets as well, making it essential for the food processing industry to adopt strong practices of food safety and quality to be competitive. Safe and effective food handling requires a structured system for controlling the quality factors involved in the process. Recently, there has been a growing call to enhance the guarantee of food safety and quality for consumers. Two essential tools for benchmarking quality and safety are traceability and certification. Increased demand for the safe food opens up immense opportunity for development of food testing labs. While there are around 80 state and 4 central food-testing laboratories in India, which over the years, have been undertaking conventional food quality assessments under the framework of the Prevention of Food Adulteration(PFA) Act,1954,they are far less than the requirement. Moreover, majority of the state laboratories are not fully geared to test a variety of food contaminants which pose serious health risks-opening up immense opportunity for development of modern food testing laboratories. In addition to the immense business opportunity that the food testing vertical provides,it is also intensely supported by government support as described.

f) **Human Resource Development:** Application of modern technology is a key imperative for the growth of food processing industry. Introduction of modern technology is expected to lead to unprecedented demand for scientists, technologists and other professionals across the agri-value chain- with the right techno-commercial expertise to effectively handle the emerging challenges of the food processing industry. The demand for high quality skilled manpower opens up opportunities for investers to establish professional training institutes catering to technical and managerial skill set requirement for verticals across the agri-value chain including procurement and commodity trading, logistics and distribution, R&D, technology management and implementation engineering and marketing among others. These educational and training initiatives can also be translated into learning centers which can be showcased as a CSR activity of big business houses. Such initiatives will lead to skill upgradation of local workforce and also ensure sufficient workforce availability to the industries in the catchment area.

6. Conclusion

India possesses remarkable strengths for supply of agricultural raw material and as policy makers are leaving no stone unturned to increase processing levels. It is the producers to link up and integrate to the demand side which would decide the entrepreneurs competitiveness in food processing industry. Some action steps that need to be taken by the entrepreneurs and policy makers in this direction are given below.

I. **Action Steps for Entrepreneurs:** As entrepreneurs try to exploit the immense business potential that the food processing sector offers in India, some critical constraints and challenges need to be kept in mind so as to realize and enhance growth. On the demand side, while the size and growth of various segments in the processed food sector are very promising, lack of critical market size for high value processed products coupled with diverse and highly segmented market are key deterrents for entrepreneurs to enter into specific segments. It is critical for investors to be very target specific and adapt their products to local tastes. This would require continual invention of products and reinvention of brands. On the supply side, it is critical for entrepreneurs to understand and address the gaps in the supply chain by developing innovative strategies and models to actualize smooth and efficient availability of raw material. It is critical for private players operating in the post harvest handling and trade of perishable to develop a sustainable long term relationship with farmers based on trust. Critical action steps for smooth sourcing operations include:

- Maintain transparency in transactions
- Facilitate in micro level planning in terms of area allocation for crops, cropping pattern etc to deliver right quality and quantity at the right time.
- Develop and disseminate technology related to production, water management, communication, transportation, quality enhancement etc. that reduces cost of operation and improves quality.

- Disseminate knowledge about quality standard.
- Act as an anchor for dissemination of market information.

II. **Action Steps for Policy Makers:** The Government of India and various state governments have taken commendable steps to promote food processing in India. Some key focus areas that need further attention include:

a) **Improve production capabilities of farmers:** The agro-climatic diversity of the country favours for production of diverse agricultural products, productivity is substantially low across various agricultural commodities. There is a huge scope to unlock the true potential of crop and livestock productivity by addressing basic issues such as availability of good planting and breeding material, efficient use of plant health chemicals and veterinary medicine, better investment by the farmer in crop cultivation and animal husbandry and enhanced quality and effectiveness of extension and technology dissemination at the farm level. Concerted efforts by policy makers and the public sector machinery in this direction are critical to sustain a successful food processing sector in the country.

Action steps to increase productivity

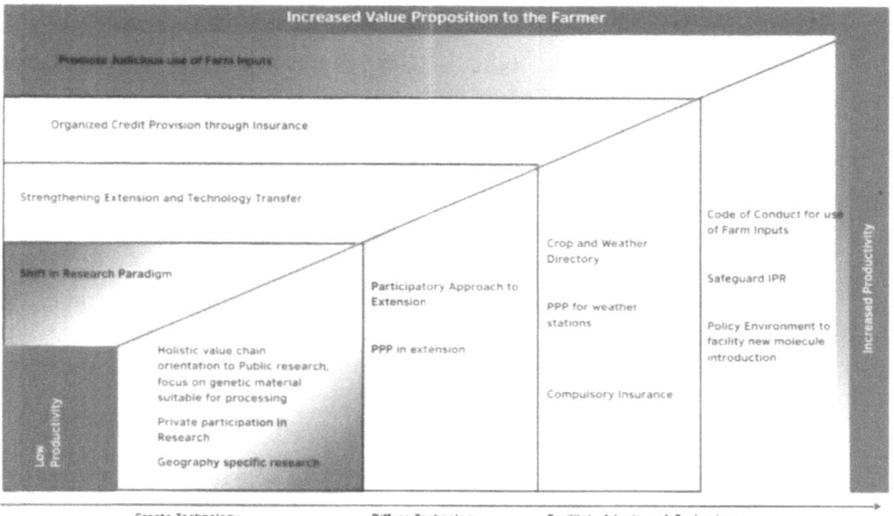

b) **Promote higher scale of operations and technology upgradation**
In order to improve the efficiency of processing sector, there is a need to increase the scale of operations, capacity utilization and operational

efficiency of the processing units. Specific anomalies of the processing sector such as the highly fragmented and unorganized industry, lower capacity utilization and non-adoption of cost effective technologies have contributed to low efficiency. While various governments have focused on protecting the small and medium enterprises, the need for scale and technology up-gradation has largely been neglected. It is imminent for policy makers to focus on attracting large business houses into food processing sector and in the process pushing for introduction of higher scale of operations and modernization of technology.

c) **Support backward integration:** Indian agriculture is dominated by small and marginal farmers with fragmented land holdings and low marketable surpluses. This has been a serious impediment in aggregation and systematic handling of agricultural produce including that of livestock(due to lack of scale of transactions). As a result small farmers tend to be left outside the current policy delivery framework and lack access to capital for crop financing and farm infrastructure, technical knowhow, quality farm inputs, market information and markets.

There is an urgent need to integrate small farmers into the value added supply chains. Recommendations in this direction are elucidated here under.

- Build organizational capital- There is a need for collective action at the farmer level to address issues of economic scale for forward linkages. The government needs to support formation of farmer associations and farmer groups which could be the stepping stones for institutionalization and consolidation of aggregation at the farm level.

- Build Market Intelligence Capital- It is essential for the government to support initiatives that upgrade farmer groups to develop expertise in market intelligence.

- Promote specific commodity clusters- To support increase in scale of aggregation, economic and uniform application of quality standards and focused market information transfer, a useful strategy could be the promotion of extensive cultivation of specific commodity in a compact geographical area. Also promoting intense reading of live stock- such as integrated dairy farms—would facilitate better control on procurement of required quality and quantity of raw material for the processing industry.

- Facilitate contract farming- It facilitates accelerated technology transfer, capital inflow and assured markets for the produce. However certain measures are required to facilitate adherence to contract farming agreements which are enlisted below.

- A model contract farming agreements need to be developed taking into account the sensitivity of such contracts to quality, prices fluctuations and inters of both the parties involved.

- There is a need to initiate and formalize a model lease agreement so as to help in aggregation of land in favour of a private player who in turn needs to pass on the benefits of consolidation and high tech agriculture to the farmer(in addition to the land lease rental)

- Rationalisation of marketing laws- There is a need to revisit the levies and taxes on the movement of agricultural produce to facilitate better private participation in aggregation and post harvest handling of agricultural produce. Policy initiatives required to facilitate efficient movement of produce from production centers to consumption centers are enumerated below:

  - Uniform implementation of the state APMC act to facilitate alternate channels of marketing.

  - Single point levy of marketing fees.

  - Single point registration for trade and transaction in more than one market area.

d) **Bridge post-harvest infrastructure gaps:** Creation of a certain level of infrastructure is the key to build efficiencies in the post-harvest handling of agricultural produce and thus increase efficiency of processing units. Infrastructure services such as roads, electricity supply and telecommunication and others are limited in the rural areas. Warehouses, cold storages and post-harvest practices are awfully inadequate in many states in India. Current Government initiatives are primarily aimed enabling private sector investment in infrastructure creation. While both the central government and state governments have floated several schemes related to marketing, infrastructure and post-harvest management in the past, some critical areas where policies review is required with specific reference to facilitating infrastructure development for food processing industry are:

  - Review Land Laws and Zoning Laws: Current land laws require conversion of agricultural land to non-agricultural land for carrying out post-harvest handling activities (including for setting up pack houses, cold stores, terminal markets and others). This exercise is time consuming and costly, making post-harvest infrastructure and handling projects inefficient. The land laws need to change such that all agriculture related post-harvest activities are permitted to be carried out without having to change the definition of the land use.

- Review Power Tariff for Post-Harvest Handling Projects: Most post-harvest handling projects such as cold storages, cold rooms, pack houses and others have power as a major cost component (energy cost makes up to 28% of the total expenses for Indian cold stores compared to 10% in the West). Industrial tariff rate is applicable for power consumption of these projects. In order to promote post-harvest infrastructure projects, it is suggested that agriculture tariff rates be applied for all post-harvest projects.

- Remove Restrictions on Multiple Subsidy Provision: Private players who have invested in post-harvest infrastructure are centers of tacit knowledge and they have to be encouraged to expand their presence in this space. Ironically, provision of subsidy for setting up post-harvest handling facility is limited to two times foe each corporate. This clause needs revision such that the subsidy provision is not capped in terms of value and number of applications per firm.

e) **Integrate food laws and regulations:** Since health and agriculture fall under the jurisdiction of state governments and union territories, the enforcement of food laws primarily resides with them. Consequently, there exists a multitude of food legislations and enforcement agencies. This proliferation of legislations has resulted in conflicting approaches, a lack of coordination, and administrative delays. There is an urgent need to rationalize numerous laws which are been complied by processors and develop a single integrated food law that governs the regulatory requirements of processed food. Introduction of Food Safety and Standards Act is a welcome step in this direction.

f) **Enable better access to credit** To enhance credit accessibility, the government has designated food processing industries as a priority sector for bank lending. Furthermore, NABARD has established a refinancing facility with a fund of INR 10 billion, specifically targeting agro-processing infrastructure and market development. However, more needs to be done to increase credit flow to the processing sector. For instance, an investment of INR 50 million in plant and machinery is set as the upper limit to qualify as priority sector credit. This limit needs to be increased substantially to promote scaled up food processing units.

g) **Human Resource Development:** As the food processing sector looks to grow exponentially in the near future, it is very essential to design and develop a mechanism to address the manpower development needs of the sector at different levels of responsibilities. Since, human resource development needs to address soft skill requirements across the value chain of processed food, policy makers need to put forward steps which would encourage state and private universities to commerce course in various vocations such as procurement, supply chain management, logistics, food packaging, processing, post-harvest technology, information technology in agriculture and other such allied fields.

Summary and Conclusion

The summary chapter serves as a concise overview, reiterating the key points discussed and providing a quick reference guide for readers. It typically covers the following aspects:

1. **Overview of Food Processing Industry**
   - **Historical Development:** A brief history of the food processing industry and its evolution over time. Tracing the evolution of food processing from traditional methods to modern, industrialized processes.
   - **Current Landscape:** Current state of the industry, including major players, market size, and key trends. : Snapshot of the current industry, including market leaders, key sectors, and global market dynamics.
   - **Evolution and Impact:** Review of the historical development of the food processing industry and its impact on food availability, safety, and variety.
   - **Current Market Structure**: Analysis of the current market structure, major industry players, and key economic indicators.

2. **Key Processes and Technologies**
   - **Processing Techniques:** Overview of various food processing techniques, such as thermal processing, freezing, dehydration, and fermentation. Detailed examination of various food processing methods such as pasteurization, canning, freeze-drying, and fermentation.
   - **Technological Innovations:** Discussion on the latest technological advancements and their impact on the industry. Overview of cutting-edge technologies like high-pressure processing, pulsed electric fields, and nanotechnology.
   - **Core Processes**: Overview of essential food processing techniques such as thermal processing, extrusion, and aseptic processing.
   - **Emerging Technologies**: Summary of emerging technologies like high-pressure processing (HPP), ultrasonic processing, and 3D food printing, highlighting their benefits and potential applications.

3. **Quality and Safety**
   - **Quality Assurance:** Methods and standards for ensuring product quality and safety.Description of quality management systems, including Total Quality Management (TQM) and Good Manufacturing Practices (GMP).
   - **Regulatory Frameworks:** Overview of key regulations governing food processing and how companies can ensure compliance. Summary of key regulations, such as the Food Safety Modernization Act (FSMA) in the US and the European Union's food safety directives.
   - **Food Safety Protocols:** Explanation of food safety protocols and standards, including the role of regulatory bodies like the FDA, EFSA, and Codex Alimentarius.
   - **Risk Management:** Strategies for managing risks related to food contamination, including the use of real-time monitoring systems and recall management procedures.

4. **Supply Chain and Logistics**
   - **Supply Chain Dynamics:** Detailed discussion on supply chain management, including sourcing, production, and distribution. Exploration of the complexities of the food supply chain, from raw material sourcing to final product distribution.
   - **Logistics Management:** Strategies for efficient logistics and minimizing supply chain disruptions. Strategies for efficient logistics, including cold chain management for perishable goods and just-in-time (JIT) inventory systems. Supply Chain Integration: Importance of integrating supply chain activities from procurement to distribution to ensure seamless operations.
   - **Cold Chain Management**: Detailed look at cold chain management practices essential for maintaining the quality and safety of perishable goods.

5. **Sustainability and Environmental Impact**
   - **Sustainable Practices:** Importance of sustainable practices in food processing and examples of successful implementation. Examples of successful sustainable practices, such as the use of renewable energy and closed-loop systems
   - **Environmental Impact:** Discussion on the environmental impact of food processing and measures to mitigate it. Discussion on the environmental challenges posed by the food processing industry and potential mitigation strategies

- **Sustainable Innovations:** Case studies of sustainable innovations in food processing, such as the use of biodegradable packaging and renewable energy sources.
- **Environmental Regulations**: Overview of environmental regulations impacting the food processing industry and strategies for compliance.

6. **Market Trends and Consumer Behavior**

- **Consumer Insights:** Analysis of consumer behavior and preferences, and their implications for the industry. Analysis of current consumer preferences, such as the demand for clean-label products, organic foods, and transparency in sourcing.
- **Market Trends:** Key market trends shaping the future of food processing, such as health and wellness, convenience foods, and plant-based alternatives. Identification of major trends, including the rise of e-commerce in food retail and the growing popularity of functional foods.
- **Consumer Preferences:** Examination of shifting consumer preferences towards organic, non-GMO, and minimally processed foods.
- **E-commerce Growth**: Impact of e-commerce on the food industry, including trends in online grocery shopping and direct-to-consumer models.

7. **Strategic Management and Leadership**

- **Leadership Skills:** Essential skills and qualities for effective leadership in the food processing industry. Key skills for effective leadership in the food processing industry, such as strategic thinking, adaptability, and innovation
- **Strategic Planning:** Importance of strategic planning and decision-making to navigate industry challenges and capitalize on opportunities. Importance of strategic planning for long-term success, including market analysis, goal setting, and performance monitoring
- **Effective Leadership:** Characteristics of effective leadership in the food processing sector, including strategic vision, adaptability, and innovation.
- **Performance Metrics:** Key performance metrics for evaluating success, such as productivity, quality, and customer satisfaction.

8. **Future Outlook**

- **Industry Forecast:** Predictions for the future of the food processing industry, including emerging trends and potential challenges.

Predictions for the future, highlighting potential growth areas, emerging technologies, and evolving consumer demands.

- **Opportunities for Growth:** Identification of growth opportunities and strategies for capitalizing on them. Identification of opportunities for growth, such as expanding into new markets, developing new product lines, and leveraging data analytics.

- **Technological Advancements**: Predictions for future technological advancements in food processing and their potential impact on the industry.

- **Global Trends**: Analysis of global trends, such as the rise of plant-based diets, increased focus on sustainability, and the impact of geopolitical factors on food trade.

Key Insights

- **Integration of Technology:** The role of technology in enhancing efficiency and productivity in food processing. This includes automation, advanced machinery, and digital tracking systems.

- **Sustainability:** Emphasis on sustainable practices, reducing waste, and ensuring environmental stewardship. This also involves sustainable sourcing of raw materials and energy-efficient processing methods.

- **Quality Control:** Importance of stringent quality control measures to ensure food safety and consistency. This includes HACCP (Hazard Analysis Critical Control Point) and other regulatory frameworks.

- **Supply Chain Management:** Effective management of the supply chain to minimize disruptions and optimize logistics, from sourcing to distribution.

- **Innovation:** Continuous innovation in product development, packaging, and processing techniques to meet evolving consumer preferences and market demands.

Challenges and Solutions

- **Regulatory Compliance:** Navigating complex regulatory landscapes and ensuring compliance with food safety standards.

- **Market Competition:** Strategies to stay competitive in a global market, including differentiation and branding.

- **Resource Management:** Efficient management of resources, including water, energy, and raw materials, to maximize profitability and sustainability.

Future Trends

- **Digital Transformation:** Adoption of Industry 4.0 technologies, such as IoT, AI, and blockchain, for enhanced transparency and efficiency.
- **Consumer Preferences:** Shifting consumer preferences towards health, wellness, and convenience foods, and how the industry can adapt.
- **Globalization:** The impact of globalization on food processing and the opportunities it presents for market expansion.
- **Personalized Nutrition:** Increasing focus on personalized nutrition and customized food products to meet individual health needs.
- **Blockchain Technology:** Use of blockchain for transparent and tamper-proof supply chain records, enhancing trust and traceability.
- **Alternative Proteins:** Growth in the market for alternative proteins, including lab-grown meat and insect-based products.
- **Artificial Intelligence:** The role of AI in optimizing production processes, improving supply chain logistics, and enhancing customer engagement through personalized marketing.
- **Health and Wellness:** The increasing focus on health and wellness driving the demand for functional foods, probiotics, and foods with specific health benefits.

Strategic Recommendations

- **Investment in R&D:** Importance of investing in research and development to foster innovation and stay ahead of the curve. : Emphasizing the need for continuous investment in research and development to foster innovation and improve processes
- **Collaboration:** Encouraging collaboration between industry stakeholders, including suppliers, manufacturers, and retailers, to create a cohesive ecosystem.
- **Capacity Building:** Building capacity through training and development programs to equip the workforce with the necessary skills and knowledge. Investing in training and development programs to build a skilled workforce capable of leveraging new technologies.
- **Collaboration:** Encouraging partnerships between academia, industry, and government to drive advancements and address common challenges.
- **Cross-functional Collaboration:** Promoting collaboration across different functions within the organization, such as R&D, marketing, and supply chain, to foster innovation and efficiency.

- **Customer-Centric Approach:** Adopting a customer-centric approach by understanding and anticipating consumer needs and preferences, and delivering products that meet those needs effectively.

Integration of Technology

- **Impact of Automation:** Automation has streamlined various stages of food processing, reducing human error and increasing efficiency. For instance, automated sorting and grading systems ensure consistent quality.
- **Digital Tracking:** Technologies like IoT (Internet of Things) enable real-time monitoring of the supply chain, ensuring traceability from farm to fork.
- **Advanced Robotics:** The integration of robotics in food processing for tasks such as packaging, palletizing, and quality control has revolutionized the industry. Robots offer precision and efficiency, reducing labor costs and enhancing productivity.
- **Data Analytics**: Utilizing big data and predictive analytics to anticipate demand, optimize production schedules, and reduce downtime. Data-driven decision-making allows for more accurate forecasting and inventory management.

Sustainability

- **Waste Reduction:** Innovations in by-product utilization and waste management, such as converting waste into bioenergy or animal feed.
- **Eco-friendly Packaging:** Adoption of biodegradable and recyclable packaging materials to reduce environmental footprint.
- **Water and Energy Efficiency:** Implementation of water recycling systems and energy-efficient equipment to minimize resource use.
- **Circular Economy:** Adoption of circular economy principles where waste from one process becomes input for another. This includes repurposing by-products and investing in technologies that support recycling and reuse.
- **Carbon Footprint Reduction**: Strategies to reduce carbon emissions through the use of renewable energy sources, energy-efficient machinery, and carbon offset programs.

Quality Control

- **Advanced Testing:** Use of rapid microbiological testing and spectroscopic methods to detect contaminants and ensure food safety.

- **Standards and Certifications:** Adherence to international standards like ISO 22000 and certifications like BRC (British Retail Consortium) to maintain high quality and safety standards.
- **Traceability Systems**: Implementation of traceability systems using barcodes, RFID tags, and blockchain to track products throughout the supply chain, ensuring transparency and quick response to food safety issues.
- **Continuous Improvement:** Encouraging a culture of continuous improvement through regular audits, employee training, and adopting best practices in quality management.

Supply Chain Management

- **Resilience Building:** Strategies to build resilient supply chains that can withstand disruptions, such as diversifying suppliers and using predictive analytics.
- **Logistics Optimization:** Use of logistics management software to optimize routes, reduce fuel consumption, and ensure timely delivery.
- **Global Sourcing:** Navigating the complexities of global sourcing, including managing risks related to geopolitical issues, tariffs, and supply chain disruptions.
- **Demand Planning:** Enhancing demand planning accuracy through integrated planning systems that align sales, inventory, and operations.

Innovation

- **Product Development:** Focus on developing new products that meet dietary trends, such as plant-based proteins, functional foods, and organic products.
- **Packaging Innovations:** Development of smart packaging that can extend shelf life, provide information on freshness, and reduce spoilage.
- **Product Personalization**: Leveraging consumer data to offer personalized food products that cater to individual dietary preferences and health needs.
- **New Ingredients**: Exploration and incorporation of novel ingredients like seaweed, algae, and insect proteins to meet the growing demand for sustainable and nutritious food options.

Challenges and Solutions

- **Regulatory Compliance:** Staying abreast of changing regulations and implementing compliance management systems to ensure adherence.

- **Market Competition:** Differentiation through unique selling propositions (USPs), such as superior quality, sustainable practices, or innovative products.
- **Resource Management:** Adopting lean manufacturing principles to reduce waste and improve resource utilization.
- **Workforce Development**: Addressing the skills gap in the food processing industry by investing in workforce training and development programs.
- **Consumer Trust**: Building consumer trust through transparency, ethical practices, and effective communication regarding food safety and quality.

3

Food Processing and Preservation

1. Introduction

India ranks second in global food production after China and holds the potential to become the largest food producer worldwide. Its food processing industry is one of the largest sectors in the country, ranking fifth in terms of production, consumption, export, and anticipated growth. With a growing population and rising disposable incomes, the food sector is experiencing significant shifts in consumption patterns.

As incomes increase, households tend to change their food preferences. Spending on staples like cereals, pulses, and edible oils decreases, while expenditure on items like milk products, meat, fruits, and beverages rises. This shift is notably influenced by the processed food market, which constitutes 32% of the overall food market, amounting to US$ 29.4 billion within an estimated US$ 91.66 billion market.

According to the Confederation of Indian Industry (CII), the food processing sector has the potential to attract US$ 33 billion in investments over the next decade and create job opportunities for 9 million individuals. However, challenges persist, particularly in food wastage. Approximately INR 13.3 billion worth of fruits and vegetables are wasted annually due to inadequate cold storage and cold chain arrangements, while around INR 44 billion worth of food grains, fruits, and vegetables meet a similar fate. Reports indicate that 18% of India's total fruit and vegetable production goes to waste, highlighting the need for expanded cold storage facilities.

Currently, India has 6,300 cold storage units with a combined capacity of 30.11 million metric tons (MMT), meeting only half of the required capacity. To bridge this gap, an additional investment of INR 55,000 crore is necessary to achieve self-sufficiency in fruit and vegetable production. To facilitate growth in the processed food sector, the government has implemented various schemes providing financial assistance for setting up and modernizing food processing units, infrastructure development, research and development, and human resource training.

The food processing industry in India encompasses a wide range of activities, including agriculture, horticulture, animal husbandry, and fisheries. It also includes sectors that manufacture edible products using agricultural inputs. According to the Ministry of Food Processing, Government of India, the key segments of this industry are dairy, fruits and vegetable processing, grain processing, meat and poultry processing, fisheries, and consumer foods such as packaged foods, beverages, and packaged drinking water. Despite its significant size, the industry remains relatively underdeveloped, processing only 2% of the country's total agricultural and food produce.

Value addition in food products is expected to rise from the current 8% to 35% by 2025, with fruit and vegetable processing increasing from 2% to 25% of total production within the same timeframe.

The dairy sector leads in processed food, with 37% of total production processed, although only 15% of this is managed by the organized sector. The Indian food processing industry is poised for substantial growth, with expected investments totaling approximately Rs 1,400 billion in the next decade.

Role of Indian Institute of Packaging for Agrifood and non-food produce

Its Objectives is

- To promote the export market by way of innovative packaging design and development.

- To promote the export of packaging materials and machinaries by way of participating overseas exhibition and organizing national and international exhibitions in India

- To increase the strength of technical manpower through packaging education in India.

- To promote packaging Industry through technical services in India.

- To upgrade the overall standards of packaging at national level.

Major activities are

- Training and education like conducts short term training programs, Certificate & Diploma courses and conferences.

- Research and development as testing and certification of packaging materials & packages, technical consultancy on package design and development, applied research on food, pharma and cosmetics. It is authorized by DG Shipping & DGCA for testing of bulk packages for carriage for export and issue certificate as a mandatory requirement.It is accredited to NABL and BIS to issue test reports. It is also to develop alternative packaging material based on jute,coir etc.It develops suitable packaging to enhance shelf life of tender coconut water sponsored by MOFPI.It develops modified packaging system for export of chilled meat products sponsored by APEDA.

- It also organizes national and international exhibitions, national packaging awards etc.

- Consultancy services: As formulates technical specifications of packages for export of fresh fruits & vegetables ,spices,tea, marine products for APEDA,MPEDA,SPICE Board,Tea Board etc respectively.It also includes technical audit of packaging systems to high light the short comings and to suggest suitable measures to the industries.

Packaging Industry

- Raw material manufacturers
- Packaging material converters
- Packaging users industry

Packaging Materials

- Scientific packaging materials like Paper,Glass,Metal and Plastic
- Traditional packaging materials, Earthen pot,Bamboo basket/box,Wooden box and Jute bags etc.
- Ancillary packaging materials like Caps & closures,labels,bopp self adhesive taps, stretch and cling films, straps, clips & hooks, likeubble films, thermocole & foam, cushioning materials.

Postharvest Handling of Fresh Produce and Agro-processing

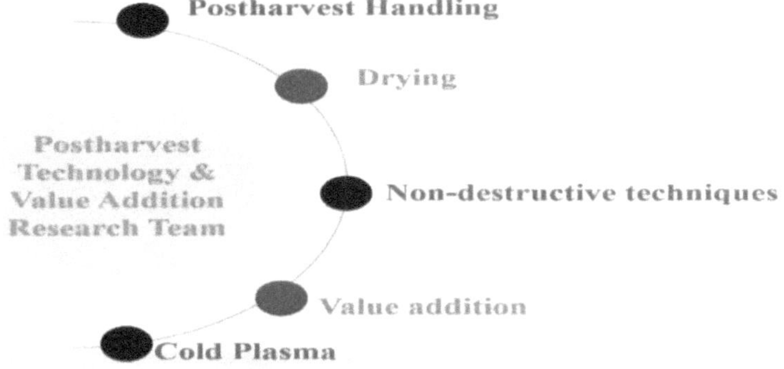

Postharvest Losses

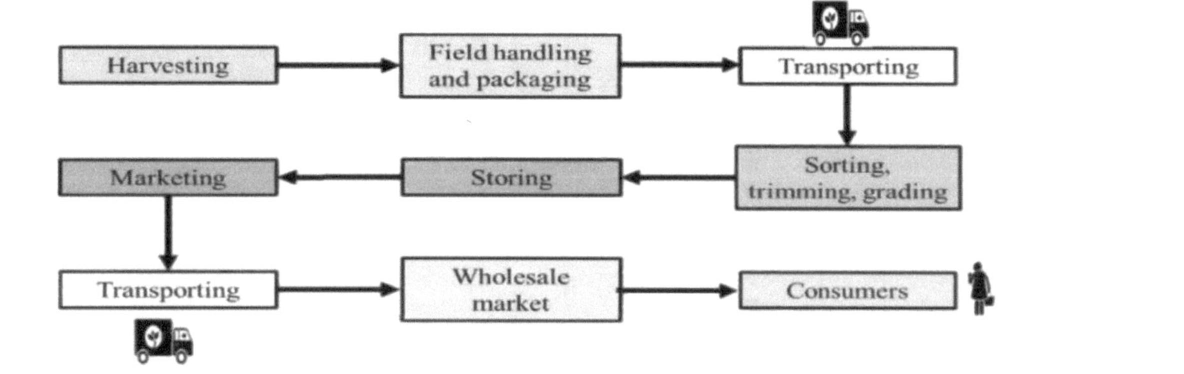

. Postharvest supply chain of fresh produce.

Postharvest Losses

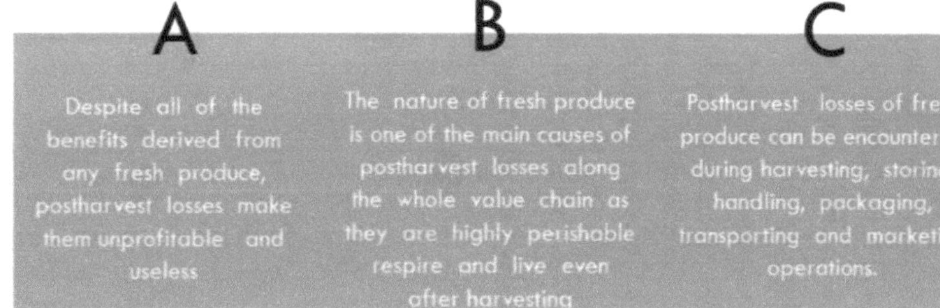

Postharvest Losses

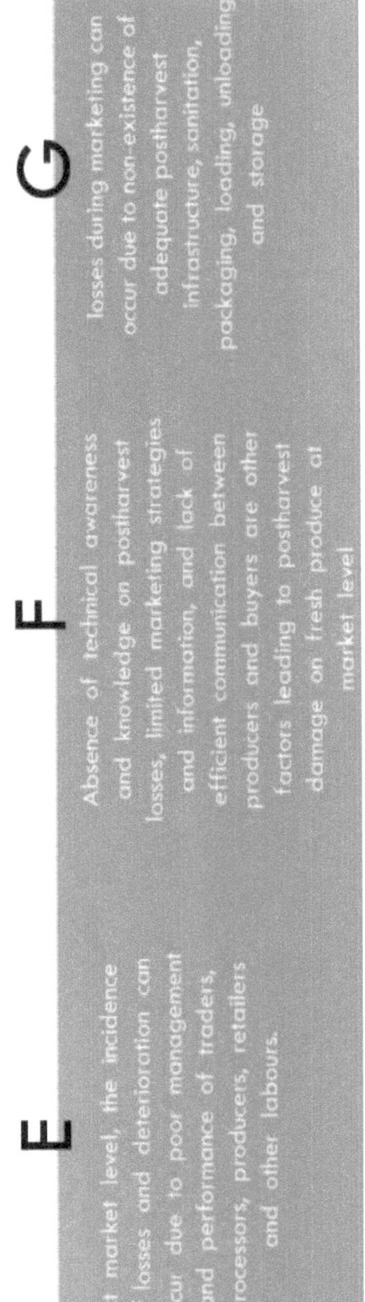

Pastharvest Losses

Packaging plays a critical role in the postharvest handling and distribution of fresh and processed food and other biomaterials. **The packaging** of fresh fruit remains vital for the long and complex journey from growers to consumers. **Packaging** provides an economic means of minimising damage and protecting packed produce during distribution.

The packages are exposed to different hazards and mechanical loadings during transportation and storage which affect the structural performance of the package components and the whole package

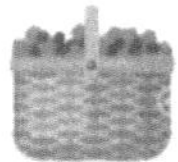

Postharvest Losses

Storage temperature is an important factor that needs to be considered during the postharvest supply chain which can be utilized to maintain the postharvest quality of fresh produce. Most food products quality parameters are highly time and **temperature-storage-dependent.**

Low-temperature storage →is the most significant factor extending the shelf-life and maintaining the quality of fresh produce due to the inhibition of metabolic activities. **High temperature** → increase the rate of respiration, transpiration, and ethylene production, therefore, the storage life of the produce progressively decreased

Postharvest Losses

Drying processes are used to preserve food products for a long period of time.

Drying is not only used to increase the shelf life of any fresh product but also to reduce the weight, volume, package, storage, and cost of transportation and to increase the productivity of marine and agriculture

Inadequate drying, lead to increase mold and or insects in the food product

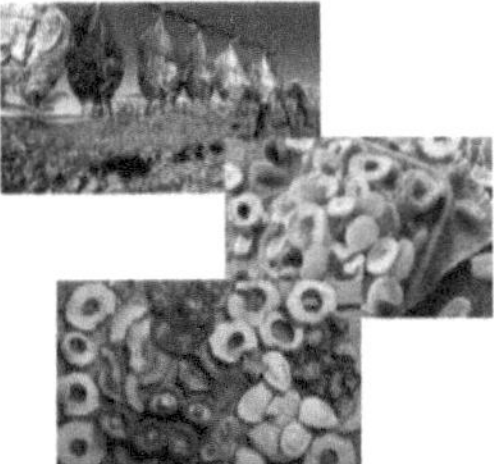

Postharvest Losses

Good handling practices (e.g. harvesting, packaging and transport) of fruits are necessary to avoid mechanical damage susceptibility.

The quality of fruits and vegetables can be substantially reduced by poor **handling**, especially if they are not consumed immediately, which is a serious food safety and economic issue.

Packing Materials

Packaging designs used: (a) MK4 box; (b) trasarrangement in MK4 box; (c) Econo box; (d) fruit packed in Plastic bags arranged in bulk inside Econo box.

Role of Handling

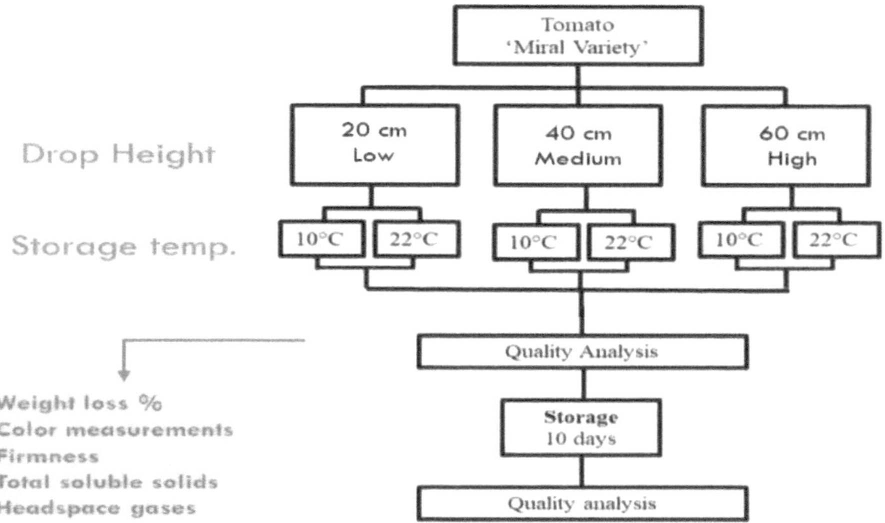

Role of Packaging

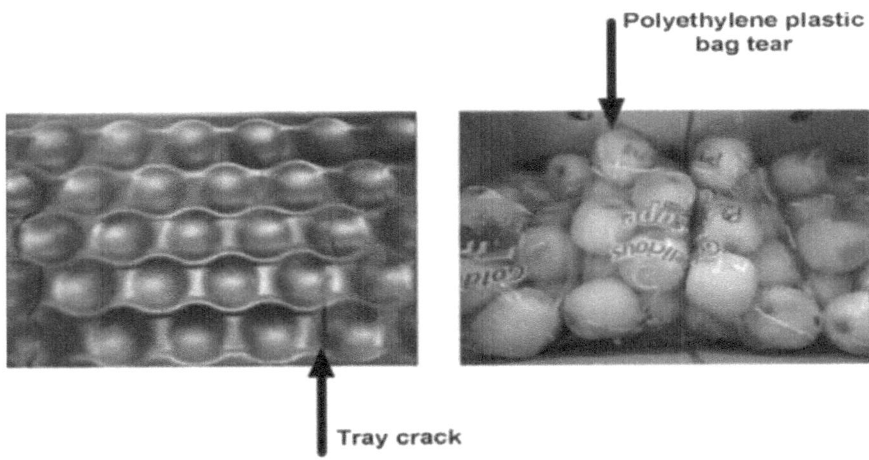

Cracked tray and torn polyethylene plastic bag after impact test.

Drying

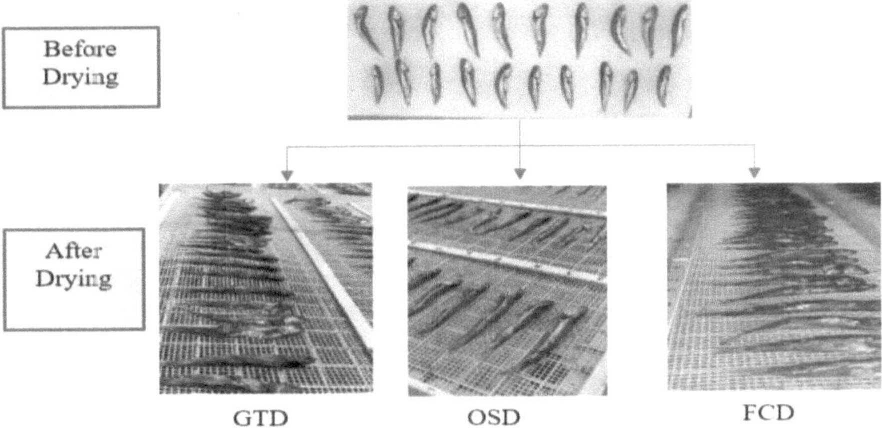

Color change of anchovy using greenhouse tunnel drier (GTD), open sun drier (OSD), and forced convective solar drier (FCD)

It is recommended to use solar dryers for better quality. The study is useful to seafood processers and policy makers to optimize fish drying and make optimum use of fisheries stock.

Tomato storage

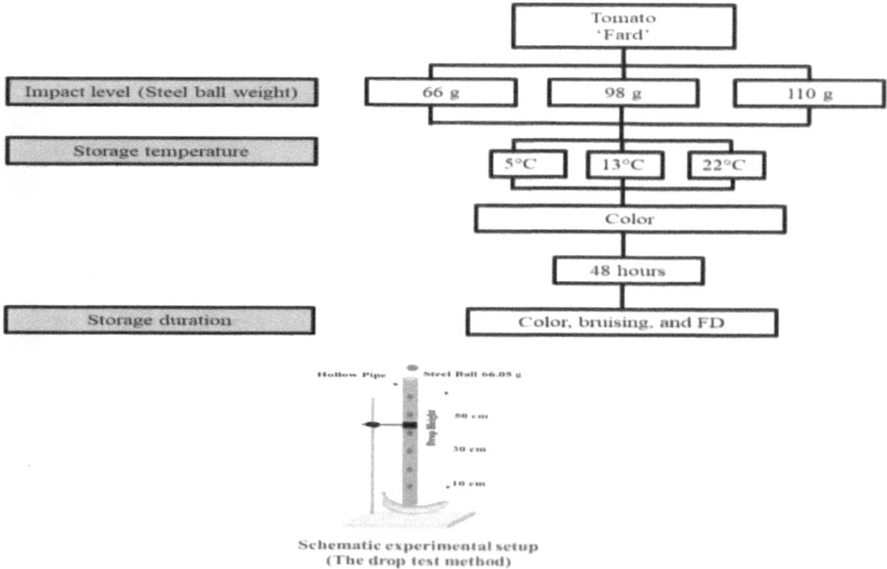

Schematic experimental setup
(The drop test method)

The study indicated that storage temperature was one of the vital factors which required high monitoring along postharvest supply chain and marketing.

The high incidence of postharvest losses is the main challenge to global food security. Postharvest losses can occur along the supply chain stages such as harvesting, storing, handling, packaging etc.Different studies have shown that inadequate postharvest processes are critical issues facing food product during the supply chain which required a huge attention to prevent and reduce.

Segmentation of different sectors in food processing industry

The Indian food processing industry is a vast and diverse sector, contributing significantly to the country's economy. To better understand its dynamics, it is essential to segment the industry into various sub-sectors.

Segmentation Based on Product Type

Fruit and Vegetable Processing: This segment includes processing activities like canning, freezing, dehydration, and juice extraction.

Meat and Poultry Processing: This involves processing of meat and poultry products, including ready-to-eat meals, sausages, and processed chicken.

Dairy Processing: This sector encompasses milk processing, production of dairy products like butter, cheese, yogurt, and milk powder.

Grain Processing: This includes milling of grains, production of flour, and other grain-based products like breakfast cereals.

Seafood Processing: This involves processing of fish, prawns, and other seafood products for domestic and export markets.

Confectionery and Bakery: This segment comprises the production of chocolates, candies, biscuits, cakes, and other bakery products.

Beverages: This includes processing and packaging of soft drinks, juices, and alcoholic beverages.

Processed Foods: This category covers a wide range of products like ready-to-eat meals, pickles, chutneys, and sauces.

Segmentation Based on Processing Level

Primary Processing: This involves initial processing activities like cleaning, sorting, grading, and packaging of raw agricultural products.

Secondary Processing: This includes value addition processes like canning, freezing, dehydration, and fermentation of processed products.

Tertiary Processing: This involves further processing of secondary products into ready-to-eat or ready-to-cook meals.

Segmentation Based on Scale of Operation

Small-Scale Units: These are typically family-owned businesses with limited investment and production capacity.

Medium-Scale Units: These units have a higher investment and production capacity compared to small-scale units.

Large-Scale Units: These are well-organized units with significant investments and advanced technology.

Segmentation Based on Ownership

Public Sector: This includes government-owned food processing units.

Private Sector: This comprises both domestic and foreign private companies operating in the food processing industry.

Cooperative Sector: This segment involves cooperative societies involved in food processing activities.

Segmentation Based on Distribution Channel

Organized Retail: This includes modern retail outlets like supermarkets and hypermarkets.

Unorganized Retail: This comprises traditional retail stores like kirana shops and local markets.

E-commerce: This involves online sales of food products.

By understanding these different segments, stakeholders can develop targeted strategies to address the specific needs and challenges of each sub-sector. This segmentation also helps in identifying growth opportunities and potential investments in the Indian food processing industry.

Primary food processing is a significant industry with a highly decentralized structure. It includes numerous rice mills, hullers, flour mills, pulse mills, and oil-seed mills, as well as thousands of bakeries, traditional food units, and fruit, vegetable, and spice processing units operating in the informal sector.

1.2 Processed Foods Scenario with respect to Specific Sectors

Industry structure and its evolving dynamics present favorable opportunities for organized entities to invest and expand their presence. As consumer preferences increasingly prioritize quality and branded products, the organized sector is expected to witness significant growth and recognition.

Dairy Sector

In the dairy industry, the unorganized sector currently dominates processing activities. However, the organized sector, which represents less than 15 percent, is expected to experience rapid expansion, particularly in urban areas. Notable products within the organized sector include ghee, butter, cheese, ice creams, milk powders, malted milk food, condensed milk, and infant foods. Prominent players, including multinational corporations like Nestle and Britannia, are venturing into emerging segments such as Ultra Heat Treatment (UHT) and flavored milk, reflecting the sector's evolving landscape.

Fruits and Vegetables

Fruit and vegetable processing in India is evenly split between the organized and unorganized sectors, with the organized sector holding a 48 percent share.

Organized entities primarily focus on products like juices and pulp concentrate, while the unorganized sector specializes in traditional items such as pickles, sauces, and squashes, with pickles being a particularly significant category.

Grains

India boasts a substantial grain production, with over 200 million tonnes annually. Wheat, rice, maize, barley, and millets are among the major grains cultivated in the country. Wheat alone accounts for about 15 percent of annual production, with 10,000 pulse mills milling approximately 75 percent of annual pulse output. The primary milling of grains is a pivotal aspect of food grain processing.

Meat and Poultry

India's vast livestock population supports meat production, with approximately 5 million tonnes produced annually. However, only a small fraction undergoes value addition, with the majority consumed raw. Poultry processing is also in its nascent stages, though the industry is witnessing growth, especially with the rise of fast food outlets. While most production remains in the unorganized sector, branded products like Venky's and Godrej's Real Chicken are gaining traction domestically.

Fish Processing

India ranks third globally in fish production, with a substantial share coming from both inland and marine resources. Processing primarily targets canned and frozen forms for export markets. Despite its vast resources, the fishery sector is perceived as underutilized, presenting opportunities for growth.

Consumer Foods

This segment includes packaged foods, aerated soft drinks, packaged drinking water, and alcoholic beverages, reflecting diverse consumer preferences and evolving lifestyles.

Packaged or Convenience Foods

This segment, which consists of bakery products, ready-to-eat snacks, chips, namkeens, and other processed foods, is experiencing steady growth driven by the demand for convenience and variety.

Aerated Soft Drinks

Global brands dominate this segment, with significant growth potential attributed to low penetration levels compared to other markets.

Packaged Drinking Water

Driven by factors like urbanization and changing lifestyles, the packaged drinking water segment is experiencing substantial growth.

Alcoholic Beverages

India ranks third globally in alcoholic beverage consumption, with spirits and beer leading the market. The sector is characterized by joint ventures and licensed production units catering to domestic and international demand.

Rice Scenario in India

Rice is a staple food for a majority of Indians, with annual production reaching 85-90 million tons. The rice milling industry, which accounts for a turnover of over Rs. 26,000 crore annually, is vital for providing staple food grain to the population. While traditional huller units prevail, there is a growing trend towards modern rice mills with higher efficiency and improved recovery rates, reflecting the industry's continuous evolution and technological advancement.

The whole grain recovery percentage further increases to 66-68% in case of miling of parboiled paddy. Thus it can be seen that there is an overall improvement of recovery of whole grains by about 10-14% if one uses rubber roll shellers for rice milling operations. The conversion ratio (i.e. recovery % of various final product and by-products for every 100kg feed of raw paddy) for these improved rice mills are as follows:

- Milled Rice   :   62-68%
- Rice Bran   :   4-5%
- Rice Husk   :   25%
- Germ Wastage :   2-8%

It has been observed that de-husking using rubber roll shellers reduces the risk of breaking the grain. This method pulls off the husk almost immediately and applies pressure through resilient surfaces across the width of the grain, where the kernels are generally more uniform compared to their length. Moreover, the process does not remove the internal epidermis of the husk. Thus the deshelled grains with their silver skin envelope are protected against scratches and keep longer and better while the silver skin and the germ increases the quantity of bran which is produced while whitening. The improved rice mills have a better husk and rice bran aspiration system. The same prevents mixing of fine brokens with rice bran. Therefore the quantity of rice bran obtained is better. It has also been observed that the location of rice mills are confined to a few selected production centers. Their development as a village level agro-processing unit is yet to take a proper shape. In the absence of village level rice milling unit, the farmers have to travel great distances for milling the rice. This leads to increased transportation and handling losses. Thus there is a need to develop improved rice mills as a village level agro-processing unit for bringing about technical up-gradation and development of the sector. Value addition and generation of gainful and sustainable employment opportunities are the other possible benefits arising out of this agro-processing industry.

Description of Rice Milling Operation (Process Defination)

The basic rice milling process consists of

- Pre-Cleaning: Remove all impurities and unfilled grains from paddy.
- De-stoning: Separate small stones from paddy.
- Parboiling: Improve the nutritional quality by gelatinizing the starch inside the rice grain, which also enhances milling recovery during de-shelling and polishing/whitening.
- Husking: Remove the husk from paddy.
- Husk Aspiration: Separate the husk from brown rice/unhusked paddy.
- Paddy Separation: Separate the unhusked paddy from brown rice.
- Whitening: Remove all or part of the bran layer and germ from brown rice.
- Polishing: Improve the appearance of milled rice by removing the remaining bran particles and polishing the exterior of the milled kernel.
- Length Grading: Separate small and large broken pieces from head rice.
- Blending: Mix head rice with a predetermined amount of broken rice as required by the customer.
- Weighing & Bagging: Prepare the milled rice for transport to the customer.

RICE MILLING OPERATION

The central government is strongly backing the development of this industry. It has repealed the Rice Milling Industry (Regulation) Act, 1958, and the Rice Milling Industry (Regulation and Licensing) Rules, 1959, effective May 27, 1998. Additionally, the rice milling sector, which was previously reserved for small-scale enterprises, has now been de-reserved. As a result, establishing a rice mill no longer requires a license or permission.

Land,layout plan and site development requirement:

The land requirement for establishing an improved rice milling unit will depend upon:

1. Whether the unit will be using a parboiling unit for pre-treatment of paddy before commencement of miling operation or it will be directly miling raw paddy.

2. Whether a single pass or a multipass miling unit is to be installed

Generally 2.00 to 2.50 acres of land is required for establishing an improved rice miling unit having an installed processing capacity of 2 MT/hr, operating for single shift/day of 8hr duration, 300 days per annum, i.e. 4800MT/annum. The land should be with proper elevation. Low lying areas should be avoided. Else proper land filling,compaction and consolidation should be done. Drainage and linkage with road and other communication should also be ensured. The layout of the rice milling plant should be done in a manner that helps in smooth operation of various unit operations in tandem to bring about optimal capacity utilization and economizing power consumption.

Civil Construction

The various construction requirement of an improved rice milling unit are follows

1. Raw paddy go-down
2. Cleaning unit
3. Drier and necessary supporting structures such as, boiler/blower system etc.
4. Milling section
5. Finished product stores
6. Machine rooms
7. Auxiliary structures such as office watch and ward etc.

Modern Rice Milling Equipments

From Paddy to Perfection: A Look Inside Modern Rice Processing

Gone are the days of manual labor and rudimentary techniques in rice production. Today, state-of-the-art processing plants utilize advanced technology to deliver high-quality, consistent rice while preserving its natural characteristics.

Here's a breakdown of these sophisticated methods

Precise Drying

Automated System: A fully mechanized system with sensor-based temperature control ensures consistent and gentle drying of paddy at a rate of 12 tonnes per hour.

Preserving Quality: This method safeguards the delicate rice grains, preventing fermentation and bacterial growth, while retaining the natural aroma.

Advanced Parboiling

Soft Water Advantage: A dedicated water treatment plant provides soft water crucial for the parboiling process, ultimately enhancing the rice's fragrance and aroma.

Sensor-Controlled Soaking: Sophisticated soaking bins with sensors precisely regulate water temperature, ensuring superior processing outcomes.

High-Capacity Milling

Equipped for Efficiency: Production capacities exceeding 10 tons per hour are achieved through pre-cleaners, de-stoners, precision sizers, graders, paddy separators, de-huskers, and magnets.

Clean and Green Design: The plant is environmentally friendly and protects against foreign particle contamination.

Sorting and Grading for Perfection

Multi-Stage Sorting: A series of color sorters and multi-sorters meticulously remove unwanted elements like glass pieces, plastic granules, foreign material, and discolored grains.

Efficient Separation: Aspirated rice huskers and paddy separators effectively remove husks and separate paddy from brown rice.

Uniformity and Yield: Plano-shifters and length graders ensure consistent grain size, while vertical abrasive polishers maximize milling efficiency and head rice yield.

International Standards for Quality

Consumer Safety: Strict adherence to international standards for paddy and milled rice guarantees that only edible rice reaches consumers.

Minimizing Waste: Improved post-harvest practices minimize waste throughout the production chain.

Enhanced Farm Yields: Agronomic practices are optimized to increase rice production at the farm level.

Transparency and Protection: Efficient processing for better milling recoveries protects consumers from price and quality manipulation.

Grading Considerations

Paddy: Factors like purity, foreign matter content, presence of defective grains, and moisture content are assessed.

Milled Rice: Grading considers the percentage of head rice, broken grains, defective grains, foreign matter, presence of paddy, and moisture content.

By employing these advanced technologies and adhering to strict quality standards, modern rice processing plants deliver high-quality, consistent rice that retains its natural taste and aroma, meeting the demands of today's consumers.

Grade specifications	Premium	Grade Grade-2	Grade-1
Head rice (min%)			
Brokens(max%)			
Brewers(max %)			
Defectives:			
Damaged grains, max%	0	0.25	0.50
Discolored grains, max%	0.50	2.00	4.00
Chalky and immature grains,max%	2.00	5.00	10.00
Red grains,max%	0	0.25	0.50
Red streaked grains,max%	1.00	3.00	5.00
Foreign matter,max%	0	0.10	0.20
Paddy,max no./kg	1	8	10
Moisture content,max%	14.00	14.00	14.00

Indian Food Processing Industries

India: A Booming Food Powerhouse with Global Potential

India is a food giant, currently ranking second in global food production after China. But there's more to the story: India has the potential to become the world's largest food producer, particularly in the agricultural and processed food sectors.

A Decade of Delicious Opportunities

Over the next ten years, India's food production is expected to double, creating exciting investment prospects across the food processing value chain. Here's where your expertise can come in:

- Food Processing Technologies: Modernize processing methods for efficiency and higher quality outputs.
- Skill Development: Train the workforce in cutting-edge food processing techniques.
- Equipment Investment: Provide the tools needed for this growing industry.

Lucrative Sub-Sectors to Explore

India's diverse food processing industry offers a rich tapestry of opportunities. Here are some key areas attracting investor interest:

- Canning: Extend shelf life and preserve food quality.
- Dairy and Food Processing: Meet the growing demand for dairy products and other processed foods.
- Specialty Processing: Cater to niche markets with unique food products.
- Packaging: Develop innovative and sustainable packaging solutions.
- Frozen Food & Refrigeration: Maintain food freshness through freezing and cold storage technologies.
- Thermo Processing: Utilize heat-based techniques for longer shelf life and improved food safety.

Beyond Production: A Growing Appetite for Health

India's consumers are increasingly health-conscious, driving rapid growth in the health food and supplement segment. This presents a lucrative market for investors in this space.

Ready to Take a Bite Out of the Global Market?

Despite being a major food producer, India's share of international food trade remains below 1.5%. This signifies immense potential for investors and exporters. Interestingly, India boasts the highest number of food processing plants outside the USA that are approved by the US Food and Drug Administration (FDA), demonstrating the industry's commitment to quality standards. India's food sector is primed for explosive growth. With its vast production potential, diverse sub-sectors, and growing consumer base, India offers a compelling opportunity for investors and exporters to be part of this exciting journey.

India's food processing landscape includes diverse areas such as fruit and vegetable processing, meat and poultry, dairy, alcoholic beverages, fisheries, plantation, grain processing, and various consumer products like confectionery, chocolates, cocoa products, soya-based items, mineral water, and high-protein foods.Our extensive database includes a broad range of suppliers, manufacturers, exporters, and importers in sectors such as food processing, dairy processing, and the beverage industry. We also cover areas like dairy plants, canning, bottling, packaging industries, and process machinery.

Promising sub-sectors within India's food processing industry include soft drink bottling, confectionery manufacturing, fishing aquaculture, grain milling and products, meat and poultry processing, alcoholic beverages, milk processing, tomato paste, fast food, ready-to-eat breakfast cereals, and more.

The Government of India's vision for the food-processing sector by 2015 includes:

- Increasing and stabilizing farmers' income
- Providing consumers with a wide variety of choices, including traditional ethnic foods
- Ensuring food safety and quality
- Promoting a dynamic food processing industry
- Enhancing competitiveness in both domestic and international markets
- Creating an attractive environment for domestic and foreign investors
- Achieving seamless integration of food processing infrastructure from farm to market
- Implementing a transparent and industry-friendly regulatory framework
- Establishing a system of standards based on scientific principles, additives, and flavors.

The following specific targets would be increased to:

	From	To
The level of processing of perishables	6%	20%
Value addition	20%	35%
Share in global food trade by the year 2015	1.5%	3%

Rice Production and processing: Rice cultivation spans diverse geographic regions and climates, encompassing over a hundred countries and occupying nearly 160 million hectares of harvested land, yielding over 700 million tons annually. The majority of rice cultivation, approximately 90%, occurs in South, Southeast, and East Asia, where around 640 million tons are produced. Rice is cultivated in four primary ecosystems, each with its own distinct growing conditions and challenges:

Irrigated: Approximately 80 million hectares of rice fields worldwide are irrigated. High-yielding regions for irrigated rice include China, Egypt, Japan, Indonesia, Vietnam, the Republic of Korea, and the Senegal River Valley in Africa.

Rainfed lowland: In this environment, rice is grown in fields enclosed by bunds, which are earthen embankments that trap rainwater during part of the cropping season. Covering about 60 million hectares globally, rainfed lowlands contribute roughly 20% to the world's rice production. Challenges such as adverse climate conditions, poor soil quality, and limited access to modern farming technologies hinder productivity in these areas.

Upland: Upland rice cultivation occurs in regions across Asia, Africa, and Latin America, occupying approximately 14 million hectares and contributing about 4% to global rice production.

Flood-prone: This ecosystem includes deepwater and floating rice environments, where specialized rice varieties are cultivated to thrive in flooded conditions. These environments, covering around 11 million hectares globally, present challenges such as deepwater flooding, prolonged flash floods, salinity in coastal areas, and problematic soils like acid-sulphate and sodic soils. Deepwater and floating rice are predominantly cultivated in floodplains and deltas of rivers such as the Irrawaddy in Myanmar, the Mekong in Vietnam and Cambodia, the Chao Phraya in Thailand, and the Niger in West Africa.

Rice cultivation involves a series of stages before it reaches consumers, including planting, nurturing, harvesting, processing, and distribution.

- Seed selection
- Land preparation
- Crop establishment
- Water management
- Nutrient management
- Pest management
- Harvesting
- Post-harvest

Post-Harvest

From Field to Fork: The Journey of Rice

Rice undergoes a transformation after harvest before reaching your plate.

Here's a breakdown of the key processing steps:

1. Drying: The Essential First Step

Drying plays a crucial role in preserving rice quality and minimizing losses. It involves reducing the moisture content of the grains to a safe level for storage, typically below 14%. This prevents spoilage from mold, bacteria, and insect activity. Delays or inadequate drying methods can significantly compromise the rice's quality and lead to waste.

2. Storage: Protecting the Harvest

Effective storage facilities are designed to keep rice safe from the elements and potential threats like pests, rodents, birds, and insects. However, the success of storage hinges on proper drying beforehand. If the rice is not dried sufficiently, even the best storage facility won't prevent deterioration. Generally, the longer rice is stored, the lower the moisture content needs to be to maintain quality.

3. Milling: Transforming Paddy into Edible Rice

Milling is the process of removing the inedible husk and bran layers from paddy rice to produce the white rice kernels we consume. Milling techniques are carefully chosen to minimize broken kernels and ensure a well-milled, clean product that meets customer preferences.

4. Moisture Content: A Balancing Act

Paddy rice is typically harvested with a high moisture content (20-25%). To ensure safe storage, this needs to be reduced significantly. Moisture content also plays a role in yield measurements, which are typically adjusted to a standardized level (around 14%) for accurate comparison.

5. Harvesting Losses: Keeping It Efficient

Physical losses during harvesting are inevitable, but can be minimized with proper techniques and machinery. These losses vary depending on the specific harvesting practices employed.

Understanding these key processing steps helps us appreciate the journey rice takes from field to table, ensuring we enjoy this staple food at its best.

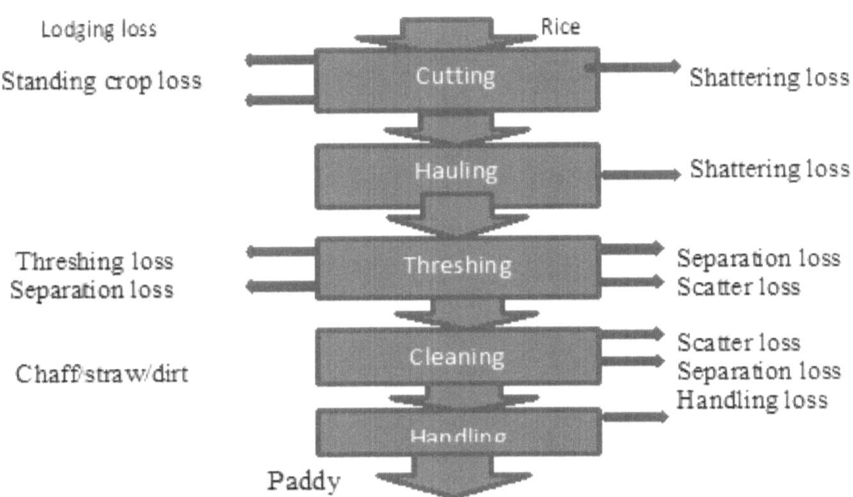

Processing and Value Addition of Millets: An Overview

- Introduction
  - Total millet cultivation area: 23-24 million hectares. Among these, small millets cover 3.5 million hectares, including 2 million hectares for ragi and 1.5 million hectares for other varieties like little, foxtail, kodo, proso, browntop, and barnyard millets.

- Small millets are cultivated across various states in India, yielding a total production of 1.78 million tonnes. The Indian government has launched significant initiatives such as INSIMP and NFSM to expand cultivation areas.
- The Government of India has established Centers of Excellence for small millets to promote processing and enhance value addition.
- Small millets are recognized as nutri-cereals due to their low glycemic index and high fiber content.
- Consumption of small millets offers numerous health benefits, including diabetic-friendly properties, reduced risk of cardiovascular diseases, and benefits for conditions like duodenal ulcers.
- Traditionally consumed by rural and tribal communities, small millets are increasingly recognized for their nutritional value.
- There is a pressing need to fully utilize small millets, which are currently underutilized.
- Increasing the utilization and value addition of small millets leads to higher returns for growers.
- Exploiting the nutritional benefits of small millets can benefit urban populations, undernourished children, and the elderly.
- Recent innovations include Britannia's successful introduction of multi-grain biscuits and Pristine Industries, Bangalore's launch of high-fiber products.
- Indira Foods, Bangalore, specializes in malted and ready-to-cook millet products.
- Exclusive restaurants focusing on millet-based foods are gaining popularity.
- Scope of Millet-Based Products

Initial studies suggest significant potential for manufacturing nutritious energy foods (high in amylase), bakery products, and breakfast cereals using millets. Extruded products made from small millets have not yet entered the market, with minimal research conducted in India on developing such products. There is a promising market outlook for instant successes like pasta/noodles and snack foods such as kurkure derived from small millets. These millets boast high-quality proteins and a balanced amino acid profile ideal for product innovation. Millet-based nutrient mixes are marketed as functional foods.

Post-harvest processing of millet

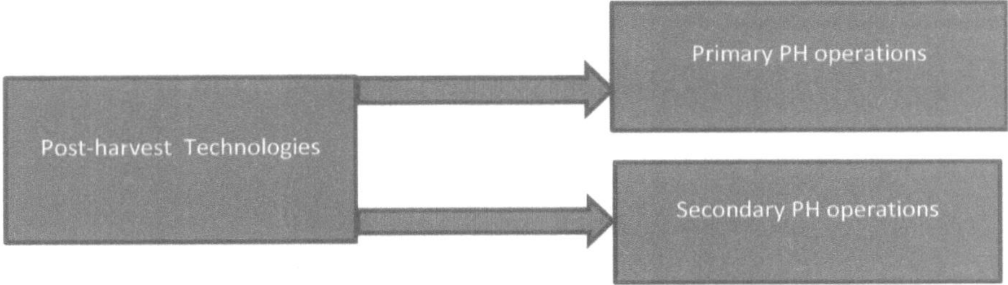

Importance of Primary Processing

Cost of ragi at village level	Rs 2200/quintal
Cleaning/pearling loss	5 kg (max)
Cleaned ragi	95 kg (min)
Cost of cleaning & pearling	Rs 50/quintal
Transportation & handling	Rs 100/quintal
Total cost	Rs 2350/quintal
Revenue	Rs 95 X 36 = Rs 3420/quintal
Profit by primary processing	3420 – 2350 = Rs 1070
In terms of investment	(1070/2350) X 100 = 45.5%
Profit from crop production	-ve for ragi

Primary Processing Machinery for millets

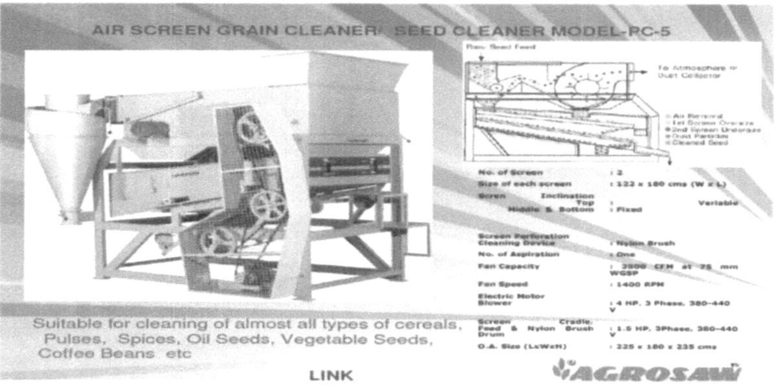
High Capacity Grain Cleaners
AIR SCREEN GRAIN CLEANER/ SEED CLEANER MODEL-PC-5
Suitable for cleaning of almost all types of cereals, Pulses, Spices, Oil Seeds, Vegetable Seeds, Coffee Beans etc
LINK
AGROSAW

Primary Processing – Pearlers & Polishers
Jowar Polisher
Ragi Pearler
Millet Rice Polisher

Dehulling Machinery for Small Millets
Kodo Dehuller
Foxtail / Little/ Proso Dehuller
Foxtail / Little/ Proso Dehuller
All Millets

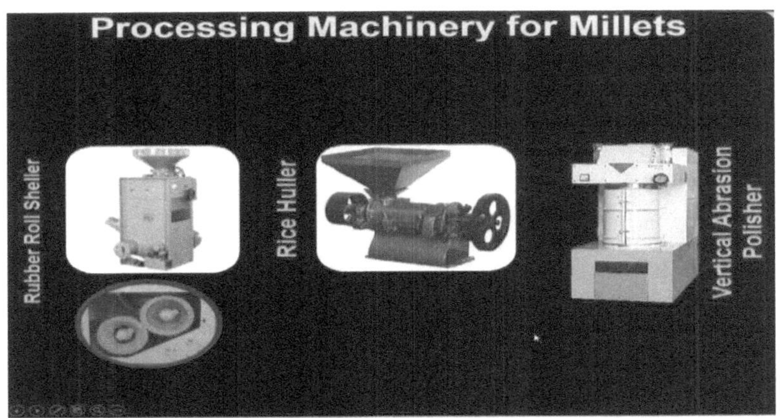

Processing Machinery for Millets
Rubber Roll Sheller
Rice Huller
Vertical Abrasion Polisher

Small Millets Processing Unit

Rotary Reel Separator
Rotary sieves

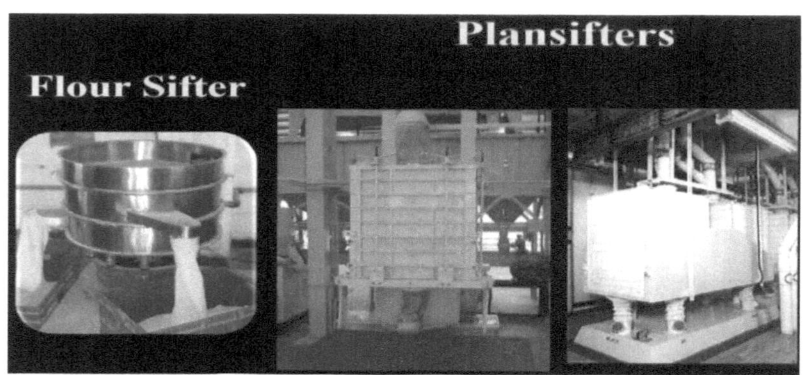
Plansifters
Flour Sifter

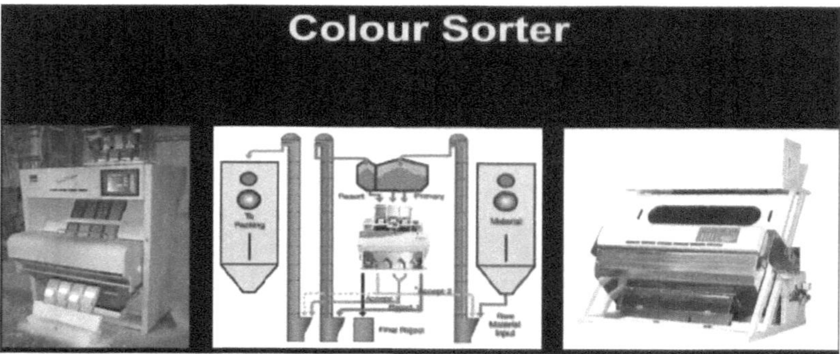
Colour Sorter

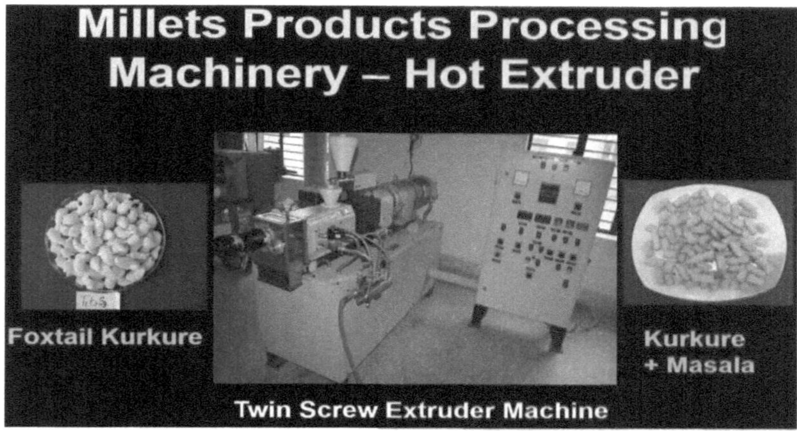
Millets Products Processing
Machinery – Hot Extruder
Foxtail Kurkure
Kurkure + Masala
Twin Screw Extruder Machine

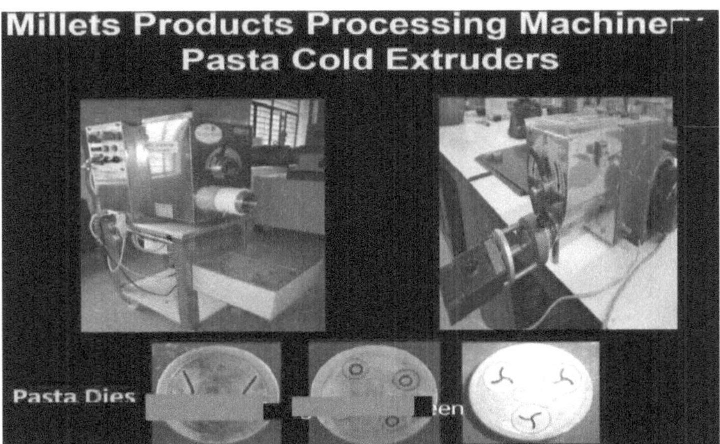

Millets Products Processing Machinery
Pasta Cold Extruders
Pasta Dies

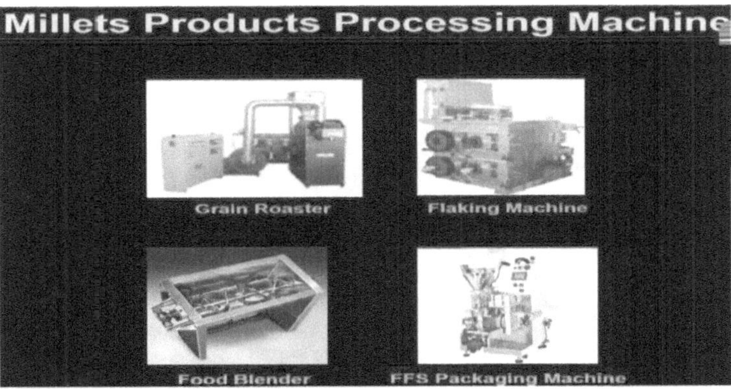

Millets Products Processing Machine
Grain Roaster
Flaking Machine
Food Blender
FFS Packaging Machine

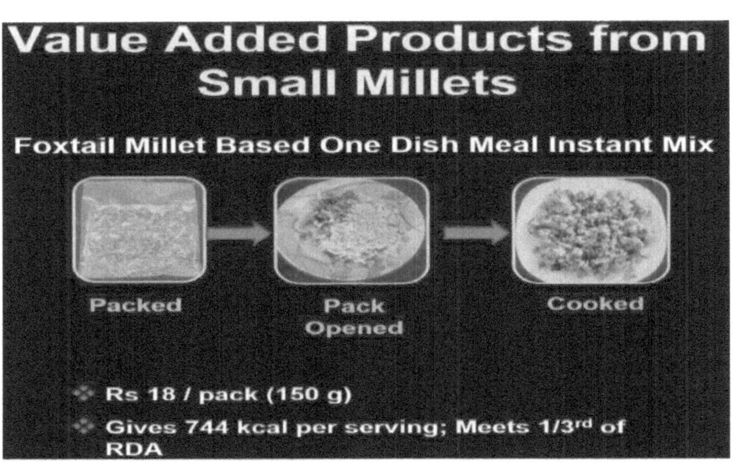

Value Added Products from Small Millets
Foxtail Millet Based One Dish Meal Instant Mix
Packed
Pack Opened
Cooked
Rs 18 / pack (150 g)
Gives 744 kcal per serving; Meets 1/3rd of RDA

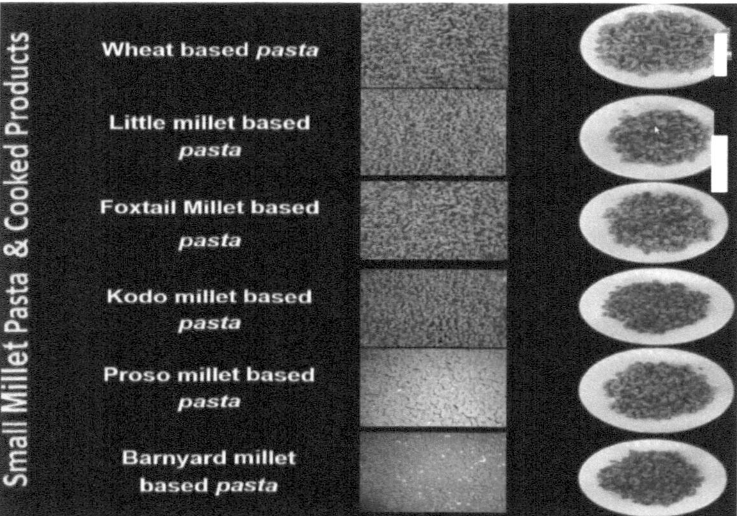

Small Millets Based
Cold Extruded Pasta Products
Barnyard millet based pasta
Foxtail millet based pasta
Kodo millet based pasta
Little millet based pasta
Foxtaile millet vermicelli
Small Millet Pasta & Cooked Products
Wheat based pasta
Little millet based pasta
Foxtail Millet based pasta
Kodo millet based pasta
Proso millet based pasta
Barnyard millet based pasta

Value Added Products from Small Millet
Foxtail millet Muruku
Barnyard millet Doughnut
Proso millet Biscuit
Kodo millet Rusk

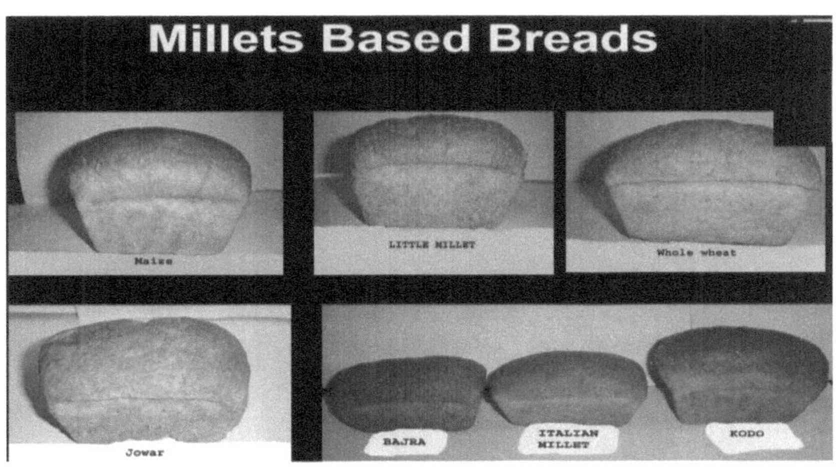
Millets Based Breads
Maize
LITTLE MILLET
Whole wheat
Jowar
BAJRA
ITALIAN MILLET
KODO

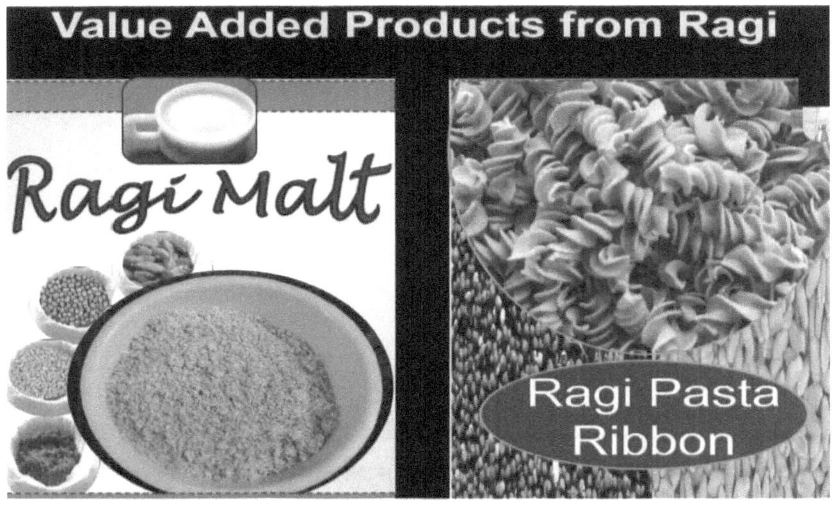
Value Added Products from Ragi
Ragi Malt
Ragi Pasta Ribbon

Ragi Mudde Machine
Ragi mudde is a staple food of
Southern Karnataka

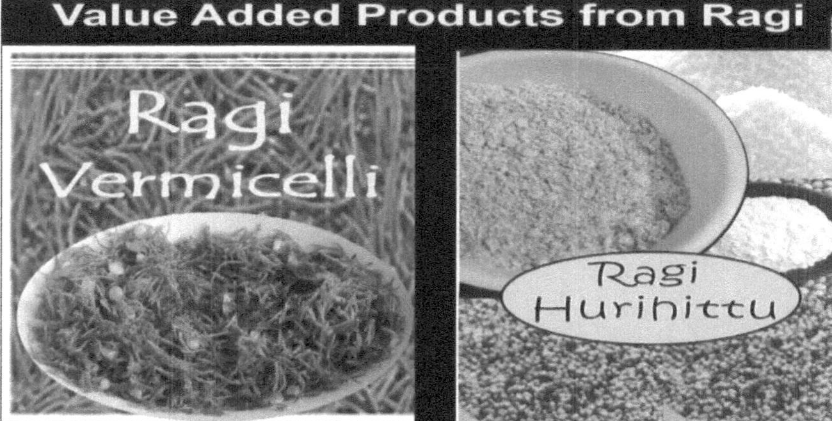
Value Added Products from Ragi
Ragi Vermicelli
Ragi Hurihittu

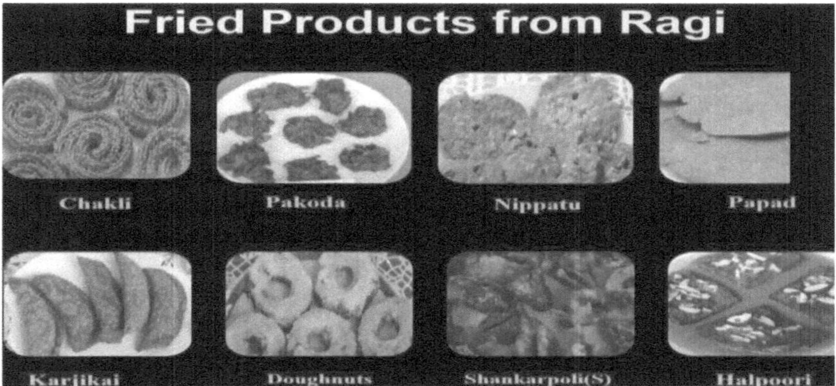
Fried Products from Ragi
Chakli
Pakoda
Nippatu
Papad
Karjikai
Doughnuts
Shankarpoli(S)
Halpoori

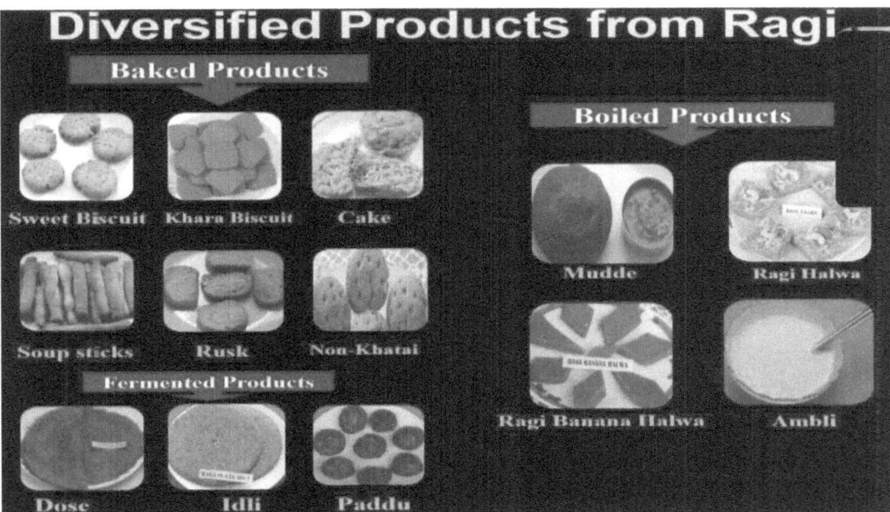

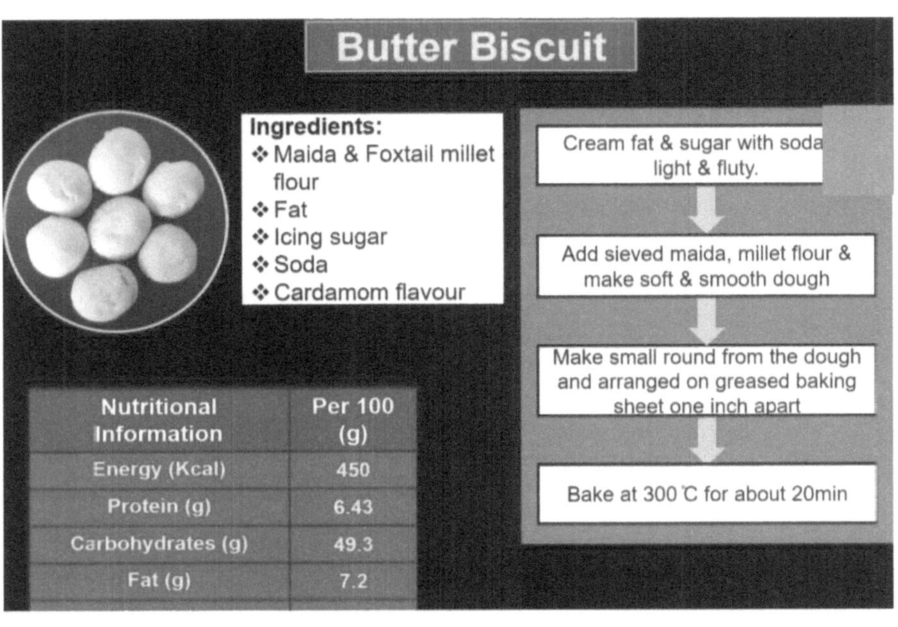

Nutritional Information	Per 100 (g)
Energy (Kcal)	450
Protein (g)	6.43
Carbohydrates (g)	49.3
Fat (g)	7.2

Foxtail millet based multi grain flour mixes with health ingredients

Formulation	Millet flour %	Foxtail Millet Flour %	Wheat flour%	Bengal Gram Flour %	Methi Seed Powder %	Jamun seed Powder %
Little millet	15	35	30	10	3	3
Kodo millet	15	35	30	10	3	3
Proso millet	25	25	30	10	3	3
Barnyard millet	25	25	30	10	3	3

Best formulations of multi-millet pasta

- BF1 (Barnyard 10%, Proso 30%, Wheat 60%)
- FF1 (Foxtail 10%, Proso 30%, Wheat 60%)
- KF3 (Kodo 10%, Proso 50%, Wheat 40%)
- LF3 (Little 10%, Proso 50%, Wheat 40%)

Butter Biscuit---

Ingredients

- Maida & Foxtail millet flour
- Fat
- Icing sugar
- Soda
- Cardamom flavor

Nutritional Information	Per 100 gm
Energy Kcal	450
Protein gm	6.43
Carbohydrates gm	49.3
Fat gm	7.2
Iron gm	1.06
Fibre mg	1.30

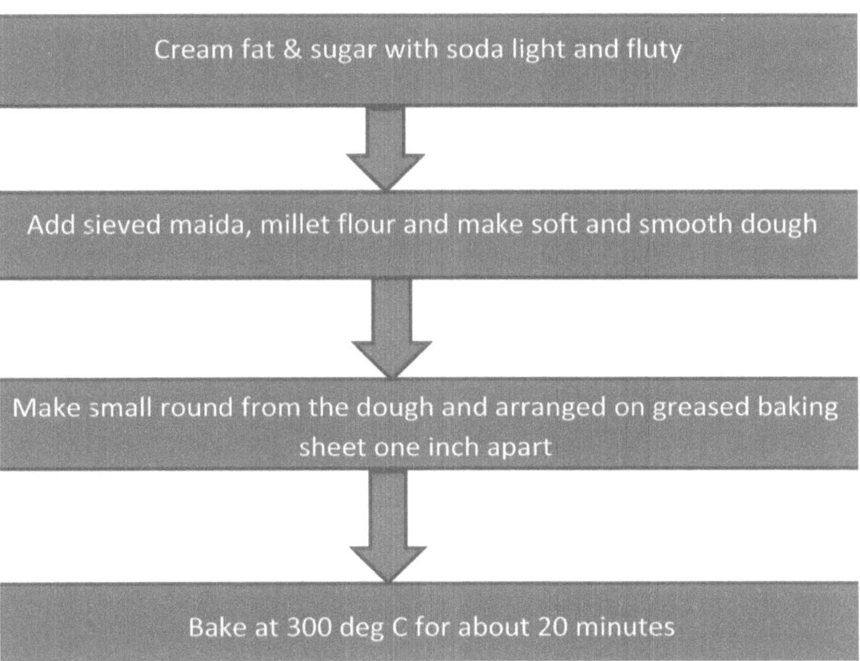

Millet based Kurkure

Ingredients

- Foxtail millet grits
- Little millet grits
- Bengal gram flour (roasted)
- Moisture content of blend

Nutritional Information	Per 100 gm
Energy (Kcal)	412
Protein (gm)	14.25
Carbohydrates (gm)	61.44
Fat (gm)	3.21
Iron (gm)	2.21
Fibre (gm)	6.82

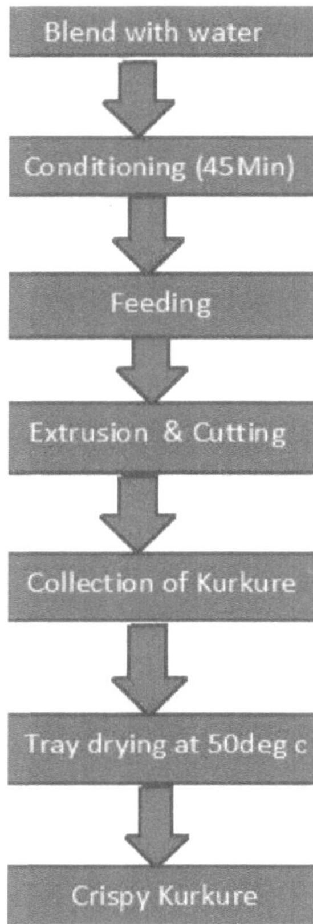

Millets Classification

Major Millets

- Pearl Millet (Bajra)
- Sorghum (Jowar)

Small (Minor) Millets

- Barnyard Millet
- Brown-top Millet
- Finger Millets (Ragi)
- Foxtail Millet
- Little Millet
- Kodo Millet
- Proso Millet

Popular Varieties

Indaf series, GPU28, GPU26, MR1, MR911 etc. besides other millets

Nutritional Status of small millet (per 100g edible portion)

Food Grain	Protein g	Carbo hydrates g	Fat g	Crude Fibre g	Mineral g	Calcium mg	Phos Phorous mg	Iron mg
Finger millet	7.3	72.0	1.3	3.6	2.7	344	283	3.9
Kodo millet	8.3	65.0	1.4	9.0	2.6	27	188	12.0
Proso millet	12.5	70.4	3.1	7.2	1.9	14	206	10.0
Foxtail millet	12.3	60.9	4.3	8.0	3.3	31	290	5.0
Little millet	7.7	67.0	4.7	7.6	1.5	17	220	6.0
Barnyard millet	6.2	65.5	2.2	9.8	4.4	11	280	15.0
Wheat	11.8	71.2	1.5	1.2	1.5	41	306	5.3
Rice	6.8	78.2	0.5	0.2	0.6	45	160	1.2

Potential of Millet-Based Products

Early research indicates substantial potential in producing nutritious energy foods (rich in amylase), bakery products, and breakfast cereals utilizing millets. Currently, extruded products from small millets are not commercially available, and research in India on their development remains limited. There is a promising market forecast for instant successes like pasta/noodles and snack foods like kurkure derived from small millets. These millets offer high-quality proteins and a balanced amino acid profile, making them ideal for innovative product development. Millet-based nutrient blends are also marketed as functional foods.

2.Post-harvest Management and Value-addition

Post-harvest management is integral to agri-produce value chain for reduction in post-harvest losses and value-addition of produce of plant origin, livestock and aquaculture. A number of equipment and structures for safe handling and shelf-life enhancement of farm produce, process protocols for value-added products, novel products and technologies for farmers and processors have been developed and commercialized through the sustained efforts of the R&D institutes. The current emphasis is on development of useful farmer centric technologies for processing in production catchments, secondary agriculture and health foods.

Cholesterol estimation in ghee

A method was developed to estimate cholesterol in ghee, using O-phthaldehyde (OPA)reagent. Benefits: Saponification of fat is achieved in 20 min.; very small amount of fat is used for saponification, and unsaponifiable material is extracted in single extraction; Small amount of extraction solvent (hexane) is used unlike conventional saponification method; It does not involve use of acetic anhydride (a controlled item) unlike Liebermann- Burchard reagent based method; The recovery of the method is 96.68 to 98.62%.In milk fat: A simple and rapid method was developed for cholesterol estimation in milk fat using enzymatic diagnostic cholesterol estimation kit.Benefits:The recovery of the cholesterol using developed method was 98.6 to 99.8% and comparable with that of direct method of cholesterol estimation usingLB reagent; The method can be easily adopted for cholesterol estimation in fresh as well as heated milk fat samples; The method is useful to serve as a substitute for acetic anhydride, which has become alimiting factor in cholesterol estimation by commonly employed LB reagent method.

Iron fortified biscuits from a composite dairy-cereal mix

Biscuits from composite wheat-pearl millet flour in combination with valuable dairy ingredients such as whey solids enriched with a suitable iron fortificant,selected on the basis of sensory evaluation was developed. The iron fortified biscuits contain 6.53 mg iron per 100 g, 18.81% fat, 12.23% protein, 1.13% ash,1.42 crude fibre, 3.2% moisture and 63.28%carbohydrates. Their shelf-life is four months without any significant change in the sensory as well as nutritional attributes. In vivo trials on Wistarrats indicated that the iron fortified biscuits helped maintain hematic status of normal animals and repair of anemic animals. The hemoglobin concentration (mg/dl)increased by 25% and 70% in normal and anaemicrats respectively. Ferritin concentration in the blood plasma also increased. The manufacturing cost of the product was `17/100 g of the product.

Process protocols

Process for high quality soy butter: Process technology for production of soy butter from roasted whole soybeans was developed. The process requires soaking, blanching, roasting, and milling of soybean. The soy butter contains 37.6% fat, 39.1% protein, 37 ppm trypsin inhibitor, no artificial preservatives, good emulsion stability and colour attributes. It is remarkably similar to peanut butter in taste and texture but has significantly lower total and saturated fat as compared to peanut butter (50% fat) and is cholesterol-free. The butter has a shelf-life of 45 days under ambient conditions and 60 days under refrigerated conditions. Soy butter, being nutritionally superior (higher protein, lower fat) to peanut butter and also free from peanut allergens, is recommended for consumption as a nutritious food.

Enhancement of shelf-life of soy paneer (tofu)and soy milk through application of selected techniques of preservation:

The main constraint in popularization of to fuhas been its poor keeping quality of few hours (3–4 h) at ambient conditions of storage and a few days (four days) under refrigeration. Shelf-life of soy paneer was enhanced through packing it inretortable pouches and autoclaving. The extended shelf-life is 18 days at room temperature and 45 days under refrigerated condition.

Mango packaging

Packaging of mango with innerlining of CFB boxes (on all sides of box except topside with flexible film) reduced the weight loss of mangoes kept at room temperature by 50% during ripening. The storage life of sapota and aonla could be extended to 3 weeks at 10°C and 12°C, respectively, by MA packing in selectively permeable film, PD-961. Matured green guava fruits could be kept in unripe green condition for one week at room temperature and three weeks at 12°C by exposing them to 500ppb 1 MCP (methyl cyclopropene). The semi-ripe (40–50%) Totapuri mango fruits withan acidity of 0.8–1.0% were found to be ideal for preservation by hurdle process. Passion fruit RTS beverage with alternate sweetener (sucralose) was comparable to that of RTS with normal sugar in taste. Osmotic pre-treatment before freezing was effectivein improving the texture, yield and quality of dehydro-frozen mango (cv. Alphonso and Totapuri) slices. The threshold level of moisture content in osmotically dehydrated slices of papaya and pineapple was found to be 14–15 and 13–14%, respectively, to prevent browning and to have better storage life and quality retention

Enhancing shelf-life of fruits

Shading the canopy from three sides enhanced fruit retention by 50%,reduces sun burning and fruit cracking by almost 40%than the open tree canopy in litchi. Litchi fruits firstpre-cooled and then packed in perforated polythenebags (200-guage) lined with litchi leaf kept better upto four days at ambient temperature. The sprays of aqueous lac formulations on pomegranate cultivar Bhagawa during fruit development stage increased shelf-life of fruits up to 17 days over the control.In apple, early variety Mollies Delicious has minimum shelf-life and its quality gets deteriorated within two weeks of harvesting. Trials were taken to increase the shelf-life of apple fruits of variety Mollies Delicious by treating with different concentrations of Aloevera gel and shrink wrapping with different sizesof semi-permeable films. The fruits coated/treated with 50% concentration of Aloe vera gel and shrink wrapped in 25 µ film stored at low temperature (5 ± 2°C) extended storage life up to 68 days.

Modified atmosphere packaging of meat emulsion

Storage of meat emulsion to make homemade convenience products under aerobic condition is notpossible without affecting its quality. Effective storage of ground meat under modified atmospheric packaging (MAP) (70% O2, 20% CO2 and 10% N2) using polyamide/polyethylene co-extruded films is possible up to 15 days at −1°C. MAP stabilizes the bright red colour of ground buffalo meat and reduces the lipidoxidation.Sheep:Nugget, salami, sausage and kofta meat products of sheep meat were prepared and evaluated for consumer acceptability. In addition, new meat.

Makhanakheermix

A ready makhanakheermix mainly consisting of ground makhana, milk powder, sugar, commonly available binder and natural flavouring agents was developed. The kheeris prepared by adding requisite amount of water in the developed mix andstirring. The shelf-life of the product is more than six months. Its proximate composition is protein 11.5%,carbohydrate 64.7%, fat 7.6%, moisture 13.9%, and minerals phosphorus, iron, calcium) 2.2%. Qualityof protein is comparable with that of fish and isbeneficial in getting immediate energy, besides having medicinal values of makhana.

Mango wine

It was developed from three mango varieties, viz. Dashehari, Langra and Chausa, using Saccharomyces cerevisiae. The product had parameter profile of 8.8°Brix TSS, 0.58% acidity, 0.97 mg/100 mlascorbic acid, 0.05% tannins, 1.04% reducing sugar,1.82% total sugar and 10.4% alcohol. Similarly, baelwine was developed using Saccharomyces cerevisiae with 14.8oBrix TSS, 0.87% acidity, 2.35 mg/100 mlascorbic acid, 0.36% tannins, 5.82% reducing sugar,6.51% total sugar and 8.6% alcohol. A partially fermented (4% alcohol), mildly spiced, anti-oxidant rich beverage having distinct flavour and taste was developed from raw mango fruits using Saccharomyces cerevisiae.

Antioxidant potential of fruit dahi

Dahi was prepared by using NCDC 167 and NCDC 261 in theratio of 1:1, incorporated with different levels of strawberry pulp/mango pulp (6–12% level). Basedon sensory evaluation, dahi incorporated with 8%strawberry pulp (corresponding to 17.8°Brix) was adjudged as best for overall acceptability.

Similarly, mangodahi showed optimum sensory quality at 8%mango pulp (20.10 Brix) fortification. The products were evaluated for their compositional parameters, physico-chemical and textural properties. The total solids for strawberry dahi and mango dahicorresponded to 18.42 and 18.39 %, pH 4.44 and 4.50, while firmnesses 0.53 and 0.58 N respectively. The antioxidant activity measured by FRAP method was 82.75, 173.94 and255.5µg Trolox equivalent/g for control, mango and strawberry fortified dahi respectively. High correlation values were observed between different methods of antioxidant capacity and between total phenolic content for different fruit dahi preparations. Further, during storage in refrigerator for three weeks, there was no significant difference in antioxidant potential of mango and strawberry fortified dahi.

Fermented butter milk drinks

Dahi was blended with cucumber juice and water (1:3) and to enhance the taste and aroma, salt @ 0.7% and steam distillateof ginger @ 6% were added to the drink. The product packed in glass bottles kept well for 15 days under refrigerated storage. Dahi, carrot extract and water were blended in a proportion of 1:1:2 and to this saltat a level of 0.6% was added. Adopting the same procedure, tomato buttermilk drink was prepared. Dahi(25 g) was blended with clarified mango juice (45 g),sugar (12%) and water (30 ml) to obtain a mango buttermilk drink. Guava extract with 1.5% total solids was blended with dahi and water (1:1:2) and salt (0.6%).Thermization and carbonation of buttermilk drinks helped to extend the shelf-life of the buttermilk drinks. These products were well accepted during sensory evaluation.

Cheese-based functional food

Cheese-based health promoting food was developed using oats. No significant difference was observed in cheese made by using three emulsifying salts of tri-sodium citrate, sodiumhexametaphosphate and di-potassium hydrogen orthophosphate. The crude fibre and ß-glucan were3.09% and 1.104%, respectively, on dry matter basis.All the samples showed an increase in pH and tyrosineduring storage at room temperature and cold store. Free fatty acid content increased from 0.209% to0.212% in tub and 0.257% in pouch packed samples of processed cheese with oats during storage in cold store. Yeast and mould counts showed an increase in all the samples irrespective of packaging materials and temperature during storage. Processed cheese with oats degraded chemically as well as microbiologically faster than control processed cheese. Tub was found more suitable than pouch packaging. The average costof production of processed cheese with oats is rs 130/kg.

Products of camel milk

Chocolate barfi, peda, skim milk powder and rasogolla were prepared from camelmilk. Chhanamade from camel milk plus cow milk (1:1 ratio) and camel milk plus buffalo milk (1:1; 1.5:1 ratios) showed good binding and tested good and had good acceptability as rasogolla.

Meat products

Cured and smoked mutton products. Cured and smoked products as restructured mutton blocks and mutton ham were developed to meet the consumer demand. Emulsion products from spent hen meat. Value-addedproducts such as emulsion stuffed capsicum, emulsion stuffed samosa, emulsion bonda and emulsion omelette etc. from spent hen meat could be produced as value-added products.

Freeze dried fish balls

They were prepared from the mince of snapper (*P. multidens*) by incorporating curry leaf, mint, turmeric, ginger, garlic and pepper. A combination of spices used in fish balls had a synergistic effect against oxidation and helped in enhancing the taste. Shelf-life of tapioca and fish curry was increased to three months at ambient storage when packed and processed as twin packs in high impact polypropylene (HIPP) thermoformed containers. These containers were further packed in three layered see-through retortable to maintain the sterility. The shelf-life of vacuum packed yellow fin tuna chunks during storage at 1–2°C in ethyl vinyl alcohol (EVOH) extended under high pressure processing at 200MPawhen compared to untreated sample.

Smoked and canned freshwater catfish

Freshwater catfishWall agoattu was smoked and canned in oil intin-free steel (TFS) cans. The meat texture of freshwater catfish is generally soft and to make it firm and non-sticky it was given the smoke treatment. The smoke treatment improved texture, appearance, odour and flavour of canned freshwater catfish. The one-hour-smoked samples gave more attractive golden brown colour and appearance with good odour flavor than two-hour-smoked samples. Nine-month shelf-life studies revealed that products remained in good condition during this period; and one-hour-smoked samples were better in sensory characteristics than two hour treated and control samples.

1. **Food Processing** Food processing encompasses a wide array of products spanning across agriculture, horticulture, plantation, animal husbandry, and fisheries & marine products. India stands as a significant global food producer, boasting abundant availability of diverse food grains, fruits, vegetables, flowers, livestock, poultry, fish, and seafood. With varied

climatic conditions and an extensive coastline, India has emerged as a major food producer offering a rich variety.

Despite its significant role, the food processing industry remains relatively underdeveloped, with only a small percentage of fruits and vegetables (2%) and milk (15%) being processed. Nevertheless, the processed food sector ranks fifth in size within the country, contributing 6.3% to GDP. It represents 13% of India's exports and constitutes 6% of total industrial investment, which is estimated at US$70 billion, including US$22 billion in value-added products.

Following India's adoption of economic liberalization, this sector has witnessed an influx of Foreign Direct Investment from various parts of the world, spanning across different sectors.

2. **Dehydrated Fruits and Vegetables** Foods are dehydrated either to preserve a perishable raw commodity to ensure its availability round the year or to reduce the cost and /or difficulty in packaging, handling, transporting and storing, by converting it to a dry solid by reducing its weight and volume. Of course, there are other benefits to the user such as price stability, and also availability for immediate use without preparation. Grapes, bananas, mango, jackfruit, pineapple, papaya among others are highly nutritious and delicious and can be used as preserved food which has got high potential. Similarly most of the vegetables are seasonal and dehydration under hygienic conditions makes them available throughout the year at a reasonable cost. These are convenient enough to be used by large scale catering establishments and for defense services and in various expeditions, etc.

3. **Fruit Based Beverages** Fruit based beverages are relished very much particularly when served chilled especially during summers. These are nutritious and healthy. Juice, Squash, Crush, Cordial and Syrups are popular fruit products. Products like syrups and squashes of orange, mango, lime, pineapple, grape, apple, etc. besides theirjam and jelly are very popular among the masses.

3. Some Success Stories

i) AMUL

The dairy development initiative in Gujarat, widely known as the "Amul Model," is a notable success story. Launched over thirty years ago, it started with just eight societies collecting a few hundred liters of milk. Over time, it has grown into a major operation, now collecting nearly seven lakh liters of milk daily from 240,000 members across 840 village societies. Today, Amul dominates 90% of the organized sector's processed butter and cheese market nationwide, significantly benefiting small-scale farmers. Dr. Kurien, the visionary behind this cooperative venture, is renowned for his commitment to social rather than financial gains, prioritizing service to the people above all else.

ii) MAFCO

The success of "MAFCO"s frozen peas market model in Maharashtra highlights the power of entrepreneurial vision. Launched eight years ago, the venture began by selling 10 tonnes of peas in its first year, increasing to 42 tonnes in the second year, 120 tonnes in the third, and continued growing thereafter. This achievement is attributed to an entrepreneur who effectively anticipated market trends and implemented successful marketing strategies. The sector holds immense potential, as demonstrated by the significant market for vegetables in West Asia, which amounts to about Rs. 36 lakhs per day for air transportation. What is needed is managerial expertise to capitalize on these opportunities by organizing small farmers effectively.

iii) "Lijjat Papad" initially was a small venture but grew in size gradually and now is a household name

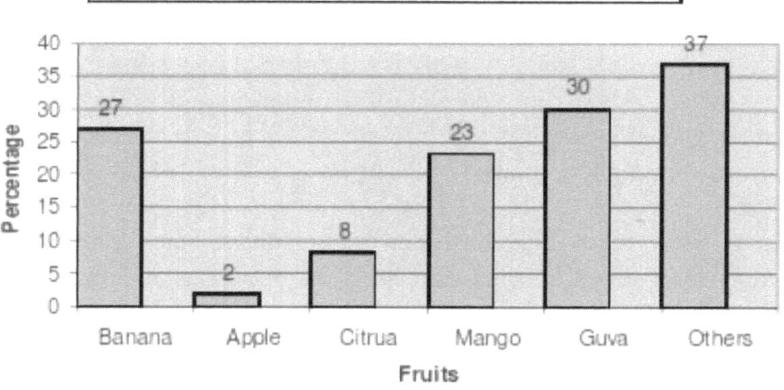

Potential Application of Eco-Friendly Packaging for Food Industry

Food and beverage packaging accounts for a substantial share, between 55% and 65%, of the $130 billion packaging market in the United States (Brody 2008). In the food processing and packaging sectors, around 15% of total variable costs are dedicated to packaging materials (Esse 2002). Sustainability has emerged as a prominent issue on the global environmental agenda, prompting academia and industry to explore sustainable alternatives aimed at conserving resources for future generations. The widespread adoption of biological, renewable materials for packaging production would address several key objectives. Historically, packaging materials have relied heavily on nonrenewable sources, with paper and board being the primary renewable options based on cellulose, the most abundant renewable polymer worldwide. While the paramount goal of food packaging remains the preservation of safety, wholesomeness, and quality, the environmental impact of packaging waste can be minimized through prudent material selection, adherence to EPA guidelines, and a reevaluation of packaging expectations with regard to environmental considerations. Collaborative efforts among industry, government, and consumers are essential for ongoing improvement, and a thorough understanding of packaging's functional characteristics is crucial to avoid well-meaning yet inadequately informed solutions that overlook both pre-consumer and post-consumer packaging factors.

CASE: Ginger

Postharvest Management

Washing and Drying

After harvesting, it's essential to trim the fibrous roots attached to the rhizomes and remove soil by washing. Subsequently, soak the rhizomes in water overnight and clean them thoroughly. To remove the skin, gently scrape it off using sharp bamboo splits or wooden splices, avoiding metallic knives as they can discolor the rhizomes. Peeling or scraping helps reduce drying time, minimizing mold growth and fermentation, although it may remove some oil constituents concentrated in the peel. Additionally, it decreases fiber content by removing the outer corky skin.

After scraping, sun-dry the rhizomes for a week, turning them frequently and rubbing them by hand to remove any remaining outer skin, resulting in unbleached ginger. Alternatively, peel the rhizomes and immerse them repeatedly in a 2% lime solution for six hours. Then, let them dry in the sun for ten days until they have a uniform coating of lime, with a moisture content of 8-10%. This process, known as bleaching, enhances the appearance, giving the ginger a light, bright color.

Mechanical drying offers rapid and more uniform drying, yielding a cleaner product compared to sun-drying, which takes 8-9 days for peeled ginger to reach the desired moisture content. To maintain quality and avoid discoloration, clean and dry the ginger as soon as possible after harvesting. During mechanical drying, ensure the temperature does not exceed 60°C.

Grading, Packing and Storage

Proper care during grading and packing is essential to maintain high-quality ginger. Dried ginger can be classified into several categories, including unpeeled, peeled, rough scraped, bleached, splits, and slices, based on the drying method. These different forms of rhizomes should be packed in jute sacks, wooden boxes, or lined corrugated cardboard boxes, depending on the transportation distance and market type. Dry slices or powder should be packaged in multi-wall laminated bags or polyethylene film pouches.

Fresh ginger should be stored in a cold room at 10-12°C with 90% relative humidity (RH). In the absence of cold storage, a zero-energy cool chamber that maintains a temperature 6-7°C lower than the outside temperature can be used. Gamma irradiation at doses of 0.05-0.06 KGy can prevent sprouting of fresh ginger. Additionally, storing fresh ginger in polyethylene bags with 2% ventilation helps prevent dehydration and mold growth.

Dried rhizomes, slices, or splits should be kept in a cold room at 10-15°C. Without cold storage, it is crucial to extract or distill dried ginger quickly, as the oil content significantly decreases after three months of room temperature storage. Gamma irradiation at doses of 5-10 KGy can inhibit mold and bacteria growth. For fumigation, ethylene oxide at a concentration of 50ppm can be used on rhizomes.

Processing

Ginger Oil : It can be prepared by steam distillation of grind paste or dried powdered ginger which is used as a flavouring agent for soft drinks, ginger beer and in food preparation. For oil extraction,dried rhizomes are ground to a coarse slurry, paste or powder, loaded into a still for distillation and steam is passed through the slurry paste/powder. This steam containing the volatile components is condensed with cold water and collected in separate container. The oil can be separated from the water upon cooling by the separatory funnel. Re-distillation can be done to increase oil yield. Usually oil yield obtained from dried rhizomes is 1.5% to 3.5% on dry weight basis and 0.4% on green weight basis depending upon variety of ginger used.

Ginger Oleoresin: It is blend of oil and resinoids. Oleorersin is obtained by extraction of dried ginger, pulverized to coarse powder with organic solvents like ethanol or acetone. Oleoresin content ranges from 3.5 to 9.5%.

Ginger Candy

Homemade Ginger Candy: A Step-by-Step Guide

Ready to tantalize your taste buds with homemade ginger candy?

Follow these steps for a delicious and rewarding experience

1. Selecting the Ginger

Choose large, mature ginger rhizomes (the root) with a low fiber content. This ensures a softer, more enjoyable candy.

2. Prep Work

Wash the ginger thoroughly to remove dirt and debris.

Peel the skin carefully using a knife or a wooden splinter.

Rinse the peeled ginger again for good measure.

3. Preparing the Ginger Pieces

Use a fork to prick the ginger pieces. This allows the sugar syrup to penetrate deeply for even flavor distribution.

Cut the ginger into bite-sized pieces, about 1-2 centimeters thick.

4. Simmering the Ginger

In a pot, boil the ginger pieces for about an hour, or until they become tender and soft.

Drain the ginger and let it dry completely in a shaded area.

5. Building the Flavor

Layer the dried ginger pieces with equal amounts of sugar in a stainless steel container.

Let this mixture sit undisturbed for 24 hours. The sugar will begin to draw out the ginger's flavor.

6. The Syrup Symphony

The next day, separate the ginger from the sugar syrup.

Add 2 grams of citric acid to the syrup and bring it to a boil.

Use a candy thermometer to monitor the sugar concentration, aiming for 60°Brix (a measure of sugar concentration).

Once the desired concentration is reached, let the syrup cool slightly.

7. Soaking and Concentration

Reintroduce the ginger pieces back into the cooled syrup and let them soak for another 24 hours. This allows the ginger to absorb the flavorful syrup.

Repeat steps 6 and 7 for the next two days, gradually increasing the sugar concentration of the syrup to 65° Brix on the second day and 75° Brix on the third day. Add 1 gram of citric acid each day before boiling the syrup.

8. Drying and Finishing Touches

After the final soaking, remove the ginger pieces from the syrup and dry them thoroughly in a preheated oven at 60°C for 6-8 hours.

Once completely dry, coat the ginger candy in your preferred topping. Options include powdered sugar, confectioner's sugar, or glucose powder. Simply sprinkle the chosen topping over the ginger and toss gently to coat evenly.

9. Storing Your Creation

Pack the finished ginger candy in airtight containers like glass jars or resealable polyethylene pouches.

Store your homemade candy in a cool, dry place to maintain its freshness and delightful taste.

Enjoy your delicious homemade ginger candy! It's a perfect treat or a thoughtful gift for those who appreciate a spicy and sweet combination.

Ginger soft drinks (RTS)

Ginger ready to serve (RTS) soft drink can be prepared by selecting healthy and blemish free rhizomes. Wash the rhizomes with water and peel with the help of wooden splinters or knives. Cut into small pieces and make pulp by passing through mixer grinder by addition of little water to facilitate easy pulping. After pulping strain the pulp and keep it for 1 hour for setting down the sediments at bottom. Then siphon off the clear juice and mix it with sugar syrup solution which can be prepared by addition of sugar+citric acid+ water @120 gm+3gm citric acid+850ml water. Strain the sugar syrup with muslin cloth to remove the impurities from dissolved sugar and mix the ginger juice pulp @ 30ml and then add the preservative potassium metabisulphite @ 40 mg/liter of RTS. Mix all the ingredients thoroughly and fill into the bottles then crown corked. The sealed bottles should be pasteurized at 85degC for 15minutes and then air cooled and can be kept for storage in cool and dry place.

Ginger Shreds: To prepare Dried Ginger

Start by washing and peeling the rhizomes. Once peeled, grate the rhizomes into small pieces.

Place the grated ginger pieces in muslin cloths and gently squeeze to remove excess juice.

Add black salt and common salt at a ratio of 4%, then spread the mixture evenly on a tray.

Dry the ginger in an oven at 60°C for two days.

Once dried, pack the ginger pieces in polyethylene pouches and store them in a cool, dry place for future use.

Ginger Pickle

Wash and peel the rhizomes, then cut them into small rectangular pieces.

Allow the pieces to dry in the shade to remove excess moisture.

Prepare a mixture of spices including ajwain, black pepper, cumin seed, chili powder, and citric acid (10 gm each for every 250 gm of ginger pieces).

Combine the spice mixture with the dried ginger pieces.

Fill glass jars with the mixture and leave them in the sun for up to two weeks, stirring occasionally.

Once the pickle is ready, store it in a cool, dry place for future use.

Ginger Chutney

It can be prepared of good quality and taste by washing ginger rhizomes (250 gm), peeling and then grinding in mixer. Tamarind (250 gm) and garlic (100 gm) should also be grind in mixer and then grinded paste of ginger ,tamarind and garlic should be mixed. This mixture should be heated to a little and add salt (100 gm). Then frying of another garlic paste (100 gm), fenugreek powder (20 gm) should be done in little mustard oil (100 gm). This fried mixture of spices should be mixed with ginger paste, sugar (500 gm) and fill into glass jar. Final product should be stored in cool and dry place.

Why the Ginger is so important for us?

- A herb with score of medicinal properties
- Cultivated in warm climatic reasons of the world
- Serves as a major cash crop in some parts / region
- Curcumin, 6-gingerol, 6-shogoals, zingiberene, bisaboline and several other lipids confers on ginger the characteristic medicinal properties
- Used as protective food and preventive stimulant spice

India's Strength

- India leads globally in ginger production, contributing approximately 32.75% of the world's total, surpassing China.
- India holds the top position as the largest producer of dry ginger worldwide.
- Over 50% of the total ginger yield originates from North Eastern states, Uttarakhand, and Sikkim.
- Significant portions of ginger cultivation in North Eastern states and Odisha adhere to organic practices.
- India has developed numerous high-yielding ginger cultivars to enhance productivity.
- The ginger sector benefits from significant research support from institutions such as the Indian Institute of Spices Research (IISR) in Kerala and State Agricultural Universities (SAUs) in regions where ginger is cultivated.

- APEDA has established Agri Export Zones in Assam, Orissa, and Sikkim to enhance ginger exports.
- The Indian Spices Board, part of the Ministry of Commerce, also offers support for expanding spice cultivation and increasing exports.

Export of ginger from India

Year	Quantity(tons)	Value(Rs.Lakh)
2003-2004	4696.5	2275.5
2004-2005	13889.9	5985.8
2005-2006	9411.3	4295.5
2006-2007	7500.1	3975.0

Why the Ginger is so Important for us ?

Orissa Scenario

- Orissa is the second largest producer of ginger in the country, which contributes approx. 10% of the total national ginger production.
- Around 17120 ha are covered under ginger and ginger cultivated area has significantly increased in last four years.
- Different ginger varieties are grown in Orissa which have less fibre content and high commercial values.
- A large tract of Koraput, Kandhamal, and Keonjhar produce ginger of different varieties like Suprabha, Suruchi, Surabhi, Kumbha etc.

Ginger contains

- Volatile oils (borneol, citral, camphene, citral, eucalyptol, linalool, phenllandrene, zingiberine and zingiberol),
- Phenols(gingerol, zingerone and shogaol)
- Alkaloid, mucilage
- Resin
- A lot of research has been carried out on the various herbal properties of the ginger.
- The herbal therapeutic benefits of ginger are mainly due to the presence of volatile oils and the high oleoresin content.
- A compound known as gingerol is an acrid chemical constituent of the ginger.

Why Value Addition?

Our Innovation focuses on improving existing processes, procedures, products or services

Value Added Products from Ginger

- Dehydrated ginger products
  - Ginger Powder
  - Ginger flakes
- Ginger Paste
- Ginger candy
- Ginger RTS
- Ginger honey
- Ginger leather
- Ginger blends
- Ginger Oil
- Ginger oleoresin

Preparation of ginger powder

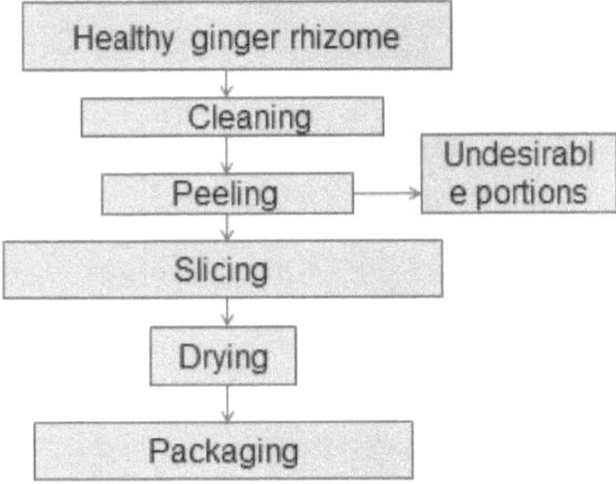

Sun drying

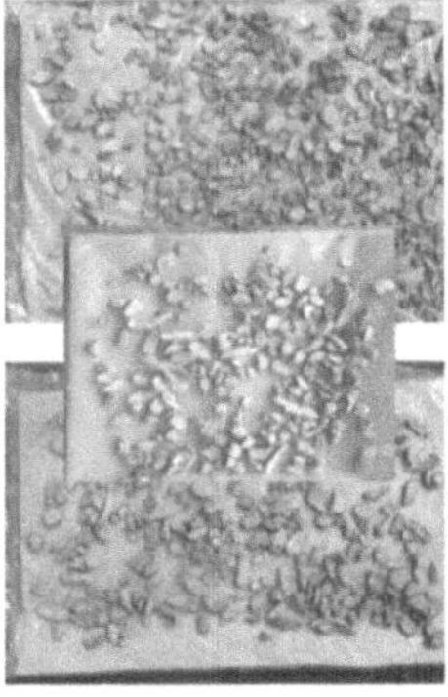

Mechanical dryer

Solar dryers

Low tunnel dryer/ Green house dryer

Dehydrated Ginger Flakes

Ginger Flakes
Developed by NAIP 2, OUAT

Ginger Powder

Ginger Powder
Developed by: NAIP 2, OUAT

Hammer mill

Hammer mill with s.s working parts required for export market

Preparation of Ginger Candy

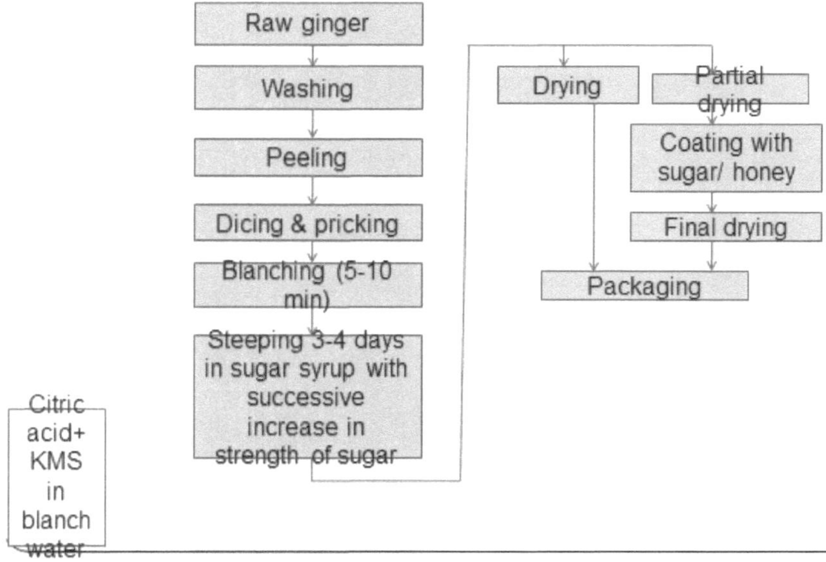

Ginger candy

Preparation of Ginger RTS

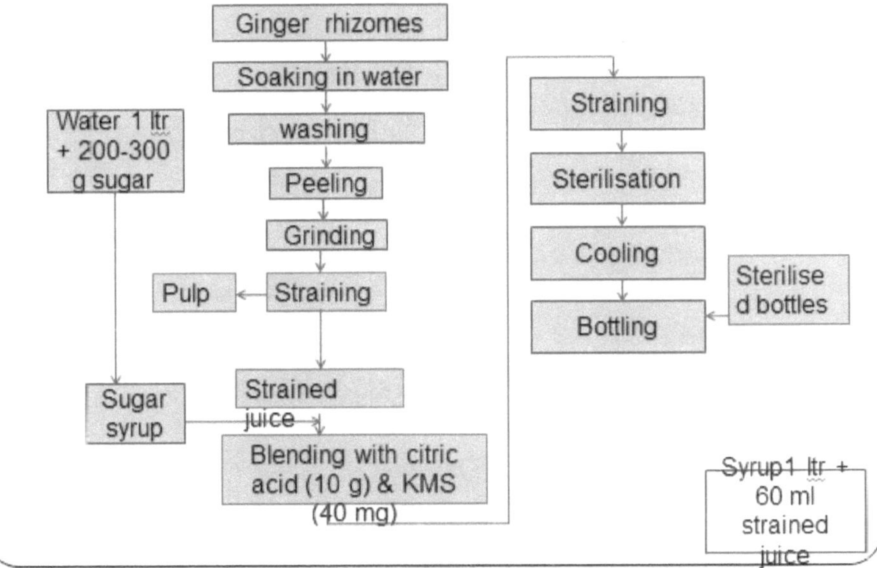

Ginger RTS

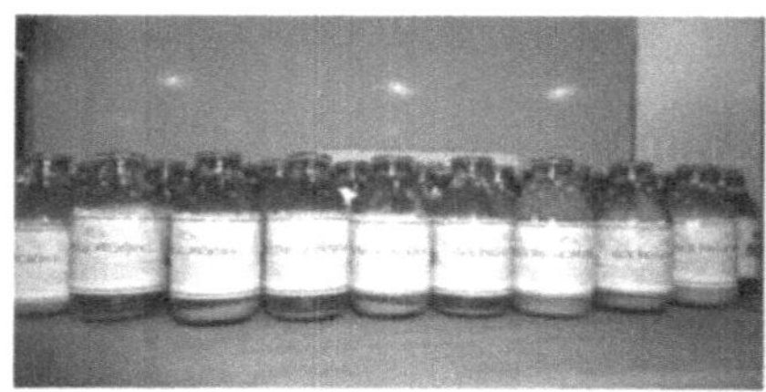

Preparation of Ginger honey

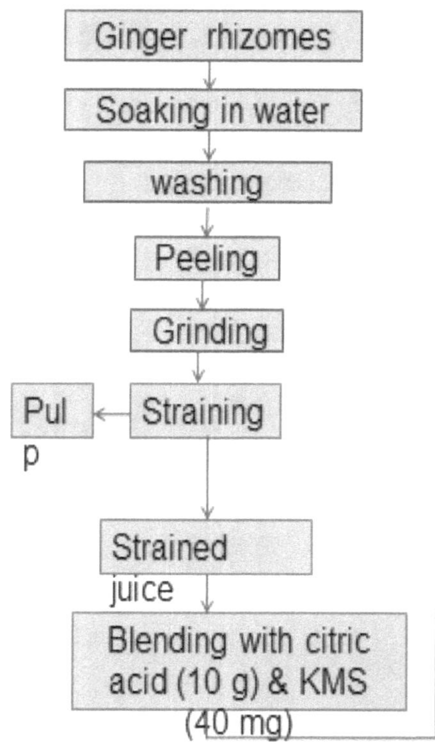

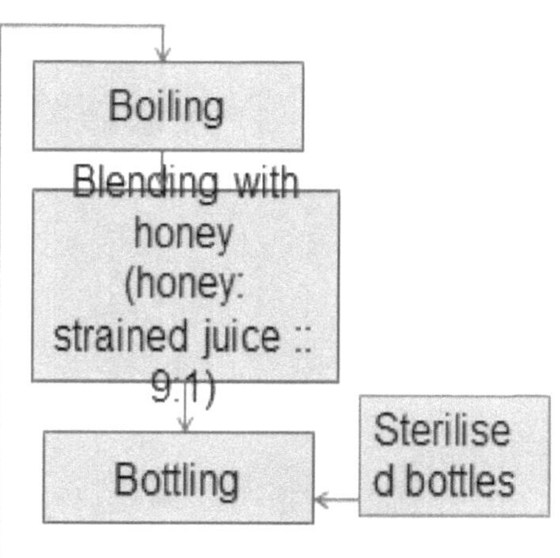

Ginger honey

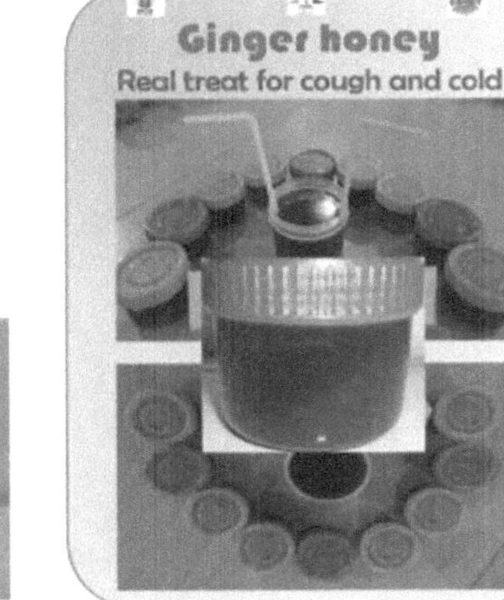

Preparation of ginger paste (water/oil based)

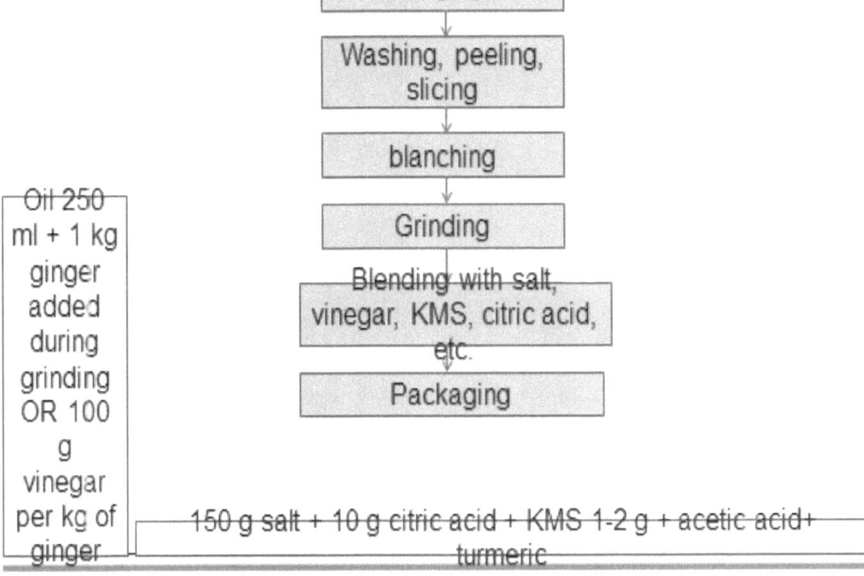

Ginger paste

Ginger paste
Developed by: NAIP-2, OUAT

Some other products

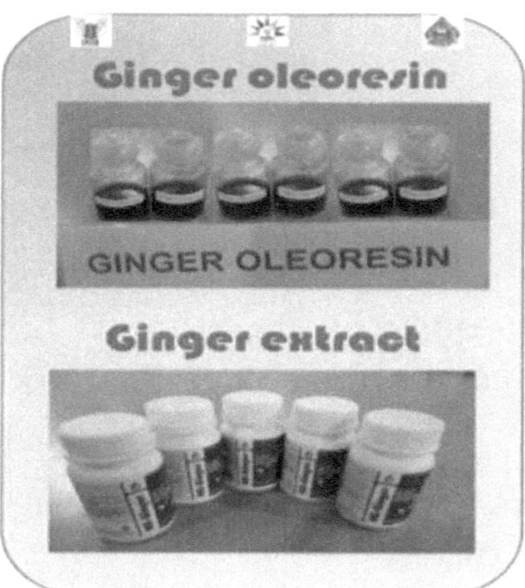

Crystallized Ginger Production Plant

• Plant and Machinery

Sr. No	Particulars	Quantity
1	Washing machine	1 no
2	peeling machine	1 no
3	Cubing machine	1 no
4	Blanching tanks	2 no
5	Steam j acketed autoclave	1 no
6	Soaking tanks	2 no
7	Discs	1 no
8	Packing machine with accessories	1 no
9	Miscellaneous allied equipments	1 no

Crystallized Ginger Production Plant

• Raw Material Requirement

Sr. No	Particulars	Quantity (Ton/annum)
1	Ginger	150
2	Sugar	75
3	Salt	20
4	Acid	2.50

Crystallized Ginger Production Plant

- Infrastructure & Facilities

Sr. No	Particulars	Requirements
1	Land	1000 sq. m
2	Building	300 sq. m
3	Power	30HP
4	Water	5000 liters per
5	Manpower	15 Personals

Crystallized Ginger Production Plant

- Estimated Cost of the Project

Sr. No	Particulars	Cost Lakh Rs)
1	land	1.00
2	Building	12.00
3	Plant & machinery	12.00
4	Misc. fixed assets	1.00
5	Preliminary & preoperative expenses	3.50
6	C ontingencies	2.00
7	Margin money for working capital	4.50
	Total	36.00

Crystallized Ginger Production Plant

- Suggested Means of Finance

Long term loans from financial institutions	24 lakhs
Equity capital	12 lakh
Total	36 Lack

Ginger Oleoresin

- A dark brown viscous liquid
- Responsible for typical ginger flavour and odour
- 1.5 to 4% (w/w)
- Used mainly by aerated water manufactures confectioners and meat packets
- It contains both volatile oil and non-volatile pungent principles.
- Advantageous over raw ginger as well as essential oils
- Hygienic
- Free from bacteria etc.
- Can be standardized for flavouring strength,

- Contain natural antioxidants,
- Free from enzymes
- Long shelf life under ideal conditions

Ginger Oleoresin Extraction

- Cleaned, fresh ginger
- Use of crusher and sieves for uniform raw material preparation
- Use of sohxlet type extractor
- Solvents: Ethanol, methanol
- Distillation of miscella at low temperature and optimum pressure
- Recovery of oleoresin

Ginger Oleoresin Extraction

- Plant and Machinery

Sr. No	Particulars	Quantity
1	Pulverizer	1 no
2	Huller	1 no
3	Boiler	1 no
4	Steam distillation plant	1 no
5	Extraction kettles	3 no
6	Tanks for storage	3 no
7	Collection condensers	2 no
S	Chilling unit	1 set
9	Lab oratory & other related equipments	1 set
10	Accessory equipments & installations	1 set

Ginger Oleoresin Extraction

- Infrastructure and Facilities

Sr. No	Particulars	Requirement
1	Land	5000 sq. m
2	Building	500 sq. m
3	Power	150 KW
4	Water	50 KL per day
5	Fuel oil	150 KL per year
6	Manpower	75 Personals

Ginger Oleoresin Extraction

• Infrastructure and Facilities

Sr. No	Particulars Requirement	
1	Land	5000 sq. m
2	Building	500 sq. m
3	Power	150KW
4	Water	50 KL per day
5	Fuel oil	150 KL per year
6	Manpower	75 Personals

Ginger Oleoresin Extraction

• Estimated Cost of the Project

Sr. No.	Particulars	Cost (Lakh Rs)
1	Land & site development	6.0
2	Buildings	22.0
3	Plant & machinery	100.0
4	Misc. fixed assets	11.0
5	Preliminary & preoperative expenses	15.0
6	Contingencies	6,0
7	Margin money for working capital	15.0
	Total	**175.00**

Ginger Oleoresin Extraction
Suggested Means of Finance

Long term loans from financial institutions	70 lakhs
Equity capital	105 lakhs
Total	175 lakhs

Ginger Oil

• Yield of ginger oil =0.5 to 3%

• Possesses only the aroma and flavor of the spice

• Used in perfymery and pharma industries where it imparts an unique individual note to composition of oriental type.

• Obtained by stem distillation of dry ginger powder.

Storage of fresh ginger

• Temerature; 7.5-10°C

• Relative Humidity: 75%

• Storage period : 16-24 weeks

Storage of dried ginger

Dried ginger is stored at ambient temperature in hermetically sealed packages.

European Spice Association (ESA) quality and sanitation specification for dry ginger

Sr.No.	Specification of Ginger	Qty
1	Extraneous matter, %	1
2	Foreign matter %	2
3	Ash % w/w max	8 (ISO)
4	Acid insoluble ash % w/w max	2 (ESA)
5	Maximum water % w/w max	12 (ISO)
6	Volatile oil	1.5 (ISO)
7	Microbes:	
	Salmonella abs in 25 g, yeast & molds	105/g target, max 106/g absolute
	E. coli	102/g target, max 103/g absolute

Source: ht:p//www.espspices.org/content/pdts/ESAQualityMinimalDocument191104.pdp
BSI : Bureau Standards Institute
ESA : European Spices Association
ISO : International Organization for Standardization

4. Sustainable Food Business

These foods have a lower environmental impact and enhance food and nutrition security, promoting a healthier life for both present and future generations. By reducing waste, food businesses can decrease their carbon footprint, save money, and improve their profitability.

Underutilised crops significantly contribute to

- Food security
- Nutritional well-being
- Therapeutic remedies
- Income generation

- Environmental benefits
- Medicinal,nutritional and economic potential is great
- Cultivated and minimal attention of climate and soil even in wastelands

Limitations

- Contains undesirable or anti-nutritional constituents
- Processing difficulties

The value addition with appropriate processing technology can assist meeting people's nutritional needs ensuring economic sustainability.

Each step adds value to the product

- Primary Processing: Involves cleaning, sorting, grading, and packing.
- Secondary Processing: Alters the original form of the product, such as milling grain into flour, splitting pulses, or roasting meat.
- Tertiary Processing: Produces high-value, ready-to-eat foods like bakery products, instant meals, and health drinks.

Value added products from cashew apple

Value added products from stone apple

PROCESSING OF ELEPHANT APPLE

Osmo-dehydration

Dried product

Packs of Dried product

Residual Osmo-syrup

Food Products from Aloe-vera Gel

Millet Based Convenient Food

Pasta maker

Hot extruder

Cold Extruder

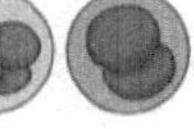

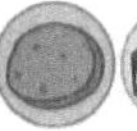

Packaging machine

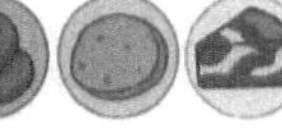

Value added products from mahua flower

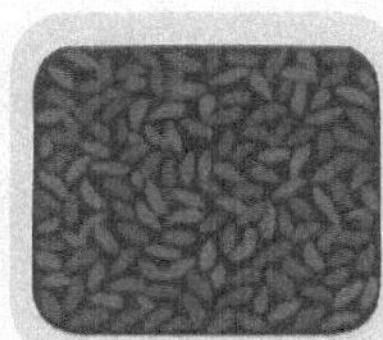

Stamen remover

Processing Machineries for mahua seeds

TUBER CROPS

Cassava

Sweet potato

Greater yam

EFY

Colocasia

Yam bean

VALUE ADDED PRODUCTS FROM SWEET POTATO
Nutritionally fortified wafers
Anthocyanin and Carotene rich functional pasta
SWEET POTATO STARCH
Tuber Starch
High fiber and high protein pasta
High fiber and high protein pasta

MINIMAL PROCESSING OF VEGETABLES
Washing
Dicing
Trimming
Centrifuge
Treatment
Shrink Wrapping

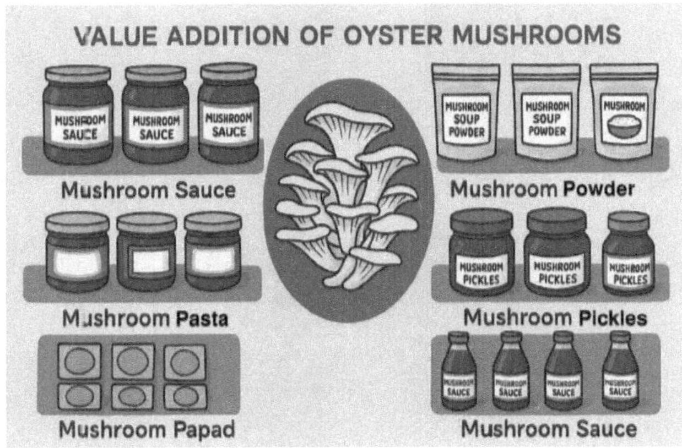

VALUE ADDITION OF OYSTER MUSHROOMS
MUSHROOM SAUCE
MUSHROOM SAUCE
MUSHROOM SAUCE
Mushroom Sauce
MUSHROOM SOUP POWDER
MUSHROOM SOUP POWDER
MUSHROOM
Mushroom Powder
Mushroom Pasta
MUSHROOM PICKLES
MUSHROOM PICKLES
MUSHROOM PICKLES
Mushroom Pickles
Mushroom Papad
MUSHROOM SAUCE
MUSHROOM SAUCE
MUSHROOM SAUCE
MUSHROOM SAUCE
Mushroom Sauce

RETORT PROCESSED PADDY STRAW MUSHROOMS

VALUE ADDED PRODUCTS FROM BAMBOO SHOOT

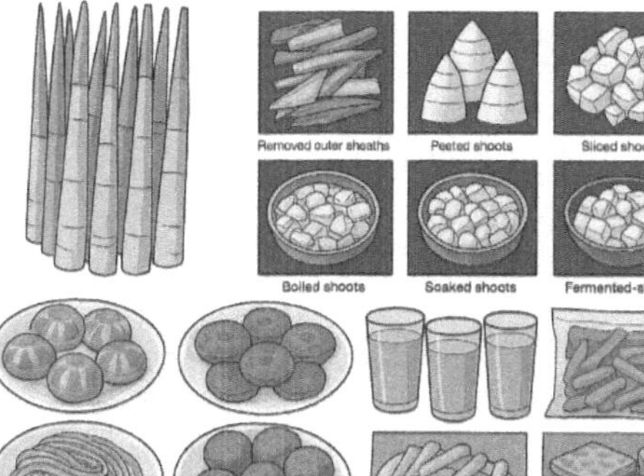

Bamboo shoot fortified convenient food

FOOD WASTE ALONG THE FOOD SUPPLY CHAIN

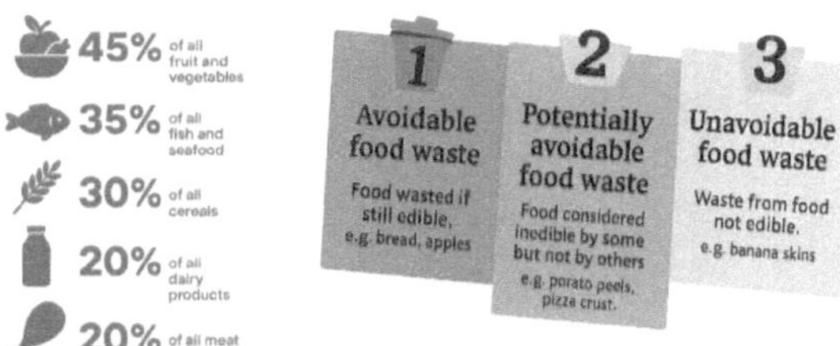

It is inefficient to use financial resources, as well as land, water, energy and labour to produce food that is ultimately wasted or lost.

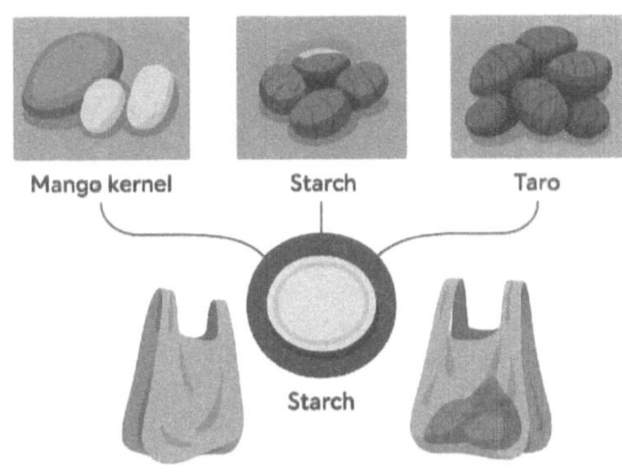

Training and Education on

- Operations and Maintenance
- Sensory profiling
- Selection of proper packaging and storage protocols
- Health hazard due to chemical use
- Adoption of FSSAI guidelines
- Appropriate certification for marketing

List of agricultural products and their cumulative loss in %

Cereals	:	4.65 to 5.99
Pulses	:	6.36 to 8.41
Oil Seeds	:	3.08 to 9.96
Fruits & Vegetable	:	4.58 to 15.88
Milk	:	0.92
Meat	:	2.71
Poultry Meat	:	6.74

5. Summary and Conclusion

Overview of Food Processing and Preservation

The chapter on food processing and preservation provides a comprehensive understanding of the techniques, principles, and innovations that ensure food safety, extend shelf life, and maintain nutritional value. This chapter delves into the historical development, technological advancements, and practical applications of various methods used in the food industry.

Historical Context and Evolution
Early Methods

Traditional Techniques: The chapter begins with an overview of early preservation methods such as drying, salting, smoking, and fermenting, which were used by ancient civilizations to prolong the usability of food.

Cultural Significance: These methods not only ensured food security but also played a role in cultural and culinary traditions.

Industrial Revolution

Technological Advancements: The Industrial Revolution marked a significant shift with the introduction of canning, pasteurization, and refrigeration. These innovations allowed for mass production and distribution of preserved foods.

Impact on Society: The ability to preserve food on a large scale contributed to urbanization, longer food supply chains, and the development of global trade.

Principles of Food Processing and Preservation

Objectives

Safety: Ensuring that food is free from harmful microorganisms & contaminants.

Shelf Life: Extending the duration for which food remains consumable without significant loss of quality.

Nutritional Value: Preserving the nutritional content of food as much as possible.

Sensory Qualities: Maintaining the taste, texture, color, and aroma that consumers expect.

Basic Concepts

Microbial Control: Understanding the role of microorganisms in food spoilage and how different preservation methods inhibit their growth.

Enzyme Activity: Methods to control enzymatic reactions that can lead to food spoilage.

Chemical Changes: Managing oxidation and other chemical reactions that can degrade food quality.

Key Techniques in Food Processing and Preservation

Thermal Processing

Pasteurization: A mild heat treatment that destroys pathogenic microorganisms and extends the shelf life of beverages and other perishables.

Sterilization: A more intense heat treatment that achieves commercial sterility, commonly used in canning.

Blanching: A pre-treatment involving brief heat exposure, mainly used for vegetables to inactivate enzymes before freezing.

Refrigeration and Freezing

Refrigeration: Slows down microbial growth and enzymatic activity, making it suitable for short- to medium-term preservation.

Freezing: Significantly slows down all biological and chemical processes, making it one of the most effective long-term preservation methods.

Dehydration

Drying: Removing moisture from food to inhibit microbial growth. Techniques include sun drying, hot air drying, and freeze-drying.

Advantages: Reduced weight and volume, making transportation and storage easier.

Chemical Preservation

Use of Preservatives: Addition of chemical agents such as salt, sugar, and acids to prevent microbial growth and spoilage.

Contemporary Practices: Use of modern preservatives like sorbates, nitrates, and sulfites.

Fermentation

Natural Preservation: Utilizing beneficial microorganisms to convert sugars into alcohol or acids, which act as natural preservatives.

Cultural Importance: Fermented foods like yogurt, cheese, sauerkraut, and kimchi play significant roles in various cuisines.

Packaging Innovations

Protective Packaging: Innovations in packaging materials and technologies that enhance food preservation, such as vacuum packing, modified atmosphere packaging (MAP), and aseptic packaging.

Environmental Considerations: Emphasis on sustainable and eco-friendly packaging solutions.

Technological Advancements and Innovations

Emerging Technologies

High-Pressure Processing (HPP): A non-thermal technique that employs high pressure to kill pathogens and extend shelf life while retaining most of the food's nutritional and sensory qualities.

Pulsed Electric Fields (PEF): Utilizes brief bursts of high voltage to disrupt microbial cells while maintaining food quality.

Ultrasound and Irradiation: Innovative methods used for microbial control and extending shelf life.

Digital Transformation

Smart Sensors: Use of sensors and IoT devices for real-time monitoring of storage conditions, ensuring optimal preservation.

Blockchain for Traceability: Enhancing transparency and traceability in the food supply chain, ensuring the integrity of preserved food products.

Case Studies and Practical Applications

Industry Examples

Dairy Processing: Techniques used in pasteurization, fermentation, and packaging of dairy products to ensure safety and quality.

Meat and Seafood: Methods like freezing, curing, and smoking used in preserving meat and seafood products.

Fruits and Vegetables: Applications of blanching, drying, and canning to extend the shelf life of produce.

Consumer Trends

Demand for Natural Preservatives: Growing consumer preference for minimally processed foods with natural preservatives.

Convenience Foods: Rise of ready-to-eat meals and snacks that require advanced preservation techniques to ensure safety and quality.

Challenges and Future Directions

Regulatory Challenges

Compliance: Navigating complex food safety regulations and standards across different regions.

Labeling: Ensuring accurate labeling of preserved foods, including information on preservatives and shelf life.

Sustainability

Reducing Waste: Innovations aimed at reducing food waste through better preservation techniques.

Eco-Friendly Practices: Emphasizing sustainability in packaging and processing methods to reduce environmental impact.

Innovation and Research

Ongoing Research: Continuous research and development efforts to discover new preservation methods and improve existing ones.

Consumer Education: Educating consumers on the benefits and safety of different preservation techniques.

Conclusion

The chapter on food processing and preservation provides a thorough understanding of the methods used to ensure food safety, extend shelf life, and maintain nutritional quality. It highlights the evolution of these techniques, the principles underlying them, and the technological advancements driving the industry forward. By addressing both traditional and modern methods, the chapter offers a comprehensive overview suitable for students, industry professionals, and anyone interested in the science and practice of food preservation.

4

Food Production and Marketing

1. Introduction

India stands as a leading global producer of agricultural and food commodities, yet less than 10% of these are processed. Anticipated growth in demand for processed foods in India presents opportunities for enhanced value addition, reduced wastage, and alternative employment avenues. Primary processing involves converting raw commodities into consumable products through steps like drying, threshing, cleaning, grading, sorting, and packing. Secondary processing focuses on creating value-added products such as bread, wine, and sausages. The rise of large-scale production of ready-to-eat foods has introduced tertiary processing as another category.

India's seafood export sector highlights its position as the 4th largest exporter globally in 2017, foremost in supplying frozen shrimp to the USA and the second largest to the European Union and Japan. The seafood industry contributes 5.15% to agriculture GDP and 1.1% to national GDP. MPEDA ensures quality control across the supply chain and conducts research and development for commercial purposes under certified authority.Exports to the US comply with the USFDA's Food Safety Modernization Act and Food Traceability Rule, necessitating comprehensive traceability from harvesting to retail, including key data elements and critical tracking events shared via traceability codes.

World Food India 2023 serves as a platform for innovation-driven solutions, transforming India's food processing supply chain ecosystem. It showcases India as a global food hub, emphasizing ready-to-eat/ready-to-cook meals, organic produce, and indigenous processed foods. The event explores investment opportunities in technology, equipment manufacturing, logistics, and cold chain infrastructure, attracting domestic and foreign investors by highlighting governmental initiatives and achievements.

Focus Pillars

- Shree Anna - Leveraging India's Superfood for the World
- Exponential Food Processing - Positioning India as the Food Hub

- Efficient Ecosystem - Harnessing Opportunities
- Strategic Segments - Focusing Potential for Growth
- Sustainable Development - Processing for Prosperity

Banking solutions for credit and other solutions

RBI Prioritizes Food Processing

The Reserve Bank of India (RBI) recognizes the critical role of the food processing industry and offers it significant financial support. Here's how:

- Priority Sector Lending: Food processing receives priority sector lending status. This means banks are encouraged to lend to businesses in this sector, making it easier for them to access credit.

- Focus on Loans: Loans for food processing units, agro-processing units, and cold chain infrastructure qualify as agricultural activities under priority sector lending. This classification allows for potentially better loan terms and conditions.

- Limit for Priority Status: Loans for food and agro-processing are considered priority sector lending up to a total sanctioned amount of ₹100 crore per borrower across the entire banking system.

- Supporting Infrastructure: Loans for developing essential agricultural infrastructure, including storage facilities (warehouses, markets, silos) and cold storage units, also fall under priority sector lending. This ensures financing for crucial storage and preservation needs.

MSMEs Included: MSMEs (Micro, Small and Medium Enterprises) involved in food processing benefit from priority sector lending as well. This expands access to credit for a wider range of businesses in the industry.

By providing these measures, the RBI aims to improve credit availability for the food processing sector, fostering its growth and development.

Digital payment solution: Banks are aggressively progressing towards providing digital solutions via, mobile wallets,digital payment platforms and other electronic payment methods tailored to meet the unique needs of the farmers and agri-entrepreneurs with its existing technological system base.

Supply chain financing; Several parties are involved in digital agriculture from distributors to input providers. In order to provide a seamless flow of products and services throughout the agricultural value chain.Banks can offer supplychain financing solutions that assist the actors in managing their working capital requirements.

Digital platform for Agribusiness: Banks can propose payment gateway for on boarding e-commerce merchants/e-tailors who develop online marketplace that links farmers with retailers,consumers and agricultural enterprises.These platforms can help with commerce and offer value added services like contract farming,market intelligence and price tracking.

Agri-tech Investments: Banks can invest through subsidiaries in Agri-tech business that are creating ground breaking approaches to digital agriculture. Banks can help the expansion of technology firms that improve the effectiveness and sustainability of agricultural practices by offering venture funding or collaborating with accelerators.

PM Formalization of Micro food enterprises(PMFME) Scheme

Implemented for a period 2020-21 to 2024-25 with an outlay of 10,000 cr to provide financial,technical and business support for upgradation of existing food processing enterpreneurs,FPOs,SHGs and co-operatives.

Loan Amount: Min.25,000/- to 9crore with a margin of 10% of project cost.

Subsidy grant:

- Individual Micro-Enterprises: Eligible for a credit-linked capital subsidy of 35% of the project cost, up to a maximum of ₹10 lakhs per unit.
- FPO/SHG/Co-operatives: Credit linked grant @35% of eligible project cost to FPOs/SHGs/Cooperatives for upgradation of their operations.
- Common Infrastructure Development: Credit linked grant @35% for common infrastructure developed by groups,Government agencies or private entities subject to maximum Rs3Cr(Technical civil work should not be more than 30% of eligible project cost.

Convergence benefit under AIF

In addition to subsidy the beneficiaries under PMFME scheme seeking credit linked subsidy would be able to avail additional benefit of interest subvention @3%.It will be applicable on the interest rate over & above the 35% of subsidy for activities covered under AIF scheme.

2. Policies and Regulation

Policy Initiatives

India's Booming Food Processing Industry: Advantages and Opportunities

India's food processing sector offers exciting opportunities due to several competitive advantages:

Government Prioritization: Recognizing its vast size and early development stage, the government prioritizes this sector. This is further emphasized by the reliance of over 70% of the population on agriculture for income. Government policies focus on commercialization, improved farm produce value, waste reduction, job creation, and export growth, aided by regulatory and tax incentives. While the sector remains largely unorganized, a growing organized segment is emerging.

Market Growth & Foreign Interest: The surge in food and agro-product popularity is evident with sales growth exceeding 150%. Foreign companies are increasingly entering the market, with well-known brands like McDonald's and KFC leading the way. Conversely, Indian food brands and FMCGs are gaining international recognition, securing shelf space in major US and European retailers. Examples include Cobra Beer, Bikanervala Foods, and ITC's Kitchen of India.

Government Support: The government offers various schemes for financial aid: setting up and modernizing food processing units, infrastructure development, research & development, and workforce training. Additionally, tax benefits incentivize new agro-processing facilities packaging fruits and vegetables.

Regulatory Reforms: Several regulatory relaxations have been implemented to ease business operations:

Waiver of excise duty on dairy machinery.

Reduced excise duty on meat, poultry, and fish products.

Exemption from licensing requirements for most processed food items.

Inclusion of food processing industries in the priority sector for bank lending.

These factors create a favorable environment for the industry's growth. The next section (2.2) will likely discuss the Food Safety and Standards Act, which plays a crucial role in ensuring food quality and consumer trust.

The Food Safety and Standards Act, 2006, aimed to consolidate and rationalize food laws by establishing unified standards for food safety. It mandates licensing or registration for all players in the food sector, enforces recall procedures for non-compliant food products, and sets up scientific panels and advisory committees to oversee food safety standards.

Objectives of FSSAI

Ensuring Safe Food for All: The Role of FSSAI

The Food Safety and Standards Authority of India (FSSAI) is a crucial organization dedicated to safeguarding public health through food safety. Its core functions encompass:

Science-Based Standards: FSSAI establishes science-backed standards for all food items. These standards define the quality and safety parameters that food products must meet to be considered fit for consumption.

Regulating the Food Chain: FSSAI oversees every stage of the food journey, from manufacturing and storage to distribution, sale, and import. This comprehensive regulation helps ensure food safety throughout the entire supply chain.

Facilitating Food Safety: Promoting food safety is a primary objective of FSSAI. They achieve this through various initiatives, such as setting hygiene standards, conducting inspections, and raising awareness among consumers and food businesses.

Beyond Core Functions

In addition to these core responsibilities, FSSAI also plays a vital role in:

Data Collection & Analysis: They gather and analyze data on food consumption, contamination levels, and emerging food safety risks. This information helps them identify potential threats and tailor their strategies accordingly.

Scientific Advice & Support: FSSAI provides scientific guidance and technical support to the government and stakeholders on matters related to food safety and nutrition. This collaborative approach strengthens food safety measures across the country.

Transforming the food safety and nutrition landscape

- Governance and Administration
- Food Standards
- Safe food practices
- Compliance-Licensing and Inspections
- Food Testing and Surveillance
- Training and Capacity Building
- Healthy diets
- Social and Behavioral change
- Consumer Focus
- Leveraging web based technology and Research focus
- International collaboration, partnership and convergence
- Partnerships and Convergence

FSSAI: Driving Innovation and Ensuring Food Quality

The Food Safety and Standards Authority of India (FSSAI) is committed to continuous improvement in food safety standards. Here's how they achieve this:

Research & Knowledge Generation

Upgrading Food Safety Standards: FSSAI actively invests in research to generate new knowledge. This knowledge helps them update and improve food safety standards to align with the latest international technical advancements. This ensures India's standards remain compatible with global best practices.

Evidence-Based Policy Making: FSSAI conducts research to support evidence-based policy making. By identifying areas for improvement through research, they can develop effective policies that ensure the highest food safety standards throughout the country.

Quality Assurance

Quality Standards & Regulations: As mandated by Chapter VIII, Section 43 of the Food Safety and Standards Act, 2006 (FSS Act), FSSAI plays a crucial role in maintaining food quality and standards.

Laboratory Network & Accreditation: FSSAI establishes procedures and guidelines for notifying, renewing, and suspending the accreditation of laboratories that test food products. This accreditation is based on the ISO 17025:2017 standard, ensuring these labs meet international benchmarks for competence and quality.

FSSAI Notified Laboratories: The FSSAI maintains a network of notified laboratories that are authorized to conduct food safety testing. This network ensures access to reliable and standardized food testing services throughout India.

By investing in research and maintaining a robust quality assurance system, FSSAI fosters a food environment that prioritizes quality and safety for all consumers.

Mobile Food Testing Laboratory

- Food Safety on wheels is doing rapid testing on spot during the districts visit.
- More than 6000 basic testing is done for the food and water samples throughout the state through mobile food testing laboratory.
- Two new MFTL will be procured for functioning at the RDC level.

Fortification-Food Fortification Resource Center

- Till now fortification of rice, milk, wheat flour, edible oil, salt
- Expansion plan under ICDS,MDM,PDS
- Regular checking by food safety officers are carried out in MDM
- Food Safty and Standards(Fortification of Foods) Regulations 2016 is followed.

Food Safety Management System

- It fosters a culture of safe food based on HACCP (Harzard Analysis and Critical Control Point). FSSAI develops guidance documents, Codes of Practices for upgrading the level of food safety implementation by the food processing sectors across the country.
- ISO Certification followed by the food chain.
- Standard Retail procedures are followed under Food Retail Regulation 2017.
- Mandatory declaration by Food Business Operators

Good Manufacturing Practices in food industry

Food Processing Levels: Ensuring Safety and Quality

Food processing involves several key levels that ensure food safety and quality:

- Personnel: This encompasses training and hygiene practices for everyone involved in handling food.

Plant & Grounds: Maintaining a clean and sanitary environment for food processing activities is crucial.

- Sanitary Operations & Facilities: Proper cleaning and disinfection procedures are essential to prevent contamination.
- Equipment & Utensils: Ensuring equipment and utensils are properly maintained and sanitized is vital.
- Processes & Control: Effective control measures are needed throughout the food processing steps.
- Warehousing & Distribution: Proper storage and transportation practices minimize the risk of spoilage and contamination.
- Maximum Defect Action Level: This establishes a threshold for defects beyond which action needs to be taken to ensure food safety.

Principles of Good Manufacturing Practices (GMP)

GMP is a framework that ensures consistent quality and safety in food production. Key principles include:

- Written Procedures: Clear and documented procedures are essential for every step of the process.
- Traceability: The ability to track the origin and movement of food products is vital for recalls and safety investigations.
- Validation: Processes and equipment are validated to ensure they consistently produce safe and high-quality food.

- Facility & Equipment Design & Maintenance: Facilities and equipment must be designed for hygiene and maintained in good working order.
- Job Competence: Personnel must be trained and qualified to perform their tasks effectively.
- Cleanliness & Sanitation: Maintaining a clean and sanitary environment is paramount.
- Component Control: Ingredients and packaging materials must be controlled and meet quality standards.

Compliance Auditing: Regular audits ensure adherence to food safety regulations.

- Elements of Good Hygiene Practices (GHP): GHP focuses on personal hygiene and food handling practices to prevent contamination throughout the food chain. Key elements include:
- Primary Production: Safe practices from farming or harvesting through initial handling are crucial.
- Establishment Design & Facilities: Facilities must be designed to promote hygiene and prevent contamination.
- Control of Operations: Processes should be controlled to minimize risks of contamination.
- Personnel Hygiene: Food handlers must practice good personal hygiene to prevent contamination.

  Transportation: Safe transportation practices minimize spoilage and contamination risks.

- Product Information & Consumer Awareness: Accurate labeling and consumer education about safe food handling practices are essential.
- Capacity Building: Providing training for food handlers about proper hygiene practices is crucial.

By adhering to these levels, principles, and elements, food processing businesses can ensure the safety and quality of their products for consumers.

Food Standards in India

FSS Regulations 2011 includes Food Product Standards and Food Additives, Packaging and Labelling, Contaminants, Toxins & Residues.

Food standards legislation criteria includes composition, appearance, freshness, source, sanitation, maxmal bacteria count,purity,maximum concentration of additives.

Scheme of Agricultural & Processed Food Export Development Authority (APEDA)

APEDA Grants Help Assess and Build Export Potential

The Agricultural & Processed Food Export Development Authority (APEDA) offers financial support to various entities interested in boosting India's food exports.

Here are the two key programs:

1. Feasibility Studies and Surveys

Who can apply? Semi-government organizations, state governments, and public sector undertakings (PSUs).

What's covered? APEDA provides grants covering 50% of the project cost, with a maximum limit of Rs. 10 lakhs per beneficiary. These grants can be used to conduct surveys, feasibility studies, and other activities to assess the potential of new food export ventures.

2. Common Infrastructure Facilities

Who can apply? Government or public sector agencies like the Airport Authority of India or Port Trusts.

What's covered? APEDA offers a 100% grant-in-aid to support the establishment of essential infrastructure facilities that benefit food exporters. These facilities could include cold storage units, testing laboratories, or export processing zones.

By providing financial assistance for pre-investment activities and infrastructure development, APEDA aims to empower various stakeholders and create a more robust ecosystem for food exports in India.

Department of Animal Husbandry, Dairying & Fisheries offers various schemes.

The Department of Animal Husbandry, Dairying & Fisheries is also involved in strengthen cold chain infrastructure in dairy sector. Milk and milk products being perishable in nature, cold chains for dairy sectors have been established with installation of Bulk Milk Coolers at village level close to the area of milk production for cooling and holding milk. The department has been implementing (i) Intensive Dairy Development Scheme (IDDS) since 1993-94 with 100 per cent grants in aid for the processing and marketing including equipment for bulk milk coolers, chilling centers, refrigerated tankers and cold storage; (ii) Strengthening infrastructure for Quality and Clean Milk Production (SIQ & CMP) since 200304 with 75 per cent grant-in-aids to profit making milk unions by the Government of India and 100 per cent for other milk unions for installation of bulk milk cooler; (iii) Dairy Entrepreneurship Development Scheme (DEDS) since 2004-05/2010-11 to encourage entrepreneurs in setting up modern dairy infrastructure for clean milk production including installation of bulk milk coolers (up to capacity of 2000 ltrs.), transportation facilities including refrigerated vans, cold storage facility for milk and milk products and dairy marketing outlets with Government of India's subsidy of 25 per cent back ended capital for general category and 33.33 per cent subsidy for SC & ST beneficiaries.

The various schemes of different Ministries/ Departments in Government of India for encouraging investments in supply chain are tabulated below:

FSSC 22000 Version 6: Navigating the path to Food Safety Excellence

Introduction to the Global Food Safety Initiative (GFSI) and FSSC 22000

In the 1990s, a series of high-profile international food safety crises, including BSE, Dioxin, and Listeria, highlighted the inconsistent standards across food manufacturing facilities. Retailers and brand manufacturers each maintained their own internal standards, leading to varying levels of compliance and eroding consumer and industry confidence. In response, global food retailers' CEOs came together to establish collaborative measures. In May 2000, they founded the Global Food Safety Initiative (GFSI), a non-profit organization dedicated to ensuring safe food for consumers worldwide.

GFSI Vision: Safe food for consumers, everywhere

- Founded in 2000 by food industry leaders.
- Benchmarking of food safety standards.
- Collaboration among global food safety experts.
- Harmonization of food safety certification schemes: BRCGS Food, FSSC 22000, SQF Code, IFS Food, Global GAP, Canada GAP, and others.

History of FSSC 22000 Food Safety Management 2001-2005

- 2001: Introduction of ISO 15161 guidelines for applying ISO 9001:2000 in the food and drink industry.
- 2005: Publication of ISO 22000:2005.
- 2005: GFSI benchmarked ISO 22000:2005 (initial rejection due to PRP).

2008-2009

- 2008: Issuance of PAS 220:2008 to establish adequate PRPs for ISO 22000:2005.
- 2009: Launch of www.fssc22000.com and establishment of FSSC 22000, consolidating previous efforts.
- 2009: Approval of FSSC 22000 by GFSI; replacement of PAS 220 with ISO/TS 22002-1.

2010-2013

- 2010: Full recognition of FSSC 22000 by GFSI.
- 2013: Reapproval by GFSI under guidance document version 6.

2018-2020

- 2018: Mandatory implementation of additional requirements in FSSC 22000 Version 4.1.
- 2018: Update of ISO 22000 to ISO 22000:2018, replacing the 2005 standard.
- 2019: Release of the FSSC 22000 certification scheme by the Foundation.
- 2020: Release of FSSC 22000 Certification scheme v5.1 following the updated GFSI benchmarking requirements.

2023

- 2023: Release of FSSC 22000 certification scheme v6.0, incorporating changes to food chain categories, additional requirements, adjustments to audit times, and enhanced documentation requirements.

Food Processing Categories: A Breakdown

This information outlines various food processing categories and their key characteristics, along with relevant standards:

Category B: Pre-processing of Plant Products

This category encompasses activities that prepare harvested plants for further processing or storage while maintaining their original whole form. Examples include fruits, vegetables, and hydrophytes. Activities include:

Cleaning, washing, rinsing

Sorting, grading, trimming

Bundling, cooling, hydro-cooking

Waxing, drenching, aeration

Preparation for storage/processing

Packing, repacking, staging, storing

Loading for transport

Standards: ISO 22000:2018, ISO/TS 22002-1:2009, FSSC 22000 (additional requirements)

Category C: Processing and Packaging

This category focuses on processing and packaging perishable food products requiring temperature control, either chilled or frozen.

Subcategories:

C0: Animal Primary Conversion: This includes initial processing, chilling, and bulk storage of animal products for further processing.

CI: Processing and Packaging of Perishable Animal Products: Examples include fish, meat, eggs, dairy, and pet food derived from animal products.

CII: Processing of Perishable Plant-Based Products: This covers processing and packaging of fruits, vegetables, grains, nuts, pulses, frozen water-based products, plant-based meat alternatives, dairy substitutes, and pet food derived from plant products.

CIII: Processing of Perishable Mixed Products: This includes processing and packaging of ready-to-eat meals like pizzas and sandwiches, along with products from off-site and industrial kitchens not intended for immediate consumption. It also covers processing perishable pet food from mixed animal and plant ingredients.

CIV: Processing of Ambient Stable Products: This category encompasses processing and packaging of food products stored and sold at room temperature, such as canned goods, biscuits, snacks, oils, beverages, pasta, flour, sugar, and ambient stable pet food.

Standards: ISO 22000:2018, ISO/TS 22002-1:2009, FSSC 22000 (additional requirements)

Category D: Processing of Feed and Animal Food

This category focuses on processing feed materials for both food-producing and non-food-producing animals (excluding household pets). Examples include meals from grains, oilseeds, and production byproducts. Activities involve processing feed mixtures with or without additives, including medicated and compound feeds.

Scope: Under ISO 22000:2018, ISO/TS 22002-6:2016, and FSSC 22000 additional requirements.

E: Catering/Food Service

Open, exposed food activities such as cooking, mixing, blending, and preparation of components and products for on-site direct consumer consumption or takeaway. Examples include restaurants, hotels, food trucks, institutions, workplaces (school or factory cafeterias), retail with onsite preparation, event catering, coffee shops, and pubs.

Scope: Under ISO 22000:2018, ISO/TS 22002-2:2013, and FSSC 22000 additional requirements.

FI: Retail/Wholesale/E-commerce

Storage and provision of finished products to customers (retail outlets, shops, wholesalers). Includes minor processing activities such as slicing, portioning, and reheating.

Scope: Under ISO 22000:2018 and FSSC 22000 additional requirements.

FII: Brokering/Trading/E-commerce

Buying and selling products on its own account without physical handling or as an agent for others, involving any item that enters the food chain.

Scope: Under ISO 22000:2018 and FSSC 22000 additional requirements.

G: Transport and Storage Services

Storage facilities and distribution vehicles for perishable food and feed, ensuring temperature integrity. Also includes storage facilities and distribution vehicles for ambient stable food and feed, and activities like relabeling and repackaging excluding open exposed product materials. Covers storage facilities and distribution vehicles for food packaging materials.

Scope: Under ISO 22000:2018, ISO/TS 22002-5:2019, and FSSC 22000 additional requirements.

I: Food Safety Standards: Beyond Processing

These regulations ensure food safety not only during processing but also in related activities:

Production of Packaging Materials: This covers the production of packaging materials intended for contact with food, animal feed, or animal food. It can include on-site production for use in the processing facility itself. These activities must comply with relevant standards like ISO 22000:2018, ISO/TS 22002-1:2009, and additional requirements of FSSC 22000.

Production of Bio-chemicals: This category encompasses the production of various food and feed additives, including processing aids (like enzymes), flavorings, vitamins, gases, minerals, and bio-cultures. Similar to packaging materials, these activities must adhere to the mentioned ISO standards and FSSC 22000 additional requirements.

FSSC 22000 Certification: Wider Applicability

The FSSC 22000 certification scheme applies to all organizations within the food and feed supply chain, regardless of factors like size, complexity, ownership structure (public or private), or profitability. This ensures consistent food safety practices across the entire supply chain.

FSSC 22000 Components: Building a Robust System

FSSC 22000 certification involves three key components:

ISO 22000:2018: This international standard provides a foundation for food safety management systems.

Sector-Specific Prerequisite Programs (PRPs): These programs address specific food safety hazards associated with different sectors within the food and feed supply chain. An example is ISO/TS 22002-1:2009, which focuses on prerequisite programs on food manufacturing.

FSSC Additional Scheme Requirements Version 5.0: These additional requirements build upon the foundation of ISO 22000 and sector-specific PRPs to ensure even more comprehensive food safety practices.

Climate Change and Management Systems: A Focus on Sustainability

Recent amendments to ISO management system standards address the growing concern of climate change. These amendments emphasize that organizations should consider climate change as a relevant external factor within their management systems. This includes:

Understanding the Organization's Context: Organizations are required to determine if climate change poses a relevant issue to their operations.

Considering Stakeholder Needs: Stakeholders, such as consumers and regulatory bodies, may have requirements related to climate change. Organizations should take these expectations into account.

The FSSC has clarified that these amendments do not require a specific implementation timeline. Existing management system practices should already incorporate these considerations for climate change.

By adhering to these comprehensive standards and addressing climate change considerations, organizations across the food and feed supply chain can contribute to a safer and more sustainable food system.

FSSC 22000 Additional Requirements

Management of Services and Purchased Materials Updates 2.5.1

- Competent laboratory analysis used for verification and/or validation of food safety.
- Documented procedures for procurement in emergency situations (applicable to FC categories C, D, I, G, and K).
- In addition to ISO/TS 22002-1:2009, Clause 9.2, a policy for the procurement of animals, fish, and seafood subject to control of prohibited substances.
- Establishment, implementation, and maintenance of a review process for product specifications to ensure ongoing compliance with food safety, legal, and customer requirements (applicable to FC categories C, D, I, G, and K).

Product Labeling and Printed Materials (2.5.2)

- Ensure products are appropriately labeled.
- Comply with applicable statutory and regulatory requirements in the country of intended sale.

Food Defense (2.5.3)

- Conduct threat assessments.
- Develop a food defense plan to safeguard against intentional malicious attacks.

Food Fraud Mitigation (2.5.4)

- Perform vulnerability assessments.
- Implement a food fraud mitigation plan to prevent fraudulent activities.

Logo Use (2.5.5)

- Certified organizations, certified bodies, and training organizations may use the logo solely for marketing activities.

Management of Services and Purchased Materials (2.5.1) (All food chain categories)

- Includes five sub-requirements that expand on ISO 22000:2018 clause 7.1.6.

Food Defense (All food chain categories)

- Requires conducting threat assessments and developing a food defense plan.

Food Fraud Mitigation (All food chain categories)

- Requires implementing a documented food fraud mitigation plan.

Logo Use (All food chain categories)

- Provides clarity on the appropriate use of the FSSC 22000 logo.

Food Defence Overview

- Food defense ensures the security of food and beverages from intentional malicious attacks, including ideologically motivated contamination.

- It is crucial for protecting businesses and consumers from internal and external threats, ranging from food tampering to potential terrorist acts.

- Requirements include conducting threat assessments, implementing mitigation measures for significant threats, and maintaining documented food defense plans.

Types of Threats Addressed

- Economically motivated adulteration
- Malicious contamination
- Extortion
- Espionage
- Counterfeiting
- Cybercrime

Guidance

- Refer to PAS 96/2017 (4th edition) for comprehensive guidance on protecting and defending food and beverages from deliberate attacks.

History of Food Fraud

- **1998:** USA - Apple juice replaced with artificially flavored sugar water.
- **2008:** China - Addition of melamine to milk powder.
- **2011:** UK - Counterfeit bottles of branded wine.
- **2013:** EU - Beef substituted with horse meat for cost-cutting reasons.
- **2013:** UK - Premium Manuka honey replaced with ordinary blended honey.

Food Fraud Mitigation: Food fraud mitigation refers to actions aimed at preventing international substitution, addition, tampering, or misrepresentation of food/feed ingredients, production processes, labeling, or information to deceive consumers for economic gain, potentially impacting consumer health.

Organizational Requirements for Food Fraud Mitigation

- Conduct food fraud vulnerability assessments.
- Develop and implement mitigation measures.
- Establish a documented food fraud mitigation plan.

VACCP Vulnerabilities: VACCP (Vulnerability Assessment Critical Control Point) focuses on preventing international adulteration and economically motivated practices such as:

- Mislabeling or misdescription.
- Varietal misdescription.
- Incorrect country of origin labeling.
- Adulteration.
- Concealment.
- Counterfeiting.
- Use of unapproved enhancements.

Steps for Conducting a Food Fraud Vulnerability Assessment

- Anticipate potential criminal actions.
- Research historical issues.
- Understand suppliers and their practices.
- Evaluate the entire supply chain, upstream and downstream.
- Stay informed through horizon scanning of current issues and sources.
- Engage a multidisciplinary team with comprehensive knowledge for effective assessment.

Management of Allergens 2.5.6 (All food chain categories)

- Conduct a risk assessment covering all potential sources of allergen cross-contamination.
- Identify and implement control measures to reduce or eliminate the risk of cross-contamination.
- Review the Allergen Management Plan annually.

Environmental Monitoring 2.5.7 (Food chain categories BIII, CI, and K)

- Develop a risk-based environmental monitoring plan.
- Establish a documented procedure to evaluate the effectiveness of all controls preventing contamination from the manufacturing environment.

Food Safety and Quality Culture 2.5.8 (All food chain categories)

- Senior management must foster a positive food safety and quality culture as part of the management system objectives.
- Support these objectives with a documented food safety and quality culture plan that includes specific targets.

Quality Control 2.5.9 (All food chain categories)

- Establish and implement a quality policy and quality objectives.
- Define and apply quality parameters aligned with product specifications for all certified products or product groups.
- Conduct analysis and evaluation of the results from defined quality control parameters.
- Incorporate quality elements into the organization's internal audit scope.

Food Safety Culture

- Emphasizes communication, training, feedback from employees, and performance measurement related to food safety activities.

FSSC 22000 Food Safety Culture Guidance Document

- Provides guidance on how GFSI guiding questions align with ISO 22000:2018 and FSSC 22000 additional requirements.

Quality Control

- The organization is mandated to
- Establish, implement, and maintain a quality policy and quality objectives.
- Define and apply quality parameters consistent with finished product specifications for all certified products or product groups, including product release criteria addressing quality control and testing.
- Analyze and evaluate the results of defined quality control parameters. These results, along with the monitoring, analysis, and evaluation of quality control parameters, are included in management review inputs.
- Ensure that quality elements specified in this section are included in the organization's internal audit scope.

Food Safety Culture

- Organizational leadership establishes the foundation and direction for its food safety culture.
- Food safety culture is grounded in shared values, beliefs, norms, mindset, behavior, and a clear vision across the organization.

- Senior management demonstrates commitment to establish, implement, maintain, and continuously improve the Food Safety Management System (FSMS) through:
  1. Effective communication.
  2. Comprehensive training programs.
  3. Soliciting feedback from employees.
  4. Performance measurement related to food-related activities.

PRP Verification 2.5.12 (For categories BIII, C, D, G, I & K)

- Implement routine site inspections and PRP checks.
- Verify that the site's production environment and processing equipment maintain suitable conditions to ensure food safety.
- Employ a risk-based approach for sampling criteria.

Product Design and Development 2.5.13 (For categories BIII, C, D, E, F, I & K)

- Establish, implement, and maintain procedures for product design and development.
- Evaluate the impact on new food safety hazards.
- Consider implications for process flow, resource and training needs, and equipment maintenance.
- Conduct production and shelf-life trials to validate product safety.

Health Status 2.5.14 (Food Chain Category D)

- Develop procedures ensuring that personnel health does not adversely affect feed production operations, subject to legal restrictions.

Equipment Management 2.5.15 (All food chain categories excluding FII)

- Specify documented purchase specifications.
- Establish and implement a risk-based change management process for new equipment.

Food Loss and Waste 2.5.16 (All food chain categories excluding I)

- Define food loss as issues occurring before reaching consumers (production, processing, storage, distribution phases) and food waste as fit-for-consumption food discarded at retail or consumption levels.
- Implement controls to reduce food loss and waste, complying with applicable legislation and ensuring updated policies.

FSSC 22000 Additional Requirements

- **Communication Requirements 2.5.17** (All food chain categories)
  - Notify the certification body within 3 working days of any events potentially affecting certification status.
- **Requirements for Organizations with Multi-site Certification 2.5.18** (Food chain categories E, F, G)
  - Incorporate internal audit requirements per ISO 22000:2018 clause 9.2.
  - Demonstrate effectiveness of corrective actions.
  - Expand scope to include transport, storage, caterers, retailers, wholesalers.
  - Mandatory application of ISO/TS 22002-5, removal of NEN/NTA 8059.
  - Updated management of services, purchased materials, and product labeling requirements.
  - Enhanced measures for warehousing, hazard control, cross-contamination prevention, PRP verification, product development, and health status.
- **Detailed Clauses in FSSC Version 6.0**
  - Validation/verification of packaging claims.
  - Criteria for using recycled materials.
  - Detailed allergen management.
  - Environmental monitoring.
  - Quality control.
  - Purchase and installation of new equipment.
  - Handling of food waste.

FSSC Audit Times

- Adjust audit times due to changes in ISO 22003-1 accreditation document and additional requirements.
- Audit times may increase for many organizations, though integrated audits with management or food safety systems could see reduced times.

Follow-up on Major Nonconformities

- FSSC 22000 version 6.0 mandates closure of major nonconformities within 26 calendar days post-audit.

- If immediate closure isn't feasible, implement temporary measures while planning permanent corrective actions.
- Agree on verification timeframe with certification body for effective implementation and certification decision based on review.

Additional Audit Documentation and Certificates

- Introduce attendance register signed by company and auditor, detailing audit start/end times and breaks.
- Senior company representative must sign integrity declaration during each audit.
- Certificates now include a QR code for enhanced traceability once issued to certified organizations.

Conclusion and Summary of Version 6.0 Changes

FSSC version 6.0, released in March 2023, introduces significant updates to certification requirements, including:

- New and revised food chain categories
- Additional compliance requirements
- Extended audit durations
- Enhanced documentation requirements
- Introduction of QR codes on certificates

Organizations must proactively familiarize themselves with these updates and undertake necessary preparations for audits under FSSC version 6.0.

FSSC version 6.0 offers a structured framework for organizations to:

- Enhance operational effectiveness
- Mitigate risks
- Contribute to sustainable practices
- Meet regulatory expectations

Section	Description	Food Chain Category Application	Changes
2.5.1	Management of Services & Purchased materials	All food chain categories	With additional requirements for category I, identified sub-categories for the requirements
2.5.2	Product Labelling and Printed Materials	All food chain categories	With additional requirements on claims on product label and for categoryI.
2.5.3	Food Defense	All food chain categories	Clarification on the requirements and specific for sub-category FII.

2.5.4	Food Fraud Mitigation	All food chain categories	Clarification on the requirements and specific requirements for sub-category FII.
2.5.5	Logo use	All food chain categories	Clarification on the use of logo.
2.5.6	Managent of Allergens	All food chain categories	Expanded requirements and clarification on the requirement and its applicability to category D.
2.5.7	Environmental Monitoring	BIll,C,I,K	Added bill and removed categories E,FI and G in the category application. Expanded requirements and clarification on the requirement.
2.5.8	Food Safety & Quality culture	All food chain categories	New requirement.Details of the requirement used to be part of a guidance document,
2.5.9	Quality control	All food chain categories	New requirement
2.5.10	Transport,storage and warehousing	All food chain categories	Added transport in the scope and expanded requirement.Incorporated previous transport & delivery require-mentfor vehicle under category FI.
2.5.11	Hazard control and measures for the preventing cross contamination.	All food chain categories excluding FII.	Extended application to all categories excluding category FII. Specified subcategory application. Incorporated previous formulation of products requirement under category D.Expanded requirement.
2.5.12	PRP Verification	BIII C,D,G,I,K	Add BIII in the category application.
2.5.13	Product Design and Development	BIII,C,D,E,F,I,K	Included in design in the scope. Added bIII in the category application. Clarification on shelf-life and with additional requirement.
2.5.14	Health Status	D	No change
2.5.15	Equipment Management	All food chain categories excluding FII	New requirement
2.5.16	Food loss and waste	All food chain categories excluding I	New requirement
2.5.17	Communication requirement	All food chain categories	New requirement
2.5.18	Requirements for organization with multi-site certification	E,F and G	Removed category A with minor clarification.

Challenges in Livestock Farming Addressed with Strategic Initiatives:

- Increase fish production per hectare through private sector initiatives to meet national benchmarks.
- Promote integrated fish farming (PAN culture) for fish fingerling rearing.
- Renovate 1,642 seasonal ponds via the NREG Programme to increase water availability by around 6,000 hectares.
- Improve fish seed production and develop supporting infrastructure for the fishery sector.
- Generate employment opportunities for fishing communities by leasing water bodies for fish farming.
- Integrate biotechnology applications into fish seed and production processes to enhance efficiency.

Infrastructure Development in Food Processing Sector

The absence of adequate infrastructure, including cold chains, packaging centers, value-added facilities, and modernized abattoirs, poses a significant challenge to the food processing sector. Enhancing general infrastructure is vital for revitalizing the industry. Recognizing this, the government has placed utmost importance on developing and expanding physical infrastructure to facilitate the rapid growth of industries. To tackle the infrastructure challenge in the food processing sector, the government has launched a scheme for infrastructure development, which includes the following components:

Food Park Scheme

Boosting Food Processing: The Role of Food Parks

The Indian government is actively promoting food processing by establishing food parks across the country. These parks address a key challenge faced by small and medium food businesses: the high cost of setting up essential infrastructure.

Shared Resources, Increased Efficiency

Food parks provide entrepreneurs with access to shared facilities, eliminating the need for individual investment. These facilities include:

Cold storage

Food testing and analysis labs

Waste treatment plants

Processing facilities

Packaging centers

Power and water supply

Training and conference facilities

Financial Assistance and Growth

The government offers financial support to establish food parks. The subsidy amount varies depending on the location, with a maximum cap. As of June 2024, over 24 mega food parks were operational with government assistance.

Taking it a Step Further: Mega Food Parks

To further enhance the food processing sector and attract foreign investment, the government is focusing on mega food parks. These larger parks aim to attract significant Foreign Direct Investment (FDI) into food processing. The government has allocated substantial funding to support the development of these mega parks.

A Brighter Future for Food Processing

By providing shared infrastructure and financial assistance, food parks are empowering small and medium food businesses. Additionally, mega food parks are expected to attract foreign investment and further accelerate the growth of India's food processing sector. This will create more opportunities for entrepreneurs and contribute to the overall development of the Indian economy.

Packaging Centres

Boosting Exports: Government Scheme Supports Food Packaging Centers

To help Indian food products compete in international markets, the government offers financial aid to establish packaging centers.

Improved Shelf Life, Wider Reach: Better packaging extends the shelf life of food products, making them suitable for export. This allows Indian businesses to reach new customers globally.

Financial Assistance: The scheme provides financial support to implementing agencies for setting up packaging centers. The subsidy covers a portion of the project cost, ranging from 25% in general areas to 33.33% in challenging locations. There's also a maximum funding cap of Rs. 20 million per project.

Open to All: Any implementing agency can apply for this assistance.

Early Success: As of now, the program has sanctioned Rs. 1450 million for a packaging center in Jammu & Kashmir, demonstrating its potential to support infrastructure development across the country.

By improving food product shelf life and providing financial aid, this scheme empowers Indian food businesses to compete on the global stage. This can lead to increased exports, economic growth, and wider availability of Indian food products for international consumers.

Integrated Cold Chain Facility

Boosting Cold Storage Infrastructure in India

The government is actively supporting the expansion of cold storage facilities across the country. This initiative aims to:

Improve Feasibility: By offering financial assistance, the program makes it easier for entrepreneurs to establish cold storage facilities.

Increase Capacity: The initiative focuses on expanding cold storage capacity to meet the growing demand for proper food storage.

Financial Support for Cold Chain Facilities

The program provides financial aid to cover a portion of the project cost for establishing cold chain facilities. The subsidy amount varies depending on the location:

25% for general areas

33.33% for challenging areas

There's also a maximum funding limit of Rs. 7.5 million per project.

Early Program Success

The initiative has already shown positive results. During the 10th Plan, funds were allocated to support the establishment of new cold storages in various states, including Gujarat, Maharashtra, Uttar Pradesh, Kerala, and more. Similarly, in the 9th Plan, assistance was provided to over 50 cold storage facilities.

By increasing cold storage capacity and making it easier to establish these facilities, this government program is helping to reduce food spoilage, improve food security, and benefit both farmers and consumers.

Value Added Centre (VAC)

Empowering Food Processors: Government Supports Value Addition

The government is launching a program to encourage food processing businesses to add more value to their products. This initiative aims to achieve several key benefits:

Improved Shelf Life: By incorporating value-added processes, food products can last longer, reducing spoilage and waste.

Higher Revenue: Value addition can translate to higher overall revenue for food processors by creating premium products.

Enhanced Traceability: The program emphasizes better traceability throughout the processing stages, ensuring food safety and quality control.

Financial Assistance for Value-Added Centers

To support the establishment and modernization of value-added centers, the program offers financial assistance. The subsidy amount varies depending on the location:

25% for projects in general areas

33.33% for projects in challenging areas

There's also a maximum funding limit of Rs. 7.5 million per project.

Early Program Examples

The program has already seen success stories. During the 10th plan, financial aid was provided to establish three value-added centers in Maharashtra, Himachal Pradesh, and Punjab, with a total allocation of Rs. 1100 million.

By providing financial support and promoting value addition, this government program empowers food processors to enhance their products, improve shelf life, and increase revenue. This can lead to a more robust food processing industry, benefiting both businesses and consumers.

Irradiation Facilities

Preserving Food with Science: Government Support for Irradiation Facilities

This program aims to extend the shelf life of food products using a safe and effective technology called food irradiation. Irradiation helps prevent:

Infestation in flour (e.g., by insects)

Sprouting in, for example, potatoes

Undesirable changes in the chemical composition of certain foods

Financial Assistance for Irradiation Facilities

The government recognizes the benefits of food irradiation and offers financial aid to establish irradiation facilities. The subsidy amount varies depending on the location:

25% for projects in general areas

33.33% for projects in challenging areas

There's also a maximum funding limit of Rs. 50 million per project.

Early Program Success

The program has already seen progress. Financial aid has been provided for four irradiation projects across different states in India, including Maharashtra, West Bengal, and Haryana, with a total allocation of Rs. 78.9 million.

By supporting the establishment of irradiation facilities, this government program helps reduce food spoilage, minimize waste, and ensure a wider availability of fresh food products for consumers.

Modernized Abattoir

The objective of the scheme is to promote scientific and hygienic practices in the slaughter process, minimizing distress to the cattle and optimizing the utilization of byproducts. Financial support, comprising 25 percent of the project cost in typical areas and 33.33 percent in challenging regions, with a cap of Rs. 40 million, is extended to local bodies for the modernization of abattoirs. To date, only one application, that of MCD Delhi, has been approved for a grant of Rs. 40 million.

Modernization of Abattoirs

a)   The aim is to modernize existing abattoirs or establish new ones, fostering scientific and hygienic slaughtering practices, implementing modern waste management technologies, enhancing byproduct utilization, providing chilling facilities, and managing retail cold chains. This is to be achieved through Public-Private Partnership (PPP) arrangements involving local bodies such as panchayats or municipalities, based on build-own-operate (BOO), build-operate-transfer (BOT), or Joint venture (JV) models. Financial assistance under the Scheme entails a grant covering 50 per cent of the total cost of plant and machinery and technical civil works for general areas, and 75 per cent for regions designated as difficult, hilly, and ITDP notified areas, with a maximum limit of Rs 15 crore per project.

b)   The Ministry initially has taken up 10 abattoir projects in the first phase. The approved 10 projects are under various stages of implementation in Dimapur (Nagaland), Kolkata (West Bengal), Ranchi (Jharkhand), Shimla (Himachal Pradesh), Hyderabad (Andhra Pradesh), Patna (Bihar), Ahmednagar (Maharashtra), Jammu (Jammu & Kashmir), Srinagar (Jammu & Kashmir) and Shillong (Meghalaya). Two of these projects viz. Dimapur and Ahmednagar have been completed and commissioned. The third project at Hyderabad is likely to be completed by December, 2011. Other projects have also received requisite approvals, including environmental clearance, and are under construction. Major challenges of the Scheme remain identification and acquisition of land and complex regulatory issues related to such projects. Considering the challenges of the sector, though, the progress of the Scheme may be considered satisfactory

Sector-Specific Government Policies

Fruits and vegetables

Setting Up a Fruit & Vegetable Processing Unit? Here's What You Need to Know

Licensing and Approvals

Most Processing Units: Good news! You don't need an industrial license to establish a fruits and vegetable processing unit in India.

100% Export-Oriented Units (EOUs): If you plan to focus solely on exports, you'll need specific government approvals.

Foreign Collaboration

Many fruits and vegetable processing industries can benefit from foreign collaboration:

Automatic Approval: You can get automatic approval for foreign technology agreements and up to 51% foreign equity participation for processing specific products.

Eligible Products: This includes items like tomatoes, mushrooms, frozen vegetables, fruits, nuts, fruit peels, fruit jellies, marmalades, fruit juices, and vegetable juices.

Regulations and Standards:

Fruit Products Order (FPO): The Fruit Products Order of 1955, issued under the Essential Commodities Act, governs this sector.

Licensing Requirement: All processing units must obtain a license under this order.

Restrictions on Certain Products: Production of some items like pickles, chutneys, tapioca sago, and tapioca flour is reserved exclusively for the small-scale sector.

Exports

Fortunately, there are no restrictions on exporting processed fruit and vegetable products from India. This allows you to freely reach international markets.

By understanding these regulations and approvals, you can navigate the process of setting up your fruit and vegetable processing unit in India with more clarity.

Fisheries

Good News for Investors: Opportunities in India's Fish Processing Industry

The Indian government welcomes foreign investment in the fish processing sector, opening doors for international collaboration and growth. Here are the key takeaways for potential investors:

Foreign Investment Allowed: You can invest freely in fish processing facilities in India.

Export Incentives: Fish processing projects that add at least 20% value to the product qualify for establishment as 100% Export Oriented Units (EOUs). This can offer specific tax and duty benefits.

Export Freedom (with one exception): You can freely export most processed fish products. However, there's a restriction on silver pomfrets under 300 grams.

Registration for Marine Products: To export marine products (fish from the ocean), your unit must register as an exporter with the Marine Products Export Development Authority (MPEDA) located in Cochin.

By investing in India's fish processing sector, you can benefit from a growing market, skilled workforce, and government support for exports.

Meat & Poultry

Setting Up a Meat Processing Unit in India? Understand the Regulations

The Indian meat processing industry offers potential, but regulations are crucial to understand. Here's a breakdown of key points:

Licensing: A license under the Meat Products Control Order (1973) is mandatory to establish a meat processing factory.

Quality and Standards: This order ensures the quality and acceptable standards for all meat products manufactured and sold in India.

Export Regulations: Exporting meat requires pre-shipment inspection and a certificate from the State Animal Husbandry Department or Directorate of Marketing and Inspection.

Restrictions on Beef: Slaughter of cows is generally prohibited, and export of beef is banned entirely.

Slaughterhouse Integration: If your processing unit is integrated with a slaughterhouse, you'll need a No Objection Certificate (NOC) from the District administration for slaughtering cattle, buffaloes, etc. Additionally, permission from civic bodies and the State Department of Animal Husbandry is required.

Understanding these regulations is essential before starting a meat processing unit in India. It's advisable to consult with relevant authorities for detailed guidance and ensure compliance.

Milk & Milk products

Navigating the Regulations for Milk and Milk Products in India

The Milk and Milk Products Order (MMPO) sets the guidelines for production in this sector. Here are key points to remember:

Smaller Units Exempt: Processing units handling less than 10,000 liters of liquid milk daily or 500 tonnes of milk solids annually are exempt from obtaining permission under the MMPO.

Foreign Investment Friendly: Good news for foreign investors! Most milk product industries, except for malted foods, allow automatic approval for foreign equity participation up to 51%.

Ice Cream Goes Big: Previously reserved for small-scale production, ice cream manufacturing is now de-reserved. This means you can establish large-scale ice cream production facilities without needing a license.

Exporting Milk Products: Following de-canalization, exports of specific milk-based products are now freely permitted. However, these units must comply with mandatory inspection requirements by agencies like the National Dairy Development Board and Export Inspection Council.

By understanding these regulations, you can navigate the Indian milk and milk product production landscape more effectively.

Grains

Deregulation Streamlines Rice Milling, Pulse Milling, and Roller Flour Industries

In 1997, significant deregulation measures were implemented to improve efficiency in the food processing sector:

Rice Milling and Pulse Milling: Previously restricted to the small-scale sector, both rice milling and pulse milling are now open to all scales of operation.

Roller Flour Mills: These mills no longer require licenses for establishment or capacity expansion, offering greater operational freedom. Additionally, they can source their wheat supply from any available source, optimizing their procurement process.

Wheat Product Manufacturing: Gone are the days of licensing and price/distribution controls! The manufacture of wheat products is now a free market, allowing for greater competition and innovation.

These reforms aim to create a more dynamic and competitive environment in the food processing sector, ultimately benefiting both businesses and consumers.

Packaged Foods

Investing in Food Processing? Understanding Key Regulations

The Indian food processing industry offers exciting opportunities for businesses.

Here's a breakdown of key regulations to consider:

Foreign Investment: Most food processing industries allow automatic approval for foreign investment up to 51% equity. Exceptions include malted foods and products reserved for small-scale production. For 100% Export Oriented Units (EOUs), specific government approval is needed.

Packaging Regulations: The Standards of Weights and Measures Act (1976) and Rules (1977) govern packaging laws for food products. These ensure accurate quantity and proper labeling for all packaged items.

Food Safety Standards: The Prevention of Food Adulteration Act (1954) and Rules (1955) set strict guidelines to prevent food adulteration and contamination. They also define permissible ingredients, prioritizing consumer health and safety.

Agmark Certification: The Agmark Rules establish quality specifications and requirements for agricultural products seeking Agmark certification, a symbol of quality and trust.

By understanding these regulations, you can navigate the Indian food processing industry with greater clarity and ensure compliance with important standards.

Government Initiative

India Welcomes Foreign Investment in Food Processing

The Indian government actively encourages foreign investment in food processing, allowing 100% FDI in this sector. This presents exciting opportunities for businesses to collaborate and grow the Indian food industry.

Strategic Locations for Processing Plants:

Agricultural Export Zones (AEZs): Setting up processing plants within these zones offers several advantages:

Simplified Sourcing: AEZs concentrate participants familiar with industry standards, making it easier to source high-quality raw materials like fruits, vegetables, flowers, or meat.

Government Incentives: Additional incentives are available for establishing processing plants within AEZs, further enhancing your investment potential.

Specialized Food Processing Hubs

Beyond location, India offers opportunities for creating specialized processing hubs catering to specific markets:

Halal Hub: Target exports to Southeast Asia and the Middle East by establishing a Halal-certified hub adhering to Islamic dietary guidelines.

Vegetarian Hub: India's large vegetarian population and growing global demand create an opportunity for a dedicated vegetarian food processing hub.

Organic Food Hub: Cater to the health-conscious markets of Europe and the US by setting up an organic food processing hub.

Seafood Hub: India boasts a rich seafood industry. A dedicated processing hub can unlock further export potential within the country.

By investing in India's food processing sector, you can leverage these strategic advantages and contribute to the growth of a dynamic food market.

3. Market Key players

Powerhouse Players and Plentiful Produce: A Look at India's F&B Industry

India's food and beverage (F&B) industry is a major player on the global stage. Leading the charge are established companies like Dabur, ITC, and Britannia, alongside international giants such as Nestle and PepsiCo.

This industry is fueled by India's rich agricultural heritage. The country is the world's:

- Largest producer of milk
- Second largest producer of fruits, vegetables, and inland fish
- Third largest producer of fish

With an annual production of 200 million tonnes of food grains, India offers not only abundant resources but also competitive pricing, making it a prime destination for processed food sourcing. This combination of strong agricultural fundamentals and established industry leaders positions India for continued growth in the F&B sector.

3.1 Cold Chain, Value Addition and Preservation Infrastructure

India's Cold Storage Challenge: Bridging the Gap

India faces a significant challenge in cold storage capacity,

with a gap estimated between 9 and 10 million tonnes. This limited capacity can lead to spoilage of perishable food items.

Government Support for Cold Storage Infrastructure

To address this gap, the government offers financial assistance to encourage the development of cold storage facilities. The program provides grants that cover a portion of the project cost:

General Areas: 50% of the total cost of plant and machinery, technical civil works, capped at a maximum of Rs. 100 million.

Northeast Region and Difficult Areas: 75% of the total project cost, capped at a maximum of Rs. 100 million.

Industry Players

Several companies are actively involved in the cold storage sector in India:

Cold Storage Manufacturers: Voltas, Blue Star, and Kirloskar Pneumatic are some leading manufacturers of cold storage equipment.

Cold Storage Facility Providers: Radhakrishna Foodland and Snowman Frozen are major players offering cold storage space for rent or lease.

Cold Chain Logistics: Companies like Concor are investing in creating a nationwide network of cold chain complexes in key cities.

By providing financial support and fostering a robust cold storage industry, the government aims to bridge the gap in storage capacity and minimize food spoilage. This can benefit farmers, food processors, and ultimately, consumers.

Third-party logistics

The transportation and cold chain management of food products require careful temperature control, as manual handling can compromise product quality and longevity. Employing logistics providers equipped with air-conditioned trucks, automated handling systems, and skilled personnel ensures end-to-end support. Additionally, implementing advanced techniques like cross-docking can reduce transit times and inventory levels.

Many companies opt to outsource their transportation needs to third-party logistics (3PL) firms, allowing them to allocate resources more effectively to their primary operations.

Collaborative efforts are gaining traction as a cost-saving strategy in logistics. Food companies are joining forces with suppliers and 3PL providers to address common challenges collectively, leveraging local cost efficiencies while maintaining overall control.

Key players in this industry include Raymond Corporation, SPS Group, SembCorp, Exel, and BAX, among others.

Retail

India's Retail Transformation: Challenges and Opportunities for Food Processing

The global retail sector is experiencing a major shift, with superstores dominating over 72% of food sales worldwide. India, however, presents a unique landscape. While the global economy is worth a staggering $7 trillion, India's retail sector boasts a vast network of around 12 million outlets.

These outlets, ranging from pushcarts and wet markets to familiar neighborhood kirana stores, often operate on a smaller scale. This fragmented retail landscape poses a challenge for the competitiveness of the Indian food processing industry. Here's why:

Limited Space: Kirana stores typically have limited space, making it difficult to stock a wide variety of processed food products.

Cold Storage Constraints: The lack of dedicated cold storage facilities in many smaller stores restricts the sale of temperature-sensitive processed food items.

Financial Constraints: Limited capital often restricts kirana stores from expanding their product offerings, hindering the adoption of a wider range of processed foods.

Despite these challenges, India's retail transformation presents an opportunity for the food processing industry. By finding innovative ways to cater to the existing retail structure, food processors can tap into this vast network and reach a wider customer base.

Despite the Indian retail sector's substantial market size of approximately $180 billion, only a mere 2% is represented by the organized sector. Enhancing the organized retail segment could catalyze growth in agriculture, food processing, and allied industries.

Key players in this sector include Bharti Airtel Group, Aditya Birla Group, Pantaloon, and Reliance, among others.

4. Challenges and opportunities

The prosperity of Indian farmers hinges on the success of the food industry, given that India's economic well-being is closely tied to agricultural incomes. As the economy becomes increasingly liberalized, the protective barriers once shielding the food and agriculture sector are being lifted, exposing it to both the opportunities and challenges of the global food economy.

Market dynamics are urging Indian agricultural producers to elevate the quality of their produce while maintaining cost competitiveness to effectively compete in the global food market. Domestically, rising per capita incomes and shifting demographic trends are fueling the demand for processed and convenient foods. Additionally, heightened consumer awareness regarding health and hygiene is driving the market towards safer food options. This transformation is sweeping across the Indian food processing sector, revolutionizing practices from farm to table. India's Food Processing Industry: A Recipe for Success

The Indian food processing industry is simmering with growth, driven by a confluence of factors:

Evolving Market: Changing consumer preferences, demographic shifts, and rapid urbanization are fueling demand for convenient, value-added food products.

Supportive Government: The Indian government's focus on this sector translates to positive policies, attracting investment and foreign direct investment (FDI).

Natural Advantages: Abundant agricultural resources and a growing pool of skilled professionals give India a competitive edge.

A Feast for Investors

With these ingredients in place, the Indian food processing sector presents a delectable opportunity for investors. Here's why:

Growth Potential: The industry is poised for significant growth, driven by the aforementioned trends.

Favorable Policies: Government initiatives are creating a business-friendly environment.

Comparative Advantage: India's natural resources and skilled workforce offer a competitive cost advantage.

By investing in India's food processing industry, you can be a part of its exciting growth story and tap into a vast market.

Challenges faced by the Indian industry

The Indian food processing industry currently grapples with a critical challenge: inadequate infrastructure, including cold chain facilities, packaging centers, value-added centers, and modernized abattoirs. Addressing this infrastructure deficit is imperative for the industry's advancement.

Additionally, several other vital initiatives are required, including:

- Promoting suitable crossbreeds while preserving indigenous livestock breeds.
- Establishing efficient livestock marketing systems.
- Encouraging rural backyard poultry farming within cooperative marketing frameworks.
- Developing cooperative dairy enterprises.
- Strengthening livestock extension services.

- Encouraging private veterinary clinic
- Institutionalising a framework for utilising synergy between restoration and creation of water bodies for water harvesting and fishery
- Provision of an insurance package to avoid distress

Strengths and opportunities that India enjoys

A Land of Opportunity: India's Food Processing Powerhouse Potential

India is a prime destination for investment in the food processing industry. Here's why:

Strong Foundation: India boasts a stable democracy, a robust legal system, and a well-developed financial and infrastructure network.

Rich Resources: Diverse agro-climatic conditions provide a vast and varied base of raw materials for food processing. While a significant portion remains unprocessed, the potential for value-added products is immense.

Growing Market: India is a demographic powerhouse with a population exceeding 1 billion, including a burgeoning middle class of 250 million.

Shifting Demands: Rapid urbanization, rising literacy rates, and increasing disposable incomes are driving a surge in demand for processed and convenient food options. On average, Indian households dedicate a significant portion of their budget to food, indicating a ready market.

Cost Advantage: India's relatively inexpensive workforce creates an opportunity for establishing large-scale, cost-effective production facilities to cater to both domestic and international markets.

Investor-Friendly Environment: The government's liberalized policies and targeted incentives for the food processing sector make India highly attractive for investment and export.

A smorgasbord of Opportunities: Investment prospects exist across various segments of the food processing industry, including:

   Fruit and vegetable processing

   Meat, fish, and poultry processing

   Packaged and convenience foods

   Beverages

   Dairy products

By capitalizing on its strong foundation, rich resources, and growing market, India is poised to become a global leader in food processing. This presents a unique opportunity for investors to be part of this exciting growth story.

Scheme of Technology Upgradation/ Establishment/ Modernization of Food Processing Industries during the 12th Plan (2013-17) for meeting the committed liabilities of 12th Plan

Food Processing Industry Gets a Boost: Scheme Extended and Merged

Good news for food processing businesses in India! The government has extended a popular scheme to help with technology upgrades and modernization. Here's a breakdown:

Scheme Extension: The Cabinet Committee on Economic Affairs approved the continuation of the "Scheme of Technology Upgradation/ Establishment/ Modernization of Food Processing Industries" into the 12th Plan period (2013-2017).

Addressing Backlog: This extension aims to address applications received during the previous 11th Plan (up to March 31, 2012) that couldn't be processed due to budget limitations. A budget of Rs. 740 crore has been allocated for this purpose.

Back-Ended Subsidy: The scheme provides financial assistance in the form of a grant disbursed after project completion.

Transition to National Mission on Food Processing (NMFP): Effective April 1, 2012, this scheme has been merged into the broader NMFP initiative.

State-Level Implementation: Under NMFP, state and union territory governments will manage the scheme's implementation going forward.

What this means for you

If you applied for assistance under the previous scheme during the 11th Plan, you may now be eligible for financial aid. Starting April 1, 2012, you'll need to contact your respective state government for application and sanction details.

By extending and merging this scheme, the government aims to provide continued support for modernization in the food processing industry.

Schemes operated by Ministry of Food Processing Industries (MoFPI)

Scheme for Technology Upgradation/ Establishment/ Modernization:

Looking to Upgrade Your Food Processing Unit? Get Government Support!

The Ministry of Food Processing Industries (MFPI) offers a grant program to help businesses modernize their operations.

Here are the key details

Who can apply? Existing food processing units are eligible for this scheme.

What's covered? Grants can cover up to 25% of the costs for:

- Plant and machinery
- Technical civil works

Grant limitations

The maximum grant amount is Rs. 50 lakh in "General Areas."

In "Difficult Areas," the grant can be higher, covering up to 33.33% of the cost or a maximum of Rs. 75 lakh.

By providing financial assistance, the MFPI aims to encourage investment in modernizing food processing facilities across India.

Establishment of Mega Food Parks

The Scheme aims to facilitate the development of comprehensive infrastructure throughout the value chain. It involves establishing a Special Purpose Vehicle to set up the Mega Food Park. Financial aid under the Scheme is provided as a one-time capital grant, covering 50% of the project cost (excluding land expenses) for general areas and 75% for difficult, hilly regions, and ITDP designated areas, with a maximum limit of Rs. 50 crore per project.

The components of the project cost include core infrastructure facilities like cleaning, grading, sorting, packing, dry and temperature controlled warehouses, ripening chambers, reefer vans etc. at collection centre and primary processing centres; buildings for common facilities like testing laboratory, sorting, grading, packing, specialized and dry warehouses, irradiation facilities, stems sterilization units, food incubation cum development centres etc. at central processing centre; factory buildings for MSMEs; basic infrastructure like roads, drainage, water supply, electricity supply, effluent treatment, parking bays; non-core infrastructure like administrative buildings, training centres, trade centre/display centres, workers hostels, canteen, marketing support system etc. not exceeding 10 per cent of project cost; hiring of domain consultants for preparation of DPRs, supply chain management It is envisaged to setup 1 Mega Food Park each for a cluster of about 3 to 4 Districts. Due care will have to be taken for smaller state and left out regions.

Establishment of Cold Chain, Value addition and Preservation Infrastructure

Building a Better Food Chain: Government Support for Cold Storage and Processing

The Indian government offers a program to support the creation of an efficient cold chain and value addition infrastructure. This initiative aims to bridge the gap between farms and consumers by minimizing food spoilage and extending shelf life.

Types of Facilities Supported

The scheme focuses on developing three key infrastructure types:

Farm Gate Processing Centers: These facilities will be located near farms and equipped with technologies for:

Weighing and sorting agricultural produce

Grading for quality control

Pre-cooling to slow spoilage

Controlled Atmosphere (CA) or Modified Atmosphere (MA) storage for extended shelf life

Individual Quick Freezing (IQF) for preserving freshness

Standard storage for products requiring less specialized environments

Mobile Pre-Cooling and Transportation: The program supports the development of mobile pre-cooling vans and reefer trucks to maintain optimal temperature during produce transportation.

Distribution Hubs: These central locations will offer advanced storage solutions, including:

CA/MA chambers for specialized storage needs

Versatile cold stores for a wider range of products

Variable humidity storage for specific produce requirements

IQF facilities for large-scale freezing

Blast freezing capabilities for rapid freezing

Financial Assistance

To encourage participation, the government provides financial aid in the form of grants. The grant covers:

50% of the total project cost (plant and machinery, technical civil works) for facilities in "General Areas."

75% of the total project cost for facilities in the Northeast Region, difficult areas, capped at a maximum of Rs. 10 crore per project.

By providing financial support for these essential infrastructure projects, the government aims to create a more robust and efficient food supply chain in India, benefiting both farmers and consumers.

Drawing from industry experience and positive feedback, the Ministry has secured approval to eliminate the ceiling on the number of cold chain projects and expand the scope of the Scheme within the allocated financial budget for the 11th Plan period. Currently, 49 cold chain projects have been green lit, meeting all eligibility criteria within the designated timeframe. Additionally, the Government has recently sanctioned another 30 projects, with individual proposals expected to receive approval by July 2012. The estimated total subsidy for these 79 projects amounts to Rs 610 crores. Among the 49 approved proposals, there is an anticipated total investment of approximately Rs. 1100 crore, which will result in the creation of an additional aggregate cold chain capacity of about 2.5 lakh MT nationwide. The majority of these projects are already in progress, with 8 projects having reached completion, and a substantial portion expected to conclude by year's end.

5. National Mission on Food Processing (NMFP)

A new scheme for 12 th Plan

Boosting Food Processing in India: Government Initiatives

The Indian government is taking several steps to strengthen the food processing sector:

National Mission on Food Processing (2012-13 onwards): This collaborative initiative with state governments aims to address various aspects of food processing, likely including infrastructure development, technology adoption, and skill development.

Enhanced Food Grain Storage: Efforts are underway to increase storage capacity for food grains across the country. This will help minimize spoilage and ensure food security.

Food Security Legislation: Subsidies are being allocated to support the efficient implementation of the proposed Food Security Legislation, aiming to provide greater access to food for citizens.

Attracting Investment: The government welcomes foreign investment by permitting 100% FDI in food processing and cold chain infrastructure. This opens doors for collaboration and innovation in the sector.

By implementing these initiatives, the government aims to create a more robust and efficient food processing industry in India, leading to benefits for both producers and consumers.

In the report of the Working Group on Food Processing Industries, it has been proposed to introduce a National Mission on Food Processing for the 12 th Plan period. The broad objectives and coverage under NMFP has been proposed as under:

Objectives of NMFP

a) To spread the message of significance of food processing for enhancing agricultural productivity and farmers income in the country.

b) To assist the state governments in creating requisite synergy between their agricultural plans and development of food processing sector.

c) To assist the state governments in addressing both institutional and infrastructural gaps along the Value Chains and thus create efficient Supply Chains for agricultural produces.

d) To promote initiatives for skill development, training and entrepreneurship which would meet needs of both post-harvest management and food processing industry.

e) To assist MSMEs in setting up/modernization of food processing units by providing need based support in terms of capital/technology/skill etc.

f) To assist food processing industry to meet requisite standards in terms of food safety laws and market demand, both domestic and international.

Major Programmes/Schemes to be covered under NMFP

a) Scheme for Technology Up-gradation / Setting up / Modernization / Expansion of Food Processing Industries

b) Scheme for supporting cold chain facilities for Non-Horticultural produces and Reefer Vehicles

c) Scheme for creating Primary Processing Centres/Collection Centres in rural areas

d) Scheme for Modernization of Abattoirs

e) Scheme for Modernization of Meat Shops

f) Scheme for Human Resource Development (HRD)

g) Scheme for Promotional Activities

h) Scheme for Up-gradation of Quality of Street Food

Table 14: Component Details of the Schemes of different Ministries/Departments for Encouraging Investments in Supply Chain

Department of Agriculture & Cooperation		
a) National Horticulture Mission (NHM) - for States other than North East and Himalayan States, Centrally sponsored scheme		
Component Details	**Maximum Permissible Cost**	**Pattern of Assistance**
1. Pack house/ On farm collection & storage unit 2. Pre-cooling unit 3. Mobile pre cooling unit	Rs. 3.00 Lakh/ per unit with size of 9Mx6M Rs. 15.00 lakh for 6 MT capacity Rs. 24.00 lakh/unit for 5 MT capacity	50% of the capital cost. Credit linked back-ended subsidy @ 40% of the cost of project in general areas and 55% in case Hilly & Scheduled areas for individual entrepreneurs.

4. Cold storage units (Const ru ct i on/e xp ans i on/ Mo dernization) 5. C.A/M.A. Storage units 6. Refer vans/ containers 7. Primary/ Mobile / Minimal processing unit 8. Ripening Chamber	Rs. 6,000 MT for 5,000 MT capacity Rs.32,000/ MT for 5000 MT capacity Rs. 24.00/ unit for 6 MT capacity Rs. 24.00 lakh/unit. Rs. 6,000/MT for 5000 MT capacity	Credit linked back-ended subsidy (a). 40% of the capital cost of project in general areas and 55% in case of Hilly & Scheduled areas in respect of only those units which adopt new technologies which are energy efficient with provision of insulation, humidity control & advance cooling system with provision of multi chambers. Technical standards, parameters & protocol issued by the Department.
9. Functional Infrastructure: for collection, sorting/ grading, packing units etc	Rs. 15.00 lakh/unit	Credit linked back-ended subsidy (a} 40% of the capital cost of project in general areas and 55 % in case of Hilly & Scheduled areas for individual entrepreneurs.
b) Horticulture Mission for North East in Himalayan States (HMNEH) - Centrally Sponsored scheme		
1. Pack house/ On farm collection & storage unit 2. Pre-cooling unit 3. Mobile pre cooling unit 4. Cold storage units (Construction/expansion/ Mo dernization) 5. C.A/M.A. Storage units 6. Refer vans/ containers 7. Primary/ Mobile / Minimal processing unit 8. Ripening Chamber 9. Functional Infrastructure: for collection, sorting/ grading, packing units etc	Rs.3.00 Lakh/ per unit with size of 9Mx6M Rs.15.00 lakh for 6 MT capacity Rs.24.00 lakh/unit for 5 MT capacity Rs.6000/MT for 5000 MT capacity Rs.32,000/ MT for 5000 MT capacity Rs.24.00/ unit for 6 MT capacity Rs.24.00 lakh/unit. Rs.6000/ MT for 5000 MT capacity Rs.15.00 lakh/unit	50% of the capital cost. Credit linked back-ended subsidy @ 55% of the project cost.

Component Details	Maximum Permissible Cost	Pattern of Assistance
		Credit linked back-ended subsidy @ 55% of the project cost which adopt new technologies which are energy efficient with provision of insulation, humidity control & advance cooling system with provision of multi chambers. Technical standards, para-meters & protocol issued by the Department to be adopted.
		Credit linked back-ended subsidy @ 55 % of the project cost.
c) National Horticulture Board (NHB) -for all States, Central Sector Scheme		
1. Cold storage units (Construction/expansion/ Modernization)	RS.6000/MT for 5000 MT capacity	Credit linked back-ended subsidy @ 40% of the capital cost of project in general areas & 55% in case of Hilly & Scheduled areas in respect of only those units which adopt new technologies which are energy efficient with provision of insulation, humidity control & advance cooling system with provision of multi chambers. Technical standards, parameters & protocol issued by the Department to be adopted.
2. C.A/M.A, Storage units	Rs.32,000/ MT for 5000 MT capacity	
3. Refer vans/containers	Rs.24.00/ unit for 6 MT capacity	
Component Details	**Maximum Permissible Cost**	**Pattern of Assistance**
Ministry of Food Processing Industries (MoFPI)		
Integrated Cold Chain, Value Added Centre, Packaging Centre and Irradiation Facilities. The components of the Scheme are at Note I :	Maximum of Rs.10.00 Crore.	Financial assistance (grant-in-aid) of 50% the total cost of plant & machinery & technical civil works in General areas & 75% for NE region & difficut areas (North East including Sikkim & J&K, Himachal Pradesh and Uttarakhand).
Ministry of Commerce - APEDA		
Common infrastructure development assistance for establishment of perishable cargo.		100% of eligible cost
Pack house and export oriented units for perishables	Rs.25.00 lakh/beneficiary	25% of the eligible cost.

Note 1: (a) A Streamlined Food Supply Chain: Facilities Supported by the Scheme

The government program aims to create a more efficient food supply chain through various infrastructure projects. Here's a breakdown of the facilities included:

1. Farm Gate Processing Centers

Located near farms, these centers offer a range of technologies for:

Weighing and Sorting: Ensuring accurate quantity and quality control.

Grading: Categorizing produce based on specific criteria.

Waxing (Optional): For certain fruits and vegetables, a protective wax coating can be applied.

Packing: Proper packaging protects produce during storage and transportation.

Pre-Cooling: Rapidly lowering the temperature to slow down spoilage.

Storage Options

Controlled Atmosphere (CA)/Modified Atmosphere (MA) cold storage: Specialized storage environments to extend shelf life.

Normal storage: Suitable for products with less stringent storage requirements.

Individual Quick Freezing (IQF): Flash-freezing individual pieces for long-term preservation.

2. Mobile Pre-Cooling and Transportation

Mobile pre-cooling vans: Maintain optimal temperature during initial produce collection and transportation.

Reefer trucks: Ensure continued temperature control for longer-distance transport.

3. Distribution Hubs

These central locations act as storage and processing centers, equipped with advanced technologies:

Multi-product and multi-CA/MA chambers: Offer a range of specialized storage environments for various products.

Variable Humidity Chambers: Maintain precise humidity levels for specific produce needs.

Packing Facility: Dedicated space for efficient and hygienic packing processes.

CIP Fog treatment (Optional): A sanitation method using fogged sanitizing solutions.

IQF facilities: Large-scale freezing capabilities for high-volume processing.

Blast freezing: Rapid freezing for maximum freshness preservation.

By supporting the development of these facilities, the program aims to minimize spoilage, extend shelf life, and create a more efficient food supply chain across India.

Given the number of schemes there needs to be better synergy between the schemes of different Departments/Ministries especially those of Department of Agriculture & Cooperation (DAC) and Ministry of Food Processing Industries (MFPI). There has been a relative neglect of the non-horticulture cold chains especially those relating to meat, poultry and fishing. State Governments need to to be actively involved in developing cold chain for these products through their Animal Husbandry & Fisheries Departments.

The Working Group on Food Processing Industries for the Twelfth Five Year Plan has

recommended launch of the **National Mission for Food Processing** (NMFP) based on the twin principles of decentralization and outreach. This has found mention in the Budget Speech 2012 of the Hon Finance Minister. It envisages a larger role of State Governments as implementing agencies in Ministry's various schemes with a three tier structure at National, States and Districts level. It is expected to be an umbrella scheme covering different aspects such as setting up /modernization of food processing industries, supporting cold chain/reefer facilities, creating primary processing centres, modernization of abattoirs/meat shops and human resources development. The Working Group has recommended a resource allocation of ₹6,533 crore for the Twelfth Plan. Out of this, ₹2,600 crore is designated for the scheme focused on technology upgradation, establishment, modernization, and expansion of food processing industries.

Applications for the grant of concessional customs duty rates under the "Project Import" Scheme for imported machinery and equipment related to the initial setup and substantial expansion of projects are governed by the provisions of the Project Import Regulation, 1986, as amended over time. These regulations allow entrepreneurs to import projects at concessional customs duty rates.

The Ministry of Food Processing Industries (MOFPI) acts as the sponsoring authority for project imports related to cold storage, cold rooms (including farm-level precooling), and industrial projects for the preservation, storage, or processing of agricultural, apiary, horticultural, dairy, poultry, aquatic and marine produce, as well as meat.

MOFPI has issued revised guidelines for sponsoring project imports, which are available on the Ministry's website under "Investor Guidance." Investors in food processing industries and cold chain logistics are encouraged to take advantage of the Project Import Scheme.

6. The Next Gen packaging

Packaging protects product from the overt and inherent adverse effects of the environment. It is for easy handling and transportation. Its primary function is to contain, protect, preserve, present and dispense whereas secondary function being easy to handle, store, open,inspect, reclose, communication mode marketing tool

Packaging development is through analyzing the buying behavior and decision making process developing collaborative packaging solutions. Plastics as the major enduse sectors in areas of agriculture production and distribution, consumer goods packaging, medical and healthcare, industrial and transportation sectors.

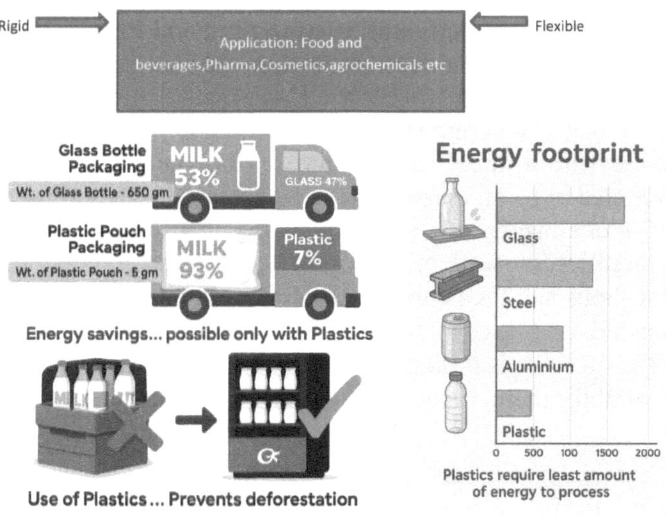

Viability of Alternatives to SUPs

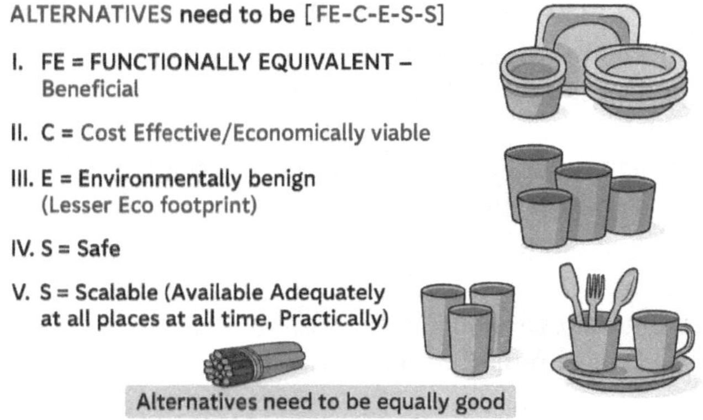

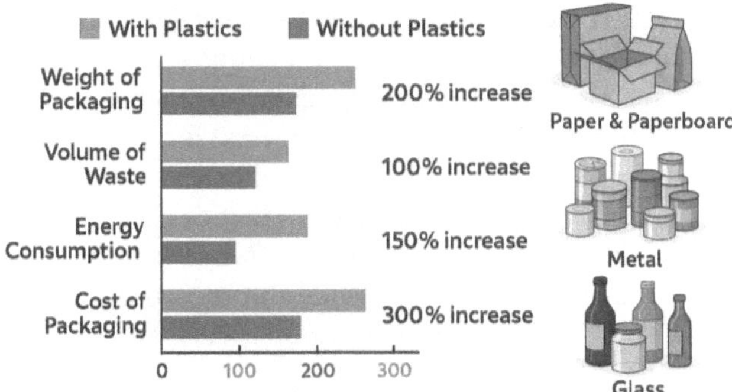

LCA Studies: Plastics are most friendly to Environment and consumer

Why plastics in packaging-

- Easy processability
- Non-staining
- Hydrolytically stable
- High modulus barrier
- Rust proof and corrosion resistant
- Resistant to oil and greases
- Resistant to acid base
- Resistant to most organic solvents

Alternatives to plastics

- Paper: deforestation,high water & chemical use,functionally not strong.
- Jute or cotton: Pressure on land,water and use of toxic chemicals
- Glass: Heavy,fragile and energy intensive.
- Metals: Heavy,energy intensive but strong
- Many other alternatives are often functionally inadequate, more expensive and of limited availability.

Single use plastics bag has lowest environmental footprint compared to paper ,cotton or biodegradable plastics as per UNEP.

Sustainable packaging development and use that is recyclable,reusable and made from rapidly renewable sources. This practice reduces the environmental impact and ecological footprint of consumers' waste.

Extended Producer Responsibility is a strategy and policy approach in which producers take responsibility for management of the disposal of products till end of life, they produce once those products are designated as no longer useful by consumers. Responsibility for disposal may be fiscal, physical or a combination of the two. EPR is the responsibility of manufacturer for production of plastic raw material, producer engaged for contract manufacturing of products using plastic packaging for a brand owner is the company which sells commodity under a registered brand, importer who imports for commercial use and brand owner to workout modality for waste collection involving urbal local body, processing and recycling. It includes product design, material sourcing, production, product use, product collection, Recycling. Manufacturers to register them selves at the PCB and provide the record of supply of RM to producer.

Conclusion

Plastics packaging reduce the environmental cost of our needs to transport and protect goods. It focus on waste management infrastructure. It invest in awareness like anti-littering and source segregation. It promote and support recycling end of life applications. The best practices and responsible use of plastics should be encouraged and enforced and manufacturers should be restricted to using 100% recyclable plastics for packaging. Sustainable approach to packaging means working to minimize or eliminate the environmental impact.

Paper boards and specialty papers packaging preparedness towards global play by ITC

- 19 years in a row carbon positive
- 17years in a row solidwaste recycling positive
- 22 years in a row water positive

Sustainable innovations in food packaging timeline-

Pre-2000

Product packaging compatibility; During this period industry focused on the printing side but also ideating materials like paper and paperboard for future needs in food packaging.

2001-2020

Virgin Grade & substance reduction: innovations in base product in previous decades gave the industry solid learning for development of products which reduces plastic use in food packaging.

2021 onwards

End of life focused innovations: At present the efforts are going on to reach the plastic packaging level barriers with sustainable alternatives.

Evolution of Foodgrade barrier technologies:

- Wax coating suitable for only low temperature food packaging
- Polyethylene Extrusion very reliable performance for food packaging but non-compostable and easy recyclable.
- Bio-polymer extrusion as good barrier properties,bio-based resins but high cost.
- Aqueous based is easy to recycling ,scalable,compostable technology is exploring.

Factors influencing barrier requirements:

Paper based product based on barrier types includes food contact safe, heat sealing, oil/grease resistance, MVTR (Moisture Vapor Transmission rate) resistance, water resistance, oxygen resistance and odor free.

- Types of food packed
- Shelf life duration
- Condition of usage like temperature
- Storage and transportation

Sustainable Packaging; FiloBev

Eco-friendly substrate to serve hot and cold beverages;

It is ecofriendly disposable and recyclable cups, designed for all uses. replaces plastics.

Recyclable under standard reclycling mechanisms as certified by CPPRI(Central Pulp and Paper Research Institute)

Compostable under industrial composting conditions as certified by CIPET(Central Institute of Plastic Engineering Technology)

Food Grade for food contact complient of US FDA,German.

Aerobically biodegradable in soil environment as certified by CIPET-ISI 7556.

Other plastic-substitution grades from PSPD

- Solid board replacing rigid plastic in point of purchase materials for indoor branding appliances.
- Anti-fungal soap wrap-paper coated with special fungicide chemical that replaces LDPE coated paper used in soap wraps.
- Paper for sticks: Paper alternative used in lollipop/candy and earbuds.
- Anti-fungal Board: Paper board coated with special fungicide chemical eliminates the need for both the plastic wrapper and LDPE coated paperboard used in soap packaging.

Food Contact Safe Packaging

- Indian FSSAI regulation for food packaging safety notifications.
- EU legislation on paper and board articles and materials
- BRC Global Standards for packaging and packaging materials
- US FDA Materials Safety Standards for direct contact packaging.

Regulation support

- Promotion of circular economy
- Use of single use plastic alternatives
- Motivating the manufacturer to produce sustainable product categories.

Ecosystem Development

- Cost optimization in sustainable packaging products to increase the viability.
- More collaborative participation of government and brandowners for accepting sustainable packaging solutions.

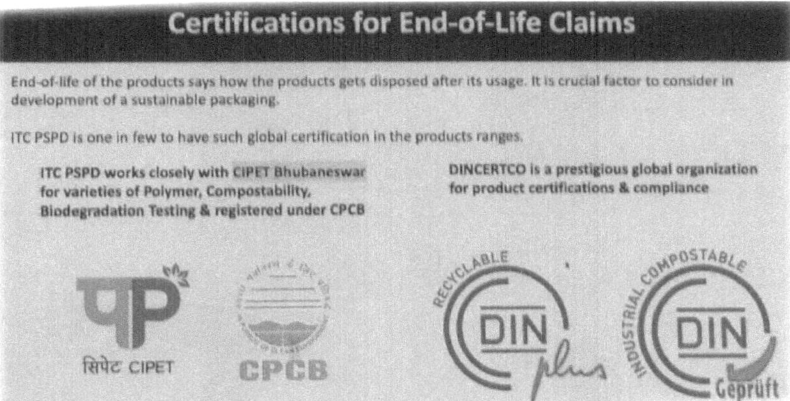

7. APEDA

APEDA's ROLE IN ENHANCING AGRICULTURAL EXPORTS"

STATUS OF APEDA

APEDA is a statutory body under the Ministry of Commerce, Govt of India. Formed by an Act of the Parliament, with Head Office in New Delhi and having branches at :

- Mumbai
- Bangalore
- Hyderabad
- Kolkata
- Guwahati

VIRTUAL OFFICES

• Kerala	Orissa
• Jammu & Kashmir	Punjab
• Tripura	Manipur
• Nagaland	Tamil Nadu
• Bihar	Uttar Pradesh
• Madhya Pradesh	Gujarat
• Chattisgarh	Goa

ORGANIZATION

- Headed by 40 Member Authority including
- 3 Members of Parliament
- 5 Representatives/UTs
- 12 Representatives of Export Trade & Industry
- 2 Specialist Scientists

FUNCTIONS OF APEDA

- **Forward Linkage.**
- Exhibitions.
- Buyer-Seller Meet.
- Delegations.
- **Backward Linkages.**
- Financial Assistance Schemes.
- Development of Standards and specifications.
- **Statutory Functions.**
- Registration.
- Database of Importers and Exporters.
- Dissemination of information pertaining to Intl Trade.
- Inspection.

(From Section 10 of the APEDA Act, 1985)

- Encouraging Export-Oriented Production
- Providing Assistance for Research and Development (R&D) and Quality Assurance
- Establishing Quality Standards and Specifications for Designated Products

- Inspecting and Certifying Meat Processing Plants, Storage Facilities, and Transportation Points
- Developing Infrastructure for Transportation, Handling, and Storage
- Enhancing Product Packaging
- Promoting and Developing Markets
- Gathering Market Intelligence through Surveys and Feasibility Studies
- Offering Training Programs on Various Aspects of Designated Product Industries

Vision

Establishing India as a supplier of quality agro and food products in the global markets.

Products Within APEDA's ambit

Floriculture

1. Cut Flowers   2. Dry Flowers 3. Seeds

Fruits & Vegetables

1. Mangoes   2. Grapes 3. Walnuts 4. Onions

5. Potatoes,   6 Pomegranate

Processed Fruits & Vegetables

1. Mango Pulp 2. Gherkins 3. Mushrooms

4. Pickle & Chutneys

Livestock Products

1. Buffalo Meat 2. Poultry Products

Other Processed Foods

1. Groundnut   2. Guargum   3. Alcoholic Beverages

Cereals

Non Basmati Rice

Non Scheduled Products

Basmati Rice, Wheat & Coarse Grains

Contribution of Various Items in Apeda's Export (2007-2008)

Value in Rs. Crores   Total : 31870.60 Crores

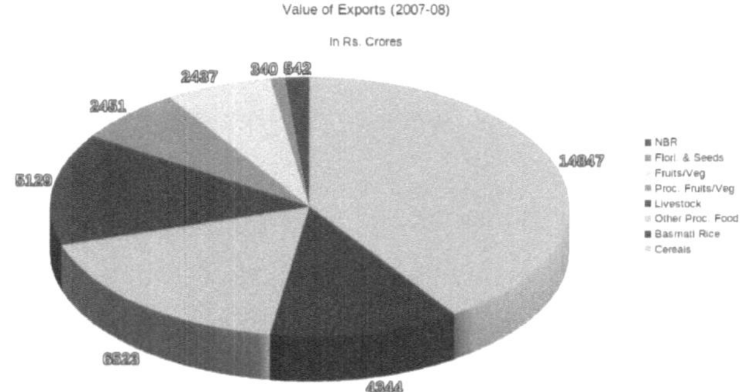

EXPORT OF APEDA PRODUCTS in 2007-08

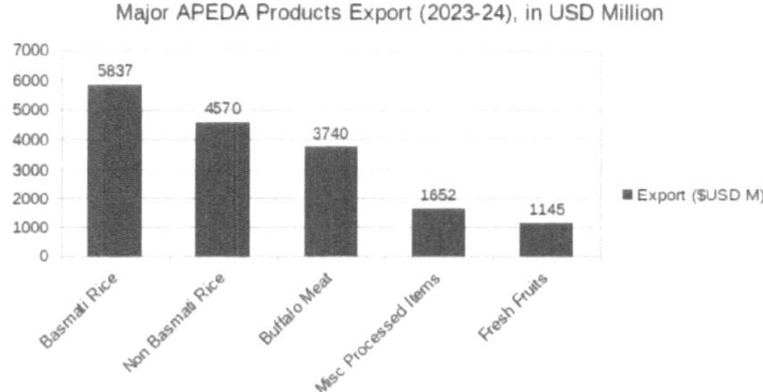

EXPORT OF APEDA PRODUCTS in 2023-24

Major Initiatives taken by APEDA

- Launching of Quality Produce of India logo
- National Programme on Organic Production was launched in April 2000
- National Organic Standards & Accreditation Policy was formulated
- Indian Organic – logo for Organic Products of India was launched
- Food Safety Programme and Food Quality Programme was introduced
- Pesticides / drug monitoring in egg products, honey, grapes,
- Gherkins and Mangoes
- Introduction of Food Quality Programmes
- Recognition Scheme for Laboratories
- Recognition Scheme for HACCP
- Accrediation system for Organic Products
- Promotion of E-commerce : Online facilities like issue of RCMC / RCAC / Monthly Party Returns / Financial Assistance Application / Virtual Trade Fair

- Recognition Scheme for Pack houses, meat/poultry units.
- Traceability
- GrapeNet
- AnarNet
- Organicproducts

India possesses significant potential for exporting processed agricultural products due to various factors:

Diverse Agro-climatic Zones: India's diverse geography enables the cultivation of a wide range of crops throughout the year. This diversity allows for the production of a variety of raw materials that can be processed into different food products.

Abundant Raw Materials: India is one of the largest producers of various agricultural commodities such as cereals, fruits, vegetables, spices, and pulses. These raw materials serve as the foundation for producing a myriad of processed products.

Expanding Food Processing Industry: The food processing sector in India is experiencing steady growth due to increasing urbanization, evolving lifestyles, and higher disposable incomes. This expansion offers significant opportunities for adding value and processing agricultural products for export.

Government Support: The Indian government has introduced various initiatives to promote food processing and facilitate exports. Key schemes include the Pradhan Mantri Kisan Sampada Yojana (PMKSY), which aims to enhance processing infrastructure, and the Agricultural Export Policy (AEP), designed to boost agricultural exports.

Technological Advancements: With advancements in technology, there's an increasing capability to process agricultural products efficiently and preserve their quality. Modern processing techniques enable the production of high-quality, shelf-stable products that meet international standards.

Quality and Safety Standards: Meeting international quality and safety standards is crucial for export competitiveness. India has been making strides in ensuring adherence to global food safety norms, enhancing the credibility of its processed agricultural products in the international market.

Growth in Global Demand: There is a growing global demand for convenience foods, ready-to-eat meals, organic products, and ethnic Indian cuisines. India can leverage its rich culinary heritage and expertise in spice processing to cater to these evolving consumer preferences worldwide.

Strategic Location: India's strategic location provides access to key markets in Asia, the Middle East, Europe, and Africa. This geographical advantage facilitates trade and enhances India's position as a supplier of processed agricultural products.

Sustainable and Organic Produce: Increasing awareness about health and sustainability has led to a rising demand for organic and sustainably sourced food products. India's vast agricultural land offers opportunities for organic farming, making it a potential hub for exporting organic processed foods.

Value Addition and Branding: By focusing on value addition, branding, and packaging, Indian processed agricultural products can differentiate themselves in the global market. Building strong brands associated with quality, authenticity, and innovation can further enhance India's export potential in this sector.

In conclusion, India's rich agricultural resources, combined with a growing food processing industry, supportive government policies, technological advancements, and evolving consumer preferences, position the country as a promising exporter of processed agricultural products on the global stage. By capitalizing on these strengths and addressing challenges such as infrastructure development and supply chain efficiency, India can significantly enhance its exports in this sector.

Financial Assistance Schemes of APEDA

(Plan Period 2007-2011)

- Scheme for Market Development
- Scheme for Infrastructure Development
- Scheme for Quality Development
- Scheme for Research & Development
- Marketing Development Assistance
- Transport Assistance (By Air & Sea)

Schemes for Market Development

APEDA Schemes for Boosting Food Exports: A Clearer Breakdown

The Agricultural & Processed Food Export Development Authority (APEDA) offers various schemes to support Indian businesses in exporting food products. Here's a simplified breakdown of the key programs:

A. Pre-Investment Activities (100% funded by APEDA): Feasibility Studies & Surveys: APEDA directly conducts these activities to assess export potential.

Market Information Development: APEDA gathers and disseminates market data on products and infrastructure.

Consultancy & Database Upgradation: APEDA manages these initiatives internally.

B. Export Promotion & Market Development:

Publicity Materials: APEDA creates brochures, advertisements, and films to promote Indian food products.

Brand Building: APEDA supports brand promotion activities for exporters, capped at 25% of the cost with a maximum of Rs. 50 lakhs.

Export Promotion Activities: APEDA organizes buyer-seller meets, trade delegations, and participation in international exhibitions.

Product Promotion: APEDA directly promotes Indian food products at fairs and events it sponsors or organizes.

C. Packaging Development: Standards & Design Development: APEDA develops and upgrades packaging standards for food exports.

Packaging Material Assistance: Registered exporters of specific products (fresh fruits, vegetables, flowers, eggs) can receive a 25% subsidy on packaging materials, capped at Rs. 5 lakhs.

D. Infrastructure Development: Financial Assistance: All infrastructure development projects receive a 25% grant from APEDA, with specific spending caps per beneficiary:

Common Infrastructure Facilities (100% funded by APEDA): Government or public sector agencies can establish facilities like cold storage units at airports or ports.

Specialized Transport Units: Grants are available for purchasing specialized vehicles for transporting animal products, horticultural, and floricultural products.

Harvest Mechanization: Financial aid supports the mechanization of harvesting processes for agricultural produce.

Storage and Grading Facilities: Grants are provided for setting up sheds for intermediate storage, grading, and cleaning operations.

Mechanized Handling Facilities: Equipment for sorting, grading, washing, waxing, ripening, packaging, and palletization can be subsidized.

Cooling Facilities: Grants are available for setting up cooling units and cold storage for storing produce.

Pre-shipment Treatment Facilities: Financial aid supports establishing facilities for fumigation, X-ray screening, hot water treatment, and water softening.

Integrated Post-Harvest Handling Systems: Grants are offered for setting up pack houses, greenhouses, or a combination of these facilities.

Advanced Treatment Facilities: Financial assistance is available for setting up vapor heat treatment, electronic beam processing, or irradiation facilities, capped at 50% of the cost.

Environmental Control Systems: Grants support establishing pollution control and effluent treatment systems.

Specialized Storage Facilities: Financial aid is available for setting up high-humidity cold storage or deep freezers.

Key Takeaways

APEDA offers a comprehensive range of programs to help Indian food exporters succeed on the global stage. These programs provide financial and informational support throughout the entire export process, from pre-investment activities to infrastructure development.

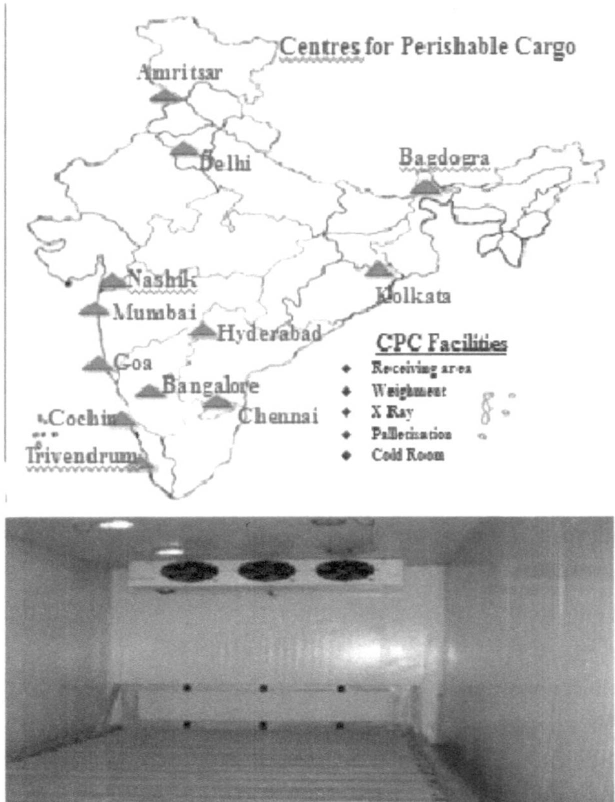

Refrigerated Trucks and Van

APEDA Schemes for Quality Development: A Clear Guide

The Agricultural & Processed Food Export Development Authority (APEDA) recognizes the importance of food quality and safety for successful exports. Here's a breakdown of their programs to support quality development:

A) Promotion of Quality & Quality Control

Laboratory Set-up & Strengthening: APEDA offers a 25% subsidy, capped at Rs. 20 lakhs, for establishing or upgrading laboratories. However, to qualify, the labs must adhere to specific quality standards.

Quality Management Systems: Financial assistance covers 50% of the cost (up to Rs. 5 lakhs) for implementing quality management systems like ISO, HACCP, TQM, KOSHER, BRC, GAP, Organic Certification, and ERP-based traceability systems. This includes consultancy, quality improvement, and certification costs.

Standardization & Quality Control Activities: APEDA manages these initiatives internally, focusing on:

- Developing quality assurance manuals, guidelines, and documents.
- Establishing standards for export testing.
- Recognizing labs for export testing.
- Certifying exporters as premium quality exporters.
- Pesticide Management programs.
- National and international standardization activities.

Lab Upgradation & Recognition: Grants are available for upgrading and recognizing labs for export testing:

- 50% of the cost for private labs.
- 100% of the cost for Central Government labs.
- 75% of the cost for State Government/University labs.
- Maximum grant amount: Rs. 50 lakhs.

Testing Services: APEDA offers a 50% subsidy (capped at Rs. 5,000 per pre-negotiated sample price) for testing water, soil, pesticide residues, veterinary drugs, hormones, toxins, and heavy metal contaminants in various agricultural products.

B) Capacity Building & Organization Management

Skill Upgradation: APEDA provides 100% funding (up to Rs. 1.5 lakhs per participant, with a maximum of 3 participants from an organization) for training programs focused on technical and management skills development, both in India and abroad.

Seminars & Group Activities: Financial assistance covers 50% of the cost (up to Rs. 1 lakh for national seminars and Rs. 2 lakhs for international seminars) for organizing seminars, group activities, and study tours within the country. APEDA also organizes its own seminars with 100% funding.

International Study Tours: APEDA sponsors or co-organizes international study tours with exporters' associations. Financial assistance is only provided for APEDA-sponsored activities (100% funding).

C) Schemes for Research & Development (APEDA Internal Schemes)

Government R&D Support: APEDA directly funds research and development activities relevant to export enhancement through government sector R&D organizations.

Exporters' R&D Support: APEDA offers financial aid (up to 50% of the project cost, capped at Rs. 20 lakhs) to exporters, trade associations, and cooperative institutions for relevant R&D projects conducted through R&D organizations in the cooperative sector.

Key Takeaways:

APEDA's Quality Development Schemes offer a comprehensive package of financial and technical support for Indian food exporters. These programs address various aspects of quality assurance, skill development, and research, ultimately leading to improved export competitiveness.

Marketing Development assistance

Participation in Trade Fair/Exhibitions abroad

Assistance will be provided for travel expenses by air, Eurorail, etc., in economy excursion class fare, as well as for the costs of the built-up finished stall, electricity, and water charges. Exporters with valid SSI registration are eligible for 90% reimbursement, while other exporters, including merchant exporters, are eligible for 75% reimbursement. This is subject to a maximum limit of ₹1.1 lakh per participation. Additionally, 25% of the cost, up to a maximum of ₹15,000, is provided for the preparation of publicity materials such as catalogs and brochures.

Transport assistance for horticulture/poultry/processed products

By Air: Fresh fruits and vegetables, Poultry-Hatching eggs, Floriculture-Cut flowers

By Sea:Fresh fruits and vegetables,Poultry-eggs , Dairy products,Processed fruits & vegetables.

8. Summary and Conclusion

Food Production

Food production encompasses the entire process from farm to table, including the cultivation, harvesting, processing, and distribution of food. It involves various agricultural practices such as crop farming, livestock rearing, aquaculture, and horticulture. Advances in technology, such as precision farming, biotechnology, and sustainable agriculture practices, have significantly improved food production efficiency and output. Food production is a complex process that involves multiple stages, from the initial planting of crops or breeding of livestock to the final preparation of food products for consumer consumption. The stages of food production include:

1. **Cultivation and Harvesting:** This stage involves planting, growing, and harvesting crops. Techniques vary from traditional methods to advanced precision agriculture, which employs technology like GPS, drones, and sensors to enhance farming efficiency and productivity.

2. **Livestock and Aquaculture**: Involves the breeding, raising, and processing of animals for meat, dairy, eggs, and other products. Aquaculture focuses on the farming of fish, shellfish, and aquatic plants, which is becoming increasingly important as a sustainable food source.

3. **Post-Harvest Handling and Processing**: After harvesting, food products undergo various processes to ensure they are safe, nutritious, and ready for market. This includes cleaning, sorting, packaging, and sometimes transforming raw materials into processed goods.

4. **Storage and Transportation**: Proper storage and transportation are crucial to maintain the quality and safety of food products. This involves the use of cold storage, logistics management, and transportation infrastructure.

5. **Technology and Innovation**: Advances in biotechnology, such as genetically modified organisms (GMOs) and biofortification, have

allowed for the development of crops that are more resistant to pests, diseases, and environmental stresses. Precision agriculture technologies, such as automated machinery and data analytics, help optimize farming operations.

Key aspects of food production include

1. **Agricultural Practices**: Traditional and modern farming techniques, soil management, irrigation methods, and crop rotation.
2. **Livestock Management**: Breeding, feeding, and healthcare of animals for meat, dairy, and other products.
3. **Aquaculture**: Farming of fish, shellfish, and other aquatic organisms.
4. **Horticulture**: Cultivation of fruits, vegetables, flowers, and ornamental plants.
5. **Biotechnology**: Use of genetic engineering, GMOs, and biofortification to enhance crop yield and nutrition.

Marketing of Food Products

The marketing of food products involves the strategies and processes used to promote and sell food to consumers. It includes market research, product development, pricing, distribution, and promotional activities. Effective marketing ensures that food products reach the target audience, meet consumer demands, and comply with regulatory standards. Food marketing encompasses the strategies used to promote and sell food products to consumers. It involves understanding consumer behavior, market trends, and competitive dynamics.

Key elements include

1. **Market Research**: Gathering data on consumer preferences, purchasing habits, and market trends to inform product development and marketing strategies. This can involve surveys, focus groups, and analysis of market data.
2. **Product Development**: Creating new food products or improving existing ones to meet consumer demands. This can include innovations in packaging, flavor profiles, nutritional content, and convenience.
3. **Branding and Positioning**: Establishing a strong brand identity and positioning products to appeal to target audiences. Effective branding can differentiate products in a crowded marketplace and build consumer loyalty.
4. **Pricing Strategies**: Determining the right price for products based on production costs, market demand, and competitor pricing. Pricing strategies can include premium pricing for high-quality products or competitive pricing to attract cost-conscious consumers.

5. **Distribution Channels**: Ensuring that products are available to consumers through various channels, including supermarkets, specialty stores, farmers' markets, and online platforms. Efficient distribution systems are critical to getting products to market quickly and maintaining freshness.

6. **Promotion and Advertising:** Leveraging a range of promotional tools and channels, including advertising, social media, public relations, and in-store promotions, to enhance visibility and boost sales. Effective marketing campaigns aim to showcase product benefits, build brand recognition, and influence consumer purchasing behavior.

Key components of food marketing include

1. **Market Research**: Understanding consumer preferences, trends, and market dynamics.

2. **Product Development**: Innovating and improving food products to meet market needs.

3. **Pricing Strategies**: Setting competitive prices to attract consumers while ensuring profitability.

4. **Distribution Channels**: Efficiently moving products from producers to consumers through wholesalers, retailers, and online platforms.

5. **Promotional Activities**: Advertising, sales promotions, public relations, and digital marketing to create awareness and drive sales.

Value Chain Integration

Value chain integration involves coordinating the activities of all stakeholders in the food production and marketing process to create value and enhance efficiency. This includes:

1. **Coordination and Collaboration**: Working together across different stages of the value chain, from farmers to processors to retailers, to streamline operations and improve product quality.

2. **Supply Chain Management**: Managing the flow of goods, information, and resources across the supply chain to minimize costs and maximize efficiency. This includes logistics, inventory management, and demand forecasting.

3. **Quality Control**: Implementing standards and practices to ensure the safety, quality, and consistency of food products. This can involve certification programs, audits, and compliance with regulatory requirements.

4. **Sustainability Practices**: Adopting sustainable practices throughout the value chain, such as reducing waste, conserving resources, and minimizing environmental impact. Sustainable value chains can contribute to long-term food security and economic viability.

Value chain integration in food production and marketing involves the coordination and collaboration among different stakeholders, from farmers to retailers, to enhance efficiency, reduce costs, and add value to the final product. This integration can lead to better quality control, improved supply chain management, and greater market access for producers.

Challenges and Opportunities

The food production and marketing sectors face several challenges, including climate change, resource scarcity, food safety concerns, and fluctuating market prices. However, there are also opportunities for growth through technological innovation, sustainable practices, and expanding global markets. The food production and marketing sectors face various challenges and opportunities, including:

1. **Climate Change**: Adapting to changing weather patterns, extreme weather events, and shifting growing seasons. This requires resilient agricultural practices and investment in research and development.

2. **Resource Scarcity**: Managing limited resources such as water, arable land, and energy. Innovative practices, such as water-efficient irrigation and renewable energy use, can mitigate resource constraints.

3. **Food Safety and Quality**: Ensuring that food products are safe to consume and meet quality standards. This involves stringent food safety regulations, traceability systems, and consumer education.

4. **Market Volatility**: Navigating fluctuations in market prices, consumer demand, and global trade dynamics. Diversification, risk management, and market intelligence can help mitigate the impact of market volatility.

5. **Technological Innovation**: Leveraging new technologies to improve efficiency, productivity, and sustainability. This includes precision agriculture, biotechnology, and digital marketing tools.

6. **Globalization and Trade**: Expanding into global markets and navigating international trade regulations and standards. Globalization offers opportunities for growth but also requires compliance with diverse regulatory environments.

9. Conclusion

The chapter on Food Production and Marketing highlights the intricate processes involved in bringing food from the farm to the consumer's table. It underscores the importance of adopting advanced agricultural techniques and effective marketing strategies to meet the growing global food demand. The integration of the value chain plays a crucial role in enhancing efficiency, ensuring food quality, and providing economic benefits to all stakeholders involved.

While challenges such as climate change and market volatility persist, the sector presents numerous opportunities for innovation and sustainability. By addressing these challenges and leveraging new technologies, the food production and marketing industries can continue to evolve, ensuring food security and meeting the nutritional needs of the global population.

It provides a comprehensive overview of the processes and strategies involved in producing and bringing food to consumers. It highlights the importance of innovation, sustainability, and collaboration across the value chain to meet the challenges of feeding a growing global population.

Effective food production relies on a combination of traditional knowledge and modern technology to optimize agricultural practices, improve yields, and ensure food security. Marketing strategies play a crucial role in connecting producers with consumers, driving demand, and fostering brand loyalty.

By addressing the challenges and leveraging opportunities in the food production and marketing sectors, stakeholders can contribute to a more sustainable, efficient, and resilient food system. This will ensure that high-quality, nutritious food is available to meet the diverse needs of consumers worldwide.

5

Case Studies in Food Industries

1. Introduction

Integrated Agro food Parks

It entails spatial clustering of different agro production and processing chains with non agro functions energy production, waste and water management. It would integrate the supply side with the demand side of food chains in an efficient manner and would include creation of modern infrastructure like farm clusters, green houses, modern livestock farm, food processing zones. R&D labs & incubators, cold storages/warehouses and pack houses. It would offer benefits like:

- Realisation of better quality and price for the produce due to migration of best international practices in production and processing.
- Development of entrepreneurship in the farmers and enabling the development of food processing industry by securing the right linkages.
- Creation of new employment opportunities for rural communities.
- Creation of innovative business models between various stake holders
- Boosting the image of our products in the international markets
- Reduction in the costs by reducing postharvest losses, transportation and energy costs

Modern Terminal Markets

It refers to the concept of hub and spoke model wherein the central market will have the state of the art infrastructure including electronic auction facility, sorting, grading and packing lines, cold storages, warehouses and ripening chambers etc. which would further be linked to a number of collection centers conveniently located in key production areas. These would allow convenient market access to farmers and facilitate in fulfilling the needs, increasing operational efficiency and effective capital utilization of investment. The benefits are:

- Multiple choices for the farmers to market their produce
- Efficient price discovery

- Faster cash settlement
- Avoid distress sale of produce by enhancing the withholding power of farmers
- Reduction in transaction cost and increased share of consumer rupee to the farmer by elimination of intermediaries and redundancies.
- Availability of graded, sorted, quality and hygienic produce to the consumers
- Reduction in wastage of produce and enabling efficient logistics.

2. Retail linkages for Food Processing Industry of Rajasthan

Rajasthan enjoys varied agro climatic conditions and grows variety of agricultural produce. It is also endowed with rich livestock state of the art infrastructure including electronic auction facility, sorting, grading, packing lines, cold storages, warehouses, ripening chambers etc. which would further be linked to a number of collection centers conveniently. There exists vast potential for processing of oilseeds, pulses, cereals, cotton,guar, fruits, vegetables, spices, condiments, milk, meat etc. in Rajastan despite low capacity utilization of some pulse mills and oil crushing industries leading to categorization of many such units as sick units. The solvent extraction of oils from soyabean and oil cakes are emerging as potential processing industry. Apart from milling of pulses, processed food item based on various pulses are coming up as a major industry in Bikaner and other areas in western Rajastan. Guar is an important crop covering 18-20 lakh hecters area annually in western Rajastan. There is lot of processing potential for guar in this area. The state produces a variety of seed spices and condiments. The advantages of organized processing of seed spices are yet to be exploited in the state as major share of seed spices move out of the state in raw form. Fruits like mango, lemon, kinnow, malta, orange, pomegranate, ber and vegetables like tomato, chillies, pea etc. hold potential for processing in the state. Organised meat processing for domestic consumption and export in an area of vital importance for value addition in the state. The current level of processing of milk to the extent of 2-3% of its production under the organized co-operative sector net work has scope for further acceleration in the state. The traditional products like 'Sojat-ki-Mahandi', Nagour-ki-Methi, 'Kanour-ki-Gulab',Bikaner-ki-Bhijia' and a host of other food and non-food products when brought under the scientific processing can pave way for further value addition for these products. The export earning through oil-cakes,leather materials, seed spices can be further promoted through accelerated technological and policy interventions.

I. Agriculture status

- Second largest producer (17.71%) of Oil seeds
- Largest producer of Rapeseed and Mustard (44.61%)
- Third largest producer of Soybean (9.18%)
- Third largest producer of Coarse Cereals (11.65%)
- Largest producer of Bajra (31.28%)
- Second largest in Spices (10.89%) Spices board to set up Spices park at Jodhpur
- Largest producer of milk (10.86%)

Food Parks in Rajasthan

The state has key clusters for agricultural development in the form of Agro Food Parks at Alwar, Jodhpur, Kota and Sriganganagar. Food parks have been developed by RIICO. Key players in processing are ITC, Reliance, Cargill, Field Fresh, Australian Wheat Board etc.

Opportunities for private investment:'

- Establishment of commercial dairy units.
- Setting up processing unit for camel milk
- Setting up livestock feed units for poultry & piggery
- Opportunities for Agro food parks

Advantages of Rajastan

- Nine agro-climatic zones and a variety of soils that support cultivation of crops.
- Availability of raw material such as millets, pulses, milk, fruits, cereals etc.
- Availability of local work force
- Proximity to NCR for a large share of food consumption
- Dairy development programme is being implemented
- Favorable policy and incentives
- Potential for solar drying and agro processing

II. Organised Retail in India

The Indian retail sector has experienced a growth rate of 10.6% and is projected to reach USD 750-850 billion by 2015. Among its segments, Food and Grocery hold the largest market share at approximately 60%. Organized retail is expected to expand from 8% to 20% by 2020. The rising demand for processed food is attributed to...

- Increasing disposable income
- Increasing urbanization,modern lifestyle and aspirations
- Increasing demand for health and functional foods
- Increasing nuclear families and working women
- Increased organized retailing

Policy support by central government

- Infrastructural development like Food parks, Cold chains, modernization of Abattoirs.
- Technology upgradation by grant of 25% of fixed investment with max. of 50lacs
- Quality control,food testing laboratories and R&D with 50-100% subsidy to private players/state government.
- HR and Institutional development: Financial assistance to set up training centers, NIFTEM,strengthening of nodal agencies and IT.
- APMC Model Act 2003
- 100% FDI in the food processing & cold chain infrastructure

FDI policy in Hulti brand retail has also good provisions to attach small and medium enterprices with big retailers. The Union Cabinet has approved and implemented a new policy that permits up to 51% Foreign Direct Investment (FDI) in multi-brand retail, aiming to facilitate the growth of the Small and Medium Enterprises (SME) segment through foreign retailers' participation. The government aims to elevate the processing level of perishable items from 6% to 20%, increase value addition from 20% to 35%, and boost India's share in global food trade from 1.5% to 3% by 2015. The policy includes the following key provisions to support Indian producers and sellers: A minimum Foreign Direct Investment (FDI) of USD 100 million and a requirement for the foreign entity to hold at least 51% stake implies that the combined minimum investment exceeds INR 1000 crore.

- 50% FDI in backend infrastructure in 3years min. investment of INR 220-250cr is to be invested in first 3 years.
- 30% of sourcing is from small industries.
- Permitted in 53cities in India with population over a million duly approved by state government.
- Multibrand retailers with FDI will not use e-commerce as compared to Indian retailers.

Apart from above state government is providing incentives under Food Processing Mission.

- Subsidy of 25% of cost of establishing, technology upgradation, modernization of processing units with a max. of 50lacs.
- Scheme for supporting cold chain facilities for non-horticultural products refer vehicle providing subsidy of 50% with a limit of 10crore.
- Support upto Rs75lakhs for HRD—
  a) Support in establishing basic infrastructure for diploma/degree programmes in food processing .
  b) For motivating entrepreneurship in processing, subsidy is provided to good training institutes/ organisations for 6weeks and one year entrepreneurship programmes.
  c) Support in establishing Food Processing Training Centers
- Support upto 50% of cost with max. limit of Rs lakh for studies/surveys, organizing seminars/workshops/exhibitions/fairs/educational trips.

III. Challenges of Food Processing

India has good contribution in world's food basket but processing industry is in nascent stage. As per the survey made by FICCI,2010, Top five challenges identified by the 125 companies in foo Limited infrastructure facilities

- National-level policy gaps in the food processing sector
- Enforcement of Food Safety Laws
- Discrepancies between central and state policies
- Shortage of skilled workforce d processing were-

Other important areas of concern identified by the companies are-

Limitations in raw material production

- Challenges in accessing credit
- R&D issues: Focus on commodities, Lack of applied research, Fragmented R&D agencies, Inadequate validation and feedback mechanisms
- Taxation concerns
- Utilization of cost-effective technologies in processing plants
- Affordable food machinery and packaging technologies
- Enhanced Market Intelligence

IV. Developing Retail Linkages

Organised and unorganized retailing will be increasing in future and there will be more and more need od modernization as consumers have become very demanding about quality, variety and service. Processors can have better margin by linking with retailers.

Sourcing of processed material by retailers—

Retailers procure processed material either from normal and known brands or from unknown brands and sell under private labels. If they procure material from known brand they can earn 15-25% margin while if they procure from unknown brands and sell under private labels then they may earn about 50% margin. Therefore, retailers try to popularize their private labels. They source the material from unknown brands in following way:

- Tie up with SMEs
- Selecting and training SMEs about quality aspects(vendor development training)
- Auditing of systems and procedures of SMEs
- Selling under private label
- Maximum profit earned by retailer

Small processors have following problems in linking with good retailers:

- Quality cannot be compromised to be sold for organized retailing
- Technology available with most of the food processing units is not comparable with large units
- Several statutory regulations and acts like packaged commodity act, weight and measures act.
- Less awareness about marketing procedures including 5 Ps
- Retailers prefer bar coding for easy procedures which most of the processors are not putting on package

All these requirements and other general problems with long gestation period,become reason of weakening small units. Generally small processors becomes manufacturer for private labeling by retailers instead of their own label or brand where margins is squeezed by retailers

To reduce the problems of processors to link themselves with retail industry, government may help them in following ways:

Training needs and advancement at processors level

- Instead of Food safety workshops for MSME, there should be training on complete branding and marketing procedures

- Government may pay for consultancy by experienced industry experts
- Government programmes should be linked with the market conditions looking at retailer requirements
- Founders and promoters of SME development should believe in R&D and innovation
- SMEs should invest in packaging and innovations

Necessity of strategic focus in Supply Chain Management

   i. Problems in Supply Chain of agri products

     a) Low productivity

     b) Quality raw material because of seasonality, perishability and variability in product

     c) Infrastructure for distribution

     d) Storage

   ii. This situation discourages processing units to reach optimum size and achieve economies of scale

  iii. Additionally, lack of consistent quality hinders small scale units to build brand equity for them selves in international and domestic markets

Raw material for processors

- Food processing units having similar/common need for raw material. Sourcing of good quality raw material is essential for such units
- Procurement managers in small units are generally not efficient
- Government may work/help as procurement window for this aggregate demand from a distant source also.

Quality

- Quality requirements/certification required by different retailers and export destinations are different
- Government may give a mark of quality to processors after auditing which should be uniform for all and acceptable by the retailers

Food Safety and Standards (Prohibition and Restrictions on Sales) Regulations, 2011

- The regulations of food safety and Standards Authority of India(FSSAI) have already been implemented in Rajastan
- Other than that BIS has also launched IS 16019:2012 named as 'Indian Standard on Food Retail Managemernt Basic Requirements'. It won't

be mandatory at present, government is considering a proposal to compulsorily implement the standards. With this processors do not need to have ISO 22000 for food safety anymore.

- Apart from that BIS has already established standards for B2B sales. As per the recipe of any food processing unit, they can have any ingredient complying with BIS Standards. So there is an opportunity with the medium processors to get engaged in B2B Business or they can opt for horizontal integration.

Challenges in HRD

The food processing industry is in urgent need of trained and skilled manpower for different levels of operations and management. There are various specific works which require training like food production, food safety awareness, auditing and inspection skills,warehousing and distribution,regulatory and trade issues,packaging,storage and safe transportation etc.

Agro based industries in Rajastan: are mainly classified into three types which are as follows.

i) Agriculture and food processing industry: Agriculture raw material and processing factories, cotton textile industry, ghani oil industry,gur and khandsari industry,pickle industry,pulse-dal industry, guar-gum industry, rice pounding industry, flour grinding industry, bee keeping fruits and vegetable industry etc.The locations of such agro-industries in the Rajastan are:

Types of industries	Locations
Ghani oil	Bharatpur, Alwar, Karauli, Kota, Baran, Jaipur, Dausa, Sriganganagar, Hanumangarh, Ajmer, Pali
Pulse-dal	Bikaner, Jodhpur, Kota, Udaipur, Rajsamand, Bhilwara, Chitorgarh Pali, Bharatpur, Hanumangarh, sikar, Jhunjhunu, Alwar
Rice pounding	Banswara, Dungarpur, Ganganagar, Bundi, Baran,Kota
Flour grinding	Working in every village of Rajastan
Guar-gum	Jaipur, Alwar, Ajmer, Sirohi, Bharatpur, Jodhpur, Bikaner, Gangnagar
Gur and Khandsari	Ganganagar, Bundi, Kota, Udaipur, Bhilwara,Jhalawar
Fruits and Vegetables	Kota, Jaipur, Jhalawar, Ganganagar
Bee-keeping	Bharatpur,Kota, Tribal areas of Rajastan
Other agriculture and	Henna in Pali, Mango papad in Banswara, Papad & bhujiya in
Food industries	Bikaner, dried methi leaves in Jodhpur, tomato in Abu-Sirohi Rose flower in Puskar,colourmaking from babul in Jaipur
ii) Milk and milk products	Dairy cooperatives in all districts of Rajastan

Commodity mix for Agri-business

Diversified cropping pattern apart from food and fodder security, the nature of commercial agriculture is also a factor. The cereal crops having processing potential include wheat, maize, barley etc. occupies 46.3% of cropped area. The ,Guar 12.2%, pulse crops with 16% and oil seeds crops with about 19.6% of gross cropped area require processing support. The state is a major producer of spices and all major vegetable crops with about 0.60% of gross cropped area are grown. Identified fruit belts for fruit crops with 0.13% of gross cropped area are already established in different parts of the state. So there is a potential fruits and vegetables hence scope exists for agro processing industries. Efforts have been made to convert western parts of the state into orchards. It has the potential for medicinal crops and spices,but however efforts to be made to upgrade marketing infrastructure though the technical support is oriented to enhance productivity of major crops.

Agro-processing potential: Spices, fruits, vegetables and raw cotton are commodities having export potential. Systematic efforts to project the state as a potential source for export of commodities like seeds, spices, meat, wool etc. The product mix of spices, oilseeds, pulses, guar, cotton, milk, wheat etc are the strength of the state for its processing. Despite low share of production of fruits and vegetables from the state many of the products are possible from fruits and vegetables from the state. The process able agricultural commodities of the state & possible products are given in the table.

Product category	Commodities	Products
Cereals	Wheat	Flour, maida, suji, instant foods & bakery
	Barley	Beer
	Maize	Starch, corn oil and flakes
Fruits	Mango	Sliced, canned & frozen mango products, beverages Chutney, jam, juice, pickle, pulp, squash
Vegetables	Tomato	Jelly, puree, paste,ketchup, sauce,soups,chutneys
	Onion	Pickle, flakes & powder
	Potato	Flakes
	Mushroom	Powder
Spices	Chilli	Powder,paste, oleoresin
	Coriander	Powder and oil
	Cumin	Seeds and Powder
	Fennel	Seeds and Powder
	Fenugreek	Seeds and powder
	Garlic	Dehydrated garlic,powder and flakes
	Ginger	Powder,paste,oleoresin,pickles ans squash
	Turmeric	Powder and pickles

Edible Oil	Mustard	Oil,soya-sauce/flour,oil cakes, protein isolate
	Groundnut	
	Soyabean	
Guar	Guar	Guar split, powder, gum, korma, churi etc.
Milk products	Milk	Milk powder, butter, ghee,ice-cream and cheese
Meat & Poultry	Meat	Meat and eggs

ACGRs of fruits and vegetables

	Area		Production		Productivity	
Year	Fruits	Vegetable	Fruits	Vegetable	Fruit	Vegetable
1990-2000	2.21	4.01	4.37	5.38	1.98	0.87
2001-2010	2.97	4.47	5.49	6.00	2.32	1.29

Percent share of expenditure on food & highvalue commodities

Year	Cereals	Pulses	Milk	Meat, fish	F&V	T. food	Non-food

RURAL

Year	Cereals	Pulses	Milk	Meat, fish	F&V	T. food	Non-food
2001-02	28.9	4.5	35.1	1.2	8.5	62.3	37.7
2007-08	27.0	3.9	30.4	1.2	11.8	53.9	46.1

URBAN

Year	Cereals	Pulses	Milk	Meat, fish	F&V	T. food	Non-food
2001-02	22.4	4.6	29.9	2.2	13.2	56.7	43.3
2007-08	23.2	0.2	29.4	2.0	15.0	42.4	57.6

Income elasticity of Fruits and Vegetables

Year	Fruits	Vegetables

RURAL

Year	Fruits	Vegetables
2004-05	1.65	0.51
2009-10	1.79	0.62

URBAN

Year	Fruits	Vegetables
2004-05	1.24	0.57
2009-10	1.68	0.68

Growth in processed fruits and vegetables sector

Year	Production of processed F & V Lakh tonnes	Installed capacity of F & V processing Lakh tonnes	Capacity utilization of fruit & Vegetables Processing in %age
2001-03	1.23	3.78	32.58
2004-06	2.10	4.78	43.93
2007-09	3.45	6.43	53.65

Constraints of F&V processing industry:

i. Highly perishable and need cold storage facility and refridgeratec transportation system

ii. Production in unorganized and tiny sectors where an economy of scale is not possible and difficult in attaining international quality

iii. High cost of raw material, machinery, packaging material, poor technology in processing/packaging/distribution, inadequate anc expensive transportation etc.

Statewise processing industry in India

Sl No.	State	No.of units
1	Andhra Pradesh	10183
2	Assam	734
3	Bihar	433
4	Chandigarh	36
5	Daman & Diu	05
6	Delhi	125
7	Pondicherry	42
8	Goa	34
9	Gujarat	1270
10	Haryana	600
11	HP	46
12	J&K	69
13	Karnataka	1221
14	Kerala	1110
15	MP	1302
16	Maharastra	2420
17	Manipur	09
18	Meghalaya	03
19	Nagaland	05
20	Orissa	425
21	Punjab	1196
22	Rajastan	515
23	TN	3792
24	Tripura	22
25	UP	2652
26	WB	1089
27	Others	09
	Total	29407

Ministry of Agriculture,GOI

SWOT Analysis of Agro-processing activity

Strength: Availability of varied raw materials

Weakness: Erratic and seasonality in availability of raw material

Opportunities: Enhancement in employment, income generation and export earnings

Threats: Quality maintenance for market competition and development of low cost processing technology.

Conclusion

There is wide scope of adding value in GDP of state by value addition in agriculture and for maximum benefits to the farmers, development of retail linkages by the help of government can create a win-win situation for farmers, processors and retailers. State government as well as central government is providing various types of support in the form of providing and facilitating training programmes, establishment of infrastructure and processing units and fiscal incentives. In the times to come,it is expected that there will be great enhancement in value addition in agriculture and systems will be developed where retailers will have more direct linkages with farmers and processors.

3. Soy Processing

Opportunity for value added food products

Properly processed soy-products are nutritious, economical and health promoting. Thus, a situation is emerging in favour of upcoming entrepreneurs to make available the properly processed soy products to the population by establishing soy food enterprises throughout the country. In spite of food grain production to the tune of 250 million metric tonnes, it is not assured of food and nutrition security. National policy on food security therefore, needs to include availability of enough food and nutritional security at affordable cost by the needy population. Being a major source of good quality protein,oil and health promoting phytochemicals, the soybean is emerging as affordable nutrious food source to Indian society. Properly processed soy products are nutrious, economical and health promoting. Thus, a situation is emerging in favour of upcoming entrepreneurs to make available the properly processed soy products to the population by establishing soy food enterprises throughout the country.Soyabean also contains some antinutrients which need to be inactivated to safe level through adequate processing. It may thus be necessary to develop a fleet of trained manpower to establish a network of cottage to small scale enterprises throughout the country for processing soybean and other agricultural produce of the area.

Soyabean and Food value

The soyabean was introduced in India mainly for taking advantage of its superior protein quality with rich content,and its adaptability towards a wide range of soil and climate. However, due to poor cooking ability on account of presence of low starch/carbohydrate, it could not find a place in the diet as dal to which the Indian population is accustomed. It therefore, demands processing appropriately for other food uses.

Nutrition composition of soybean and parts

Part	%	Protein%	Oil%	Ash%	Carbohydrates%
Soy	100.0	40.0	21.0	4.9	34.0
Coty	90.0	43.0	23.0	5.0	29.0
Hull	7.3	8.8	1.0	4.3	86.0
Hypocotyl	2.4	41.0	11.0	4.4	4.3

Health and Soybean: The people now readily accept that plant foods contain a host of biologically active non-nutritive components called phytochemicals which improve health and reduce disease risk in a number of ways.

How people use Soybean: It is seen that to derive the nutrition and health benefits of soybean, some people mix raw soybean with cereals,get it milled and use for food purpose. This is not a correct approach.

How to use soyabean for food: Only properly processed soybean should be made part of daily diet for deriving nutritional and health benefits. Soybean can be very easily processed at domestic level or properly processed soy products can be purchased from open market. Approach for domestic scale soybean processing is described as follows:

Consumption of raw/unprocessed soybean is not good for health.

Domestic scale method for processing of soybean for fullfat soy flour

Following two approaches are suggested giving sequential steps.

Hot water Blanching

- Cleaning of soybean to remove impurities, immature and damaged grains
- Drying in sun/oven
- Dehusking/splitting by adjusting clearance in commercial chakki as is done in Bengal gram dal making
- Taking one kg dal to 3litre of water as proportion,first boil water and then add soydal to it and continue boiling for 30minutes
- Drain the water after boiling and dry the splits

- Processed soysplits are ready for:
- Mixing with cereals in the proportion of 1 kg dal and 9 kg cereal (wheat, jowar or bajra etc) for miling to set protein enriched cereal flour

  OR
- Miling in chakki and soyflour obtained can be mixed with cereal flour in the proportion of 1 soyflour: 9wheat flour to get protein enriched cereal flour.

Soaking and Steaming

- Cleaning of soybean to remove impurities immature and damaged grains
- Cleaned soybean are soaked for 2-3 hours in clean potable water in the proportion of 1kg soybean into 3 litre of water and husk is removed by gentle hand-rubbing
- After soaking,the water is drained and the soaked soybean are steamed/cooked in pressure cooker upto 6-7 whistles
- The steamed/cooked soybean be dried in shed by spreading in a tray for about one hour for removal of surface moisture.

Properly processed soybean only should be made part of the diet for nutritional and health benefits

- Sun drying of shed dried soybean for about 8-10 hours
- Processed soy splits are ready for:
- Mixing with cereals in the proportion of 1 kg dal and 9kg cereal (Wheat, Jowar or bajra etc.) for milling to get protein enriched cereal flour.

  OR
- Milling in chakki and soyflour obtained can be mixed with cereal flour in the proportion of 1 soyflour: 9 wheat flour to get protein enriched cerealflour.

Uses of Full Fat Soyflour

Protein enriched soyflour can be used for preparation of chapatti,poori,paratha etc. and in bakery products. Alternatively the soyflour can also be mixed with besan in 1:1 proportion and used in preparation of conventional snack foods like sev,chakli,pakoda etc.

Shelf Life

The shelflife of packed soyflour in polythene packet is upto 2 months.However, after opening of the packet,it should be consumed within 15 days irrespective of opening it after one month storage or 15 days storage.

Caution

Use of unprocessed soybean is not recommended for Health reasons. Producers of soybean and others can easily follow this approach of processing at domestic level.

Soy food products

Soy protein products find wide application as a versatile ingredient virtually in every food system including bakery,breakfast cereals,beverages,infant formula,dairy and meat analog as :

- Most of the soy products can be used as ingredients in other foods.
- Various soy foods are manufactured e.g. oil, traditional soy foods like soy flour, soy milk, soy paneer, soy nuts,soybean sprouts, soy sauce and soy protein concentrates, protein isolates and textured soy protein products.
- Oil is used in food products. Soy-meal is used in processing industries.
- Soy flour is used in supplementation of cereal flours for preparation of chapatti, roti and different bakery products for protein enhancement.

Full fat soy flour(FFSF)

One of the simplest products is in the form of full fat soy flour(40% protein,20% oil) for use in combination with cereals and pulses. 10% addition of soy flour is recommended to start with and can be increased up to 20%. Preparation and use of recipes from soy-cereal/pulse blended flour does not demand any change in the traditional food habits of the people.

Soymilk

Soymilk is the water extract of soybean. One kg of dry soybean yields 6-8litres of soy milk nutritionally comparable with dairy milk etc. Soy milk can be prepared by different methods and substituted in diets of patients who have allergy to milk protein. Soy milk is the base material for preparation of variety of soy based dairy analogs like soy paneer, curd, shrikhand, lassi, matha,amrakhand etc. Heat treated okara, the by-product of soy milk unit can be used in preparation of GulabJamun,halwa, pakoda,biscuits etc. Homemade soymilk is considered healthier because it is fresh and does not contain additives and preservatives. If properly prepared in the morning,the soymilk will be safe to use all day even if there is no refrigeration available. If properly cooled after boiling and stored in clean containers in the coldest part of refrigerator, refrigerated soymilk can be kept for about 10 days under refrigeration. Soymilk can be added with food flavours like cardamom,fruit, (mango, apple, litchi) chocolate etc. and used as beverage. The flavoured soymilk when served chilled is a highly acceptable.

Soypaneer(tofu)

Also known as bean curd or soy cheese, tofu is low in cholesterol and calories and high in vitamins. It is a complete food supplement that can be consumed without any worry of side effects, unlike cottage cheese. It is prepared by using soymilk. Tofu can be eaten as it is, mixed with salads, fried or prepared in almost any way one prepares cottage cheese. From one kg of soybean about 1.5 to 2 kg soypaneer can be obtained. The yield of soy paneer depends on the variety and quality of soybean seed and coagulant used. At 72% moisture,it contains about 14% protein and 9% fat. Soypaneer has great potential to be a substitute to milk paneer,in near future for low and middle income groups. Soypaneer can be used in vegetable curry, paneer-pakoda,paneer-paratha, cutlets, bread rolls etc. Soy-products are nutritious and consumption of these in daily diet will supply the necessary nutrition to safeguard the consumer health. These products have gained popularity among the users due to the reasons of nutrition and cost effectiveness.

Soy products Variety

Soydal(instant), soyflakes	Soymilk,Soypaneer(tofu)
Soyflour, Soyfortified biscuits sweet	Soy-yogurt, Soy ice cream
Soyfortified bread and muffins/cup cake	Tempeh. Soy-sattu, Okara based
Soyfortified bun,Soynuts(roasted/fried)	Burfi & Gulabjamun, Soy sauce
Soy amrakhand, Soy based Rasogulla,Soy dhokla,Soy idli and chakli	Soy shrikhand, Soy Suji, Soy based sweet, analog, Soy sev, Soy dosa

Soy products Variety

Nutritional composition of various soyfoods

Soy products	Protein%	Fat%
Full fat soyflour	38-41	19-20
Medium fat soyflour	45-48	6-8
Defatted soyflour	52-53	0.5-0.9
Soy sattu	22	8.6
Soy milk	3.5	3.4
Soy shrikhand	10-13	8-11
Soy amrakhand	7.3-8.7	9.4-13
Soy paneer	14	9
Soy biscuits	11-12	24
Soy nuts	45	26

Sprouted Soybean and its application

Soybean on sprouting has reduced levels of antinutrients like tripsin inhibitor, phytic acid and flatulents. The sprouts are removed and the desprouted beans can be used for making flour with reduced levels of antinutrients.

Medium fat soy flour

It is obtained after mechanical expression of soy oil. Soybean being a hard seed is difficult for mechanical expelling by conventional methods. It is processed for oil extraction mainly by solvent process, which requires high capital investment. Therefore, a technology for extrusion as pretreatment for an effective expelling was perfected at commercial scale of 2 t/day capacity. In this process the soybean is first dry extruded to make it soft and then oil expression by mechanical press. The cake after cooling is ground to get medium fat soyflour which contain 45-46% protein and 6-8% oil. Both the products are chemical free and fit for human consumption.

Defatted soyflour

Soybean oil industry produces about 4.0 million tonnes of soymeal containing 50-52% protein annually. Some part of this is being converted to good quality defatted soyflour. It can be used for supplementation of wheat flour and marketed as protein rich cereal flour.

Soy Suji

Pre-cooking of the clean soybean followed by size reduction and sieving are the unit operations. The product can be used for supplementation of wheat suji up to 30% in preparation of good quality nutritious products like halwa, laddu, upma etc.

Soy nuts

It is whole soy/split based ready to eat product. Ordinarily involves only frying of soaked whole soy/dehulled cotyledons to desired crispiness. High degree of consumer acceptability and are consumed as snacks. It is a high protein containing nutritious product and can be very much suitable for combating protein calorie malnutrition.

Soy fortified bakery and other products

Process technology has been developed for soy supplemented sweet, salty biscuits with both fullfatsoyflour and defatted soyflour at 30% supplementation level. Soy-millet based biscuits have also been developed for nutrition enhancement purposes.

Raw material availability

MP,Maharastra, Rajastan, Karnataka, AP and Chattisgarh are the major producers of soybean and serve as a potential part of the country for soy food industry. Maharastra contributes to over 34% of national soybean production with very good distribution among the districts.

Status of Food Processing Industries

- Size of food market in India—Rs 860000 crores
- Primarily processed food market—Rs 280000 crores
- Value added processed food market—Rs 180000 crores
- The sector attracted a total investment of Rs 38531 crores during the 9th plan
- Investment during the 10th plan is estimated at Rs 62105 crores
- Industry growth rate during the last five years is estimated at 7.14% against GDP of 6.2%
- Investment required during next ten years—Rs 150000 crores

Districtwise soybean production in Maharastra State(2010-11)

District	Production in 1000 tn	District	Production in 1000 tn
Ahmednagar	90.8	Latur	431.8
Akola	238.4	Nandurbar	53.6
Amaravati	444.5	Nagpur	287.1
Aurangabad	16.4	Nanded	268.4
Beed	96.6	Nasik	80.9
Bhandara	12.1	Osmanabad	111.4
Buldhana	416.1	Parbhani	165.2
Chandrapur	148.6	Pune	5.8
Dhule	47.1	Sangli	119.6
Gadchiroli	3.1	Satara	65.4
Hingoli	237.4	Solapur	5.3
Jalna	80.0	Wardha	151.6
Jalgaon	26.2	Washim	298.7
Kolhapur	137.1		

Soybean Processing Equipment

Variety of equipment have been developed/ are commercially available for establishment of soy processing units for manufacture of different nutritious food products based on soybean. The CIAE Bhopal can supply many of those suitable for cottage scale enterprise. Upcoming entrepreneurs can purchase those.

Soy Processing Equipment for Food uses of Soybean

Cleaner-Grader	Plate type wet grinder
Manual dehuller	Modified oil expeller
Power operated dehuller	Low cost steam generator
Blancher	Soybean cake grinder
Natural convection tray dryer	Dough mixture
Forced convection tray dryer	Lever type paneer pressing device
Multipurpose LSU type dryer	Screw type paneer pressing device
Three-roller flaking machine	Cottage level soy paneer plant
Two-stage roller mill for soyflake	Low cost single screw forming extruder Dough mixer (lab scale)

Soyfood Promotion

The upcoming entrepreneurs are encouraged for establishment of soy food enterprises in different parts of the country to make available variety of properly processed nutritious soy food products to the population. Women are the food and nutrition provider in a household, the force behind cultivating the taste and food habits. Therefore, women are also being made aeare of the nutritional and health benefits of soybean and encouraged to process and use soybean at domestic level.

The image and the acceptance of soy as food have been significantly improved these days. Promotion of soyfoods in India will lead to the attainment of better health and happiness to population.

Commercial availability of Soy foods

India being a non-traditional soybean producing and consuming country, there have been initial difficulties in promotion of soy-products. However, now, variety of soy food products are commercially available in the market and the people have accepted them on health and economic grounds. Out of various soyfoods developed at CIAE, full fat soy flour, soyfortified biscuits and muffins, soypaneer and soynuts have good acceptance by the consumers and the demand for these products is increasing with time.

Soy food enterprises have great potential for income and employment generation for the unemployed. A modest investment of Rs 50000 to 3 lakhs can fetch annual profit of Rs 1lakh to 3 lakh per year. To enable the upcoming enterpreneurs with technical skills for proper processing of soybean for variety of food uses, training activity is organized every month and the applicants are required to apply in advance.

Future Potential of Soyfood industry

With growing population, the demand for nutritious food is increasing. However, those who need nutrition cannot afford costly nutritious food raw materials/food products. Soybean thus is a viable and affordable alternative food resource for everyone. The future of soyfood industry targeted for common population is bound to be bright provided properly processed affordable safe and nutritious soy foods are made available to the population. Large number of small capacity soy processing units can be established in villages to cater to around 65% population of the country and in towns and cities for remaining 35% population. The countrywide scatter of soyfood processing units thus can serve as a source of gainful employment generation locally and thereby minimize migration to cities, apart from nutrition status improvement of population of the country. The upcoming entrepreneurs from different states should come forward to establish the soyfood based enterprises and take advantage of potential available for the purpose.

4. Spices Processing Technologies and Opportunities

Introduction: India is the largest producer of spices(Annual Production in 2023 is around 11.1million metric tons in compared to 10.87 million tonnes. The annual yield of spices in India has also increased from 1.63 tonnes per hectare in 2005 to 2.5 tonnes per hectare in 2020-2021. After consuming more than 70% of the spices produced, we still manage to be the largest exporter of spices in all its forms raw,ground and processed as active ingredient isolates. We makeup 48% of the total world trade quantity and 43% of the value. The industry has shown stunning progress over the last 5 years-there has been a 120% increase in revenues. The demand for and awareness about spices is at its peak. Spices are finding newer applications in food. Research that shout out the potential of spices in healing/preventing diseases and promoting good health further strengthen the cause of spices, the skin recuperation properties of turmeric, Mental fatigue tackling properties of Black Pepper and more. Amid the progress and ambitious vision are challenges that threaten to wipe out the industry.

  i)   Sustainability of spice production
 ii)   Slow progress in the farm
iii)   Farm grade quality issues
 iv)   Striking the right balance on regulations
  v)   Blocked communication channels
 vi)   Low productivity in agriculture

The Indian Spice Industry and Food Safety is an area of major concern for the industry from the point of view of providing food safe, wholesome spices to all consumers and also meeting the stringent food regulations of the countries India exports to. High precision analytical capabilities can trace contaminants setting high standards for the industry. Food safety hazards lurk at different points on the supply chain ,right from the supply of agricultural inputs to consumption. The challenges that the industry faces include:

i)   Creating safe spices by working out improvements in agriculture and the supply chain.

ii) Meeting global expectations

iii) Making the formulators realize, the importance of a consultative approach setting realistic standards suitable to a particular growing area.

iv) Harmonisation of testing methods and food safety standards

Types of Food safety risks

i)   Microbial Pathogens-Bacteria, Parasites, Fungi

ii) Toxins flatoxins, Ochratoxins, environmental toxins like lead, Mercury and Arsenic

iii) Pesticide residue, Ethion, Endosulfan etc.

iv) Illegal dyes-Sudan, para red, rhodamine, malachite green

v)   Other contaminants/adulterants-white oil, saw dust

Indian Spice Industry Sustainability

Businesses that have their base in agriculture look into the future with concern. Where will our raw material come from? What about quality? Will it be pestcidefree?How long can be sustain our supplies? How do we reduce the ecological and social impact of our actions insuring the future?

The spice industry has time and again tried to answer these questions and realized that it can not be achieved single handedly. It needs passion and dedicated efforts. Deliberations between industry experts and the support of the government i. e. Spice Board help form the World Spice Organisation(WSO) to bring changes with headquarters in India. The industry scenario is bleak for overwhelming regulations,rising demand vs. raw material storage,reducing productivity,rising prices, reducing quality and active ingredient content, contaminants like pesticide,illegal dyes etc.WSO for Global Food Safety and sustainability. The solution to industry challenges lie in the farm focusing its activities in spice growing areas fulfilling CSR towards the farmer and environment.

1. Spice Oleoresins: Extracts are prepared from Chilli (Capsicum annum L and Capsicum Frutescence L) and Turmeric (Curcuma Longa L). Also from Black Pepper, Cassia, Celery, Cinnamon, Coriander, Cumin, Ginger, Mace, Ajowan etc. Spice Oleoresins generally are the natural extracts from spices using a group of polar & nonpolar solvents.

Spices in powder/pellet form are extracted using solvents to recover all the essential components of spices which are responsible for the Flavor, Aroma and Taste of the spices and leftover contains only fiber and cellulose material which will have fuel and manure applications. Chilli contains Capsaicin responsible for the heat/pungency and Capsanthin and relative Xanthophylls responsible for Natural red colour. As for as Turmeric is concerned the essential component is oil and Curcumin is the yellow natural colour. Solvent extraction removes these essentials completely leaving behind fiber material only after extraction and the concentration is in the range of 5-8% of the spice only.

Advantages: There are many advantages in using spice oleoresins instead of original spices. Spices naturally occur with wide variations as an important quality parameters due to source of raw material,soil where it is grown,season etc. Oleoresins are of universally accepted consistent quality. The shelf life of raw spices is relatively smaller. The essential components of the spice gradually degrade during storage due to temperature,humidity and esposure to light. The spice oleoresins generally have shelf life than 1 year and the essentialsremain constant. The cost of spices is not directly proportional to the important quality parameters for which they are sold and thus it cecomes costlier to use spices in place of oleoresins. It is economical to use Spice oleorasins than spices. One kg of Capsicum oleoresin replaces appox. 40 kg of an averaged quality Chilli.

Transportation Costs: It is very economical to transport spice oleoresins when compared with spices/powder as it saves 90% with respect to the transportation costs.

Applications

Hot Chilli Capsicum oleoresin 10%, 20% and 40% and natural Capsaicin 95%.

Capsicum oleoresin 0.5 MSHU, 1 MHU and 2 MSHU are used to impart heat to food products. Capsicum oleoresin 10% and above are used in the manufacture of self defense pepper sprays, pharmaceutically for preparing pain balms, arthritis pain releasers etc. Also the Capsicum oleoresin of higher pungency is used in preparing natural pesticide based and anti-termite paints for ships. Natural Capsaicin has been found to be very effective medicine for colon cancer.

Paprika oleoresin on the other hand is the natural red colour from Chilli devoid of heat and has main use as food colour as the artificial colours have carcinogenic effects when used in food and pharmacy components. Also Paprika oleoresin is used in animal feed to get colour of egg yolk. Turmeric oleoresin has Curcumin 95% which is not only used as food colouring but also has nutraceutical and pharmaceutical applications as antioxidants, cosmetic applications. Curcumin is used for curing various cancer diseases. Both Curcumin and Capsanthin have provitamin-A activity. Even the waste material after extraction containing fiber and cellulose material from spice are use full as fuel due to their high calorific value. Briquetted spice wastes are used as biofuels in thermal, cement industries.

Market

All spice oleoresins have tremendous export potential and are exported. Globally 2000-2400 tons of oleoresins paprika of various ASTA colours is used for different purposes and 1200-1500 tons of Capsicum oleoresins of various pungency levels are marketed globally,annually. Curcumin has demand both in domestic and export market.

Process details

Raw spice is cleaned,ground, palletized/flaked and subjected to solvent extraction. Hexane +Acetone mixture is used for the extraction of Chilli and Acetone/Ethyl acetone is used to extract Turmeric. The extract thus obtained is called miscella. It is subjected to solvent evaporation and recovery and the desolventised product is called semi finished product. This is further subjected to liquid extraction using Methanol in case of Chilli and Isopropanol in the case of turmeric. Methanol extraction results to separate colour from pungency and colour or Paprika oleoresin is produced. By treating with Isopropanol,Curcumin gets precipitated. The finished products are subjected to vaccum distillation or drying to get products with residual solvent levels below 25 PPM, as specified by US-FDA. Centrifugation method is used wherever necessary to remove sediment in oleoresin. Different batches of the products are blended to meet desired specifications of the customer and packed in international standard packing materials such as food grade metal drums,HDPE pails,can and barrels etc. Curcumin is packed in food grade poly propylene bags which are further packed in open top barrels with lids.

2. High efficiency Size Reduction Equipments

For fine grinding of a wide range of materials such as Spices, Food products, Sugar, Pesticides, Chemicals, Dyes & Pigments, Power paint and Food items (Sugar, Spices, Wheat and many other materials). RIECO offers

- Micro-Pulveriser
- Air Classifying Mills
- Universal Mills
- Micron Separator

RIECO can design, engineer and commission specialized plants for Spices grinding such as Red Chilly, Coriander, Turmeric as well as Mixed Spices. To ensure the production capacity a n indepth study of various spices and their behavior at different temperatures has been undertaken at our lab. That is certified by DST. Trials and experiments have been conducted and the results compiled and analysed. All this scientific data has then been put to use while designing the equipment depending on the application and the client's requirement. Many a times,our existing clients have partnered with us in this developmental activity and have reaped the benefits of new advancements. For instance, we have now developed a sophisticated system that can grind spices in controlled atmosphere. This new development is finding many takers already.

Process description

A project will envisage setting up of a spices grinding unit (for Cumin, Turmeric, Chilly etc.). This ia a new concept in spice processing, which results into higher production with better quality of the end product not just in terms of aroma but also the much desired colour, than any conventional spice grinding unit. RIECO technology uses chilled air at 15-17 degrees to control the grinding chamber, the result of which is reduction in loss of volatile or essential oils in the spices and higher production rate. This grinding method enhances aroma by reducing the loss of essential oils, which typically ranges from approximately 3-10%, contrasting with conventional processing where losses can be as high as approximately 15-43%. This type of technology is particularly important for Cumin processing. Spices are ground to a uniform fineness of 500 microns as compared to a size range of anywhere between 600 to 1000 microns using conventional grinding processes.

Advantages of Technology

It has been developed taking into consideration aspects to produce the best possible produce from the equipment. At the same time due consideration has been given to minimizing industrial hazards while designing the equipment.

- Spices processed using cool-grinding retain natural colour to a far greater extent, as compared to those ground with conventional process. This is especially critical with products like Chilly and Turmeric powder.

- Finer particle size with uniformity can be achieved.
- Losses of natural aroma are greatly reduced.
- The overall grinding capacity can be increased by 1.5 times, as process equipment won't experience thermal fatigue from heating up.
- Fire risks too are eliminated as temperature during processing is controlled.
- This method of grinding enhances unlocking of the natural flavor aiding easy dispersion of the same and controlling the flavor strength.

3. Spice Oils, Extracts by Supercritical Extraction

Supercritical fluid extraction technology is an alternative method for new applications in food processing. This is the eco friendly green process. This is the effective separation technique. A supercritical fluid is derived from a combination of gas and liquid. When either a gas or liquid is compressed under pressure and heated to its critical point, it transitions into a phase known as a supercritical fluid. The critical temperature and pressure required for this transition are specific to each pure substance. In the supercritical state, the fluid exhibits characteristics of both a gas and a liquid. Supercritical extraction is ideal process for:

- Extraction of essential oils from flowers, herbs and spices.
- Extraction of food flavours from herbs and spices.
- Medicinal extracts for health food industries
- Removal of natural pesticides
- Extraction of natural food colouring, antioxidants and vitamins.

Some common solvents used in SCF state are

Carbon dioxide, Ethane, Ethylene, Propane, Propylene, Benzene, Toluene, Chlorotrifluoromethene, Tricholoromethane, Nitrous oxide, Ammonia and water.

With this technology spice oil and Oleoresins can be extracted

Equipment Providers in India

   i)   Chemtron Science Laboratories,Navi Mumbai

  ii)   Sanjivani Phytopharma P Ltd.

 iii)   Pioneer Enterprise

4. Steam Sterilisation

It has become an unavoidable issue with Spices and food products and it forces industry to revisit their entire production lines in order to comply with the ever-increasing requirements of Food Safety Standards. Consumers turn increasingly to food products with a guaranted or organic origin. Recent sterilization processes such as ethylene oxide or ionization are incompatible with these demands, encouraging the development of innovative processes based on traditional methods such as steam. The REVTECH technology uses steam for its efficiency in the elimination of bacteria and clean electric energy in order to heat the product. Overall steam consumption is therefore significantly less than competing technology, resulting in improved product quality, especially in the domain of aromatically rich herbs,spices etc. Less steam will be injected into the system, lower will be the leaching effect of the steam on the surface of the product. Even the most fragile products such as oregano see colour maintained after treatment. Last year some famous spice company round the world successfully trusted in innovative Revtech technology such as the Russian/Thailand leader. Investment costs and operating costs are particularly low with REVTECH technology. The quality of products treated with the REVTECH process is significantly improved when compared to products treated in traditional systems such as steam-heated autoclaves. As heat is provided by contact with the tube and steam is used only for its steam sterilization properties,wetting of the product is minimal flavor loss is kept well within the allowed standards. For drying and cooling,TPC is associated with vibrations to obtain high coefficients of thermal transfer between the material and the heated tube. The amount of air used is reduced to levels necessary only for the removal of humidity released by the material itself. A water/ethylene glycol mix is used in the cooling system to remove heat and to obtain a constant temperature of the materials as it leaves the system.

Results: TPC   <10000 cfu/gm

Enterobacteriaceae < 100 cfu/gm

Yeast   <100 cfu/gm

Mould   <100 cfu/gm

Coli forms   < 100 cfu/gm

Salmonella   <100 cfu/gm

5. Spice Drying

The processing and trading of spices have long been vital industries. Even today, the spice trade significantly influences the economies of many countries. In India, it has evolved from a small-scale operation to a lucrative business with considerable export potential. Proper cleaning of the crop before processing is crucial. Initially, dust and dirt must be thoroughly removed. Improper drying procedures can result in mold growth, potentially reducing the sale value by nearly 50%. Moreover, inadequate washing and drying can lead to the growth of food-poisoning bacteria on certain spices, posing a genuine health risk. Spices have been dried throughout history as the spices are hygroscopic by nature. They absorb moisture from the air, so drying is done to extract the unwanted moisture or dry the water particles. Drying of spices helps in retaining their aroma and flavor, it also helps in storage. To retain the flavor, aroma colour, freshness and to reduce product spoilage, spice have to be dried at low temperature. Once dried and powered, being highly hygroscopic, spices absorb moisture from the surrounding air during packaging and storage.

Methods of Drying

In the earlier days and even now in some areas, the produce is typically dried in the sun. However, this is not practical and effective anymore, as huge batches need to processed to highest quality atandard. During sun drying, dust and dirt are blown onto the crop and unexpected rainstorms can rewet the crop. A solar sryer avoids these problems and is sometimes promoted as an alternative to sun drying. Solar dryers are commonly small cabinets crafted from locally available materials such as bamboo, coir fiber, or nylon weave. However, this approach is not always efficient or commercially sustainable. During the wet season or periods of high humidity, which frequently align with spice harvesting, solar dryers or sun drying methods cannot be effectively utilized. Thus, one needs a dryer which can dry the spices continuously without being effected by the weather or humidity at low temperatures. The spice crop cannot be overheated (the max. air temperature for frying pepper and cardamom is 50 deg.C). Neither should it be over dried as it effects the final quality of the spice. The final moisture content for various spices are shown in table below.

Spices	Max. Final moisture content in% (wet basis)
Mace	6
Nutmeg,Cloves	8
Turmeric, Coriander	9
Cinnamon	11
Pepper,Chillies ginger	12
Cardamom	13

The drying of certain spices requires special conditions. For example, cardamom has to be dried in the dark so that the green colour is retained. Inadequately dried cardamom causes mould,making it unfit for processing. For longer shelf life and aroma the moisture content of the cardamom has to be brought down to 10%. Even the leaves of cinnamom possess a substantial amount of aromatic volatiles which are lost if the leaves are dried at temp. higher than 15 deg C.

The leaves have to retain their green colour for marketability. Drying chillis is one of the most important steps in processing. The desired moisture content of chillis is 8 to 10%. Recommended Relative Humidity and temperature conditions for some common spices –

Cardmom	30-35%	28°C
Dry Garlic	65-70%	0°C
Dry Onion	50-55%	10-20°C
Cinnamom	40.00%	15°C
Chillis	18020%	45-50°C
Spices	R H %	Temperature

The simplest and most cost effective method of drying spices at low temperature irrespective of ambient conditions outside is with a Dryer using desiccant dehumidifiocation.

Drying by Dehumidification

Dehumidifying dryers work on the principle of maximizing evaporative potential at the desired low temperatures by physically removing moisture from the air. In a typical arrangement, a dehumidifier along with a cooling apparatus, if required, is connected to a suitable drying chamber. Process air from the dehumidifier is circulated through the chamber and usually brought back to form a closed loop. The system is sized for optimum moisture removal rate having regards to product characteristics and energy required for drying. Moisture is removed by direct physical adsorption and works independent of dewpoint of the air being dried. Such dehudifiers can maintain relative humidity of 1% or lower at any temp. for which the system is needed.

Though drying is most important process in spice processing, it is not the only process which needs effective humidity control.

Dried and powdered spices being highly hygroscopic absorb moisture from the surrounding air when humidity is highand becomes sticky. This inhibits their free flow through the packaging machine. The damp powder also sticks to the wrapping paper slowing the process and creating hygiene problems. This not only creates operational problems but also reduces shelf life of product. So humidity should be controlled not only during drying but during packaging and storage also to get final quality. Thus it is equally impottant to surround the spices with dry air to retain the colour,aroma and increase its shelf life. To retain the flavor,aroma,colour,freshness and to reduce product spoilage,spices have not only to be dried at low temp. but once dried and powdered, need to protected against absorbing moisture from the surrounding air during packaging and storage. Dehumidification of the air surrounding the packaging and storage keeps the sry letting production and packaging equipment run effectively.

Desiccant Dehumidifiers can be effectively used to dry the following products

- Spices, Asafoetida, Dry fruits
- Almond, Pista, Cashew
- Chillies, Cardamom, Onion
- Garlic, Ginger, Grapes

6. Spices Park

The Spices Board of India operates as the statutory commodity board under the Ministry of Commerce & Industry, tasked with promoting spice product exports. India stands as the world's largest producer, consumer, and exporter of spices, contributing over 65% of various spice varieties out of the 109 listed by ISO. With the global spice trade estimated at 1.10 million tonnes valued at $3750 million, India commands a significant share of 48% in quantity and 43% in value. However, the evolving quality standards demanded by major consuming regions like Europe and the USA pose challenges, necessitating adherence to stringent quality stipulations. India has responded to these demands through quality improvement programs initiated by the Board, but future trends indicate a need for compliance with internationally accepted food safety standards to sustain and increase export share.

Concept Plan

A Spices Park is conceptualized as an industrial hub dedicated to processing and adding value to spices and spice products, aligning with international standards. The concept of regional crop-specific Spices Parks integrates cultivation, post-harvesting, processing, value addition, packaging, storage, and exports, meeting the quality specifications of consuming nations.

Facilities

The primary aim is to offer common infrastructure for post-harvest and processing operations of spices, fostering rural employment through backward integration. These parks feature processing facilities meeting global standards, enabling cleaning, grading, sorting, grinding, packing, and warehousing. Additionally, common infrastructure like roads, water supply systems, power stations, fire control systems, weighing bridges, effluent treatment plants, and quality labs are developed. Educational services are provided, offering training programs on Good Agricultural Practices, post-harvest operations, advanced processing practices, and global food safety and quality standards. The establishment of Spices Parks aligns with the government's commitment to agricultural growth and supporting farmers, aiming to streamline supply chains and ensure better pricing for produce by enabling direct sales to exporters through enhanced processing facilities.

Public Private Participation: Under the concept of the Spices Park, the Board will allot the land available in the Park to prospective private entrepreneurs for developing their own processing units for value addition and higher end processing. The land will be allotted for a period of 30 years initially and it can be extended on mutually agreed conditions. The Private entrepreneurs will develop their processing plants by availing the common facilities in the Spices Park. The grower community can make use of these facilities for selling their produce directly to the exporters so that they can avail the premium price for their produces. On the other side the exporters can develop a link with reliable farming community for an uninterrupted supply of farm fresh raw material for their business. Currently, the Board had released an advertisement for allotting the land in the Park. The response from the trading community is encouraging and as on date Expression of Interest was received from more than 31 companies for taking land in the park. The address list of the companies submitted the EOI is attached. Under the concept of the Spices Park, the Board will allot the land available in the Park to prospective private enterpreneurs for developing their own processing units for value addition and higher end processing. The land will be allotted for a period of 30 years initially and it can be extended on mutually agreed conditions. The Private entrepreneurs will develop their processing plants by availing the common facilities in the Spices Park. The grower community can make use of these facilities for selling their produce directly to the exporters so that they can avail the premium price for their produces. On the other side the exporters can develop a link with reliable farming community for an uninterrupted supply of farm fresh raw material for their business. Currently, the Board had released an advertisement for allotting the land in the Park. The response from the trading community is encouraging and as on date around 31 companies for taking land in the park.

Locations of establishment of Spices parks in the country

The Board is in the process of establishing Spices Parks across the major producing/market centers. The mission is to establish at least one Spice park in each State of the Country by the end of the XII plan period. The location of the Parks and Spices currently established/in process are as follows.

Sl No.	Location/State	Spices covered	Status
1.	Chhindwara, MP	Garlic & Chilly	Started
2.	Puttady, Kerela	Pepper & Cardamom	Started
3.	Jodhpur, Rajastan	Cumin, Coriander & Fenugreek	Completed

4.	Guntur, AP	Chilli	Operational
5.	Sivaganga, Tamilnadu	Turmeric, Chilli & Coriander	Operational
6.	Guna, MP	Coriander, Fenugreek & Garlic	Operational
7.	Kota, Rajastan	Coriander, Cumin	Operational
8.	Mehsana, Gujarat	Cumin, Fennel & Coriander	For land clearance
9.	Hamirpur, HP	Ginger & Turmeric	Waiting for Land
10.	Raebareli, UP	Mint	Waiting for Land

5. Millet Processing

Post Harvesting in State of Odisha

Procurement of Ragi through Women Self Help Groups/Farmer Producer Organisations

- Ragi procurement centers through MPAS
- TDCCOL Central Godown at District level
- Child Development Project Officer for ICDS as per Indent
- To SHG for Laddu making
- To Anganwadies
  OR
- To Civil supplies Officer for PDS as per indent
- To Fair price shops
- Beneficiaries carrying Ragi to home

Different Activities undertaken by FPOs

Different activities	Present status
Bio Input	169
CHCs	51
CMSC	86
Seed Village Program (Kharif)	122
Ragi Procurement	84
Organic Cluster	8
Destoner cum grader	18
Dehuller	11

Millet based Value Addition and Sale Outlets with WSHGs

- Kiosks at Block towns and Tribal Haat locations serving breakfast and snacks items,
- Mobile sales units at district and town levels selling dry and value added products made by SHGs and FPOs.

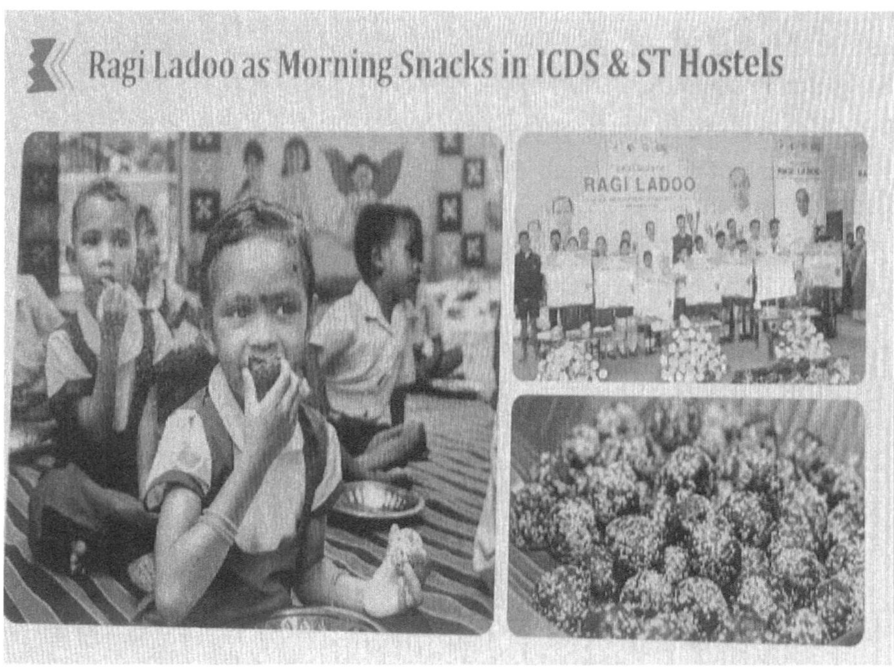

Way Forward

- Millet Service Center(MSC)
- Mini Millet Factory

6. ANOLE

Value addition of Anole (Phyllanthus emblica) at Udaipur district of Rajastan

A value chain includes all activities necessary to take a product or service from its initial concept through various production stages, involving physical transformation and the incorporation of different goods and services, until it reaches the final customer and is ultimately disposed of. Participants in this chain, who engage in transactions as the product advances, include input suppliers, farmers, traders, processors, transporters, wholesalers, retailers, and final consumers. Value chain analysis employs both qualitative and quantitative tools, beginning with a qualitative assessment followed by a quantitative approach.

Aonla is a deciduous tree of family phyllanthaceac. It fruits are rich in Vitamin C and highly valued for indigenous medicines. Its consumption is useful in hemorrhages, diarrhea, decentry, anemia, jaundice and cough. In Rajastan aravali belt is the main producing area of aonla including districts Udaipur, Sirohi, Chittorgarh, Bhilwara, Rajsamand, Dungarpur and Banswara. In Rajastan nearly 200 hectares area is under this crop. This case study was conducted at Hinta village of tehsil Vallabhnagar of Udaipur district. Aonla can be processed to make candy,murabba,aonla powder and juice. The per hectare costs and returns from preparation of all these products are presented. The per quintal cost of processing aonla for candy preparation including marketing cost is Rs. 5700/- while the returns from sale of one quintal of candy is Rs. 12000/-.

This gives a profit of Rs. 6300/-. Considering the yield of aonla as 200 quintals per hectare, the net returns from processing of aonla for making candy from one hectare of land is Rs. 12,60,000/-.

Per hectare value addition in Aonla through preparation of candy:

Sl.No.	Particulars	Quantity (Qt)	Value (Rs)
A	Cost		
1.	Raw aonla	1.00	700.00
2.	Sugar	1.00	4000.00
3.	Fuel @ 7 kg. LPG/Qt.		
Boiling of Aonla	7.00 kg	200.00	
4.	Casual labour	Half day	100.00
5.	Fixed cost (depreciation, interest, salary of labour etc.)	--	200.00
6.	Marketing cost (packing, transportation, buying/selling etc.)	--	500.00
	Total Cost		5700.00
B.	Returns		
1.	Main product (candy) @ Rs 100/ kg	1.20	12,000.00
2.	Net returns per quintal		
(Total returns-Total cost)	--	12000- 5700=6300	
3.	Per ha total cost,if yield/ha is		
200 qt/ha	--	11,40,000.00	

4.	Net returns per hectare		
Total returns-total cost)	--	12,60,000.00	
The per quintal and per hectare net returns from value addition in aonla by processing it into murabba are Rs 4800 and Rs 960000			
Per hectare value addition in Aonla through preparation of Murabba			
Sl.No.	Particulars	Quantity(qt)	Value(Rs)
A	cost		
1.	Raw Aonla	1.00	700.00
2.	Sugar	1.00	4000.00
3.	Fuel@7kg.LPG/Qt.boiling of Aonla		
7.00 kg	200.00		
4.	Casual labour	Half day	100.00
5.	Fixed cost (depreciation,interest on fixed capital,salary of permanent labour etc.)	--	200.00
6.	Marketing cost(packing, transportation,buying/selling etc.)	--	500.00
	Total Cost		5700.00
B	Returns		
1.	Main product(muraba) @Rs 70/kg	1.50	10,500.00
2.	Net returns per quintal		
(Total returns-Total cost)	--	10500-5700	
=4800			
3.	Per ha total cost,if yield per ha is 200qt/ha	--	11,40,000.00
4.	Net returns per hectare		
(Total returns-Total cost)	--	21,00,000-11,40,000 =9,60,000	

The per quintal and per hectare net returns from value addition in aonla by processing it into aonla powder are Rs 6500 and Rs 13,00,000

Per hectare value addition in aonla through preparation of aonla powder

Sl. No.	Particulars	Quantity (qt)	Value (Rs)
A	Cost		
1.	Raw aonla	1.00	700.00
2.	Casual labour	Half day	100.00
3.	Fixed cost(depreciation, interest on fixed capital, Salary of permanent labours etc.)	--	200.00
4.	Marketing Cost (Packing, transportation,buying/selling etc.)	--	500.00
	Total cost		1500.00
B	Returns		
1.	Main product(aonla powder)@rs400/kg	0.20	8000.00
2.	Net returns per quintal		
(Total returns-Total cost)	--	8000-1500=6500	
3.	Per ha total cost,if yield per ha is 200qt/ha	--	3,00,000.00
4.	Net returns per hectare		
(Total returns-Total cost)	-- 16,00,000-3,00,000=13,00,000		

The per quintal and per hectare net returns from value addition in aonla by processing it into aonla juice are Rs1980 and Rs 3,96,000

Per hectare value addition in aonla through preparation of aonla juice:

Sl. No.	Particulars	Quantity (qt)	Value (Rs)
A	Cost		
1.	Raw aonla	1.00	700.00
2.	Preservatives	20gm	20.00
3.	Casual labour	Half day	100.00
4.	Fixed Cost (Depreciation, interest on fixed capital, salary of permanent labour etc.0	--	200.00
5.	Marketing Cost		
(packing,transportation, buying/selling etc.)	--	500.00	
	Total Cost		1520.00
B	Returns		
1.	Main product (juice) Main Product@Rs500ml@ Rs50/lit		
By product @ 500gm @Rs10/kg	50.00		
50.00	2500.00		

1000.00			
2.	Net returns per quintal		
(total returns-total cost)	--	3500-1520 = 1980	
3.	Per ha total cost, it yield per ha is 200qt/ha	--	3,04,000.00
4.	Net returns per hectare		
(Total returns-total cost)	--	7,00,000-3,04,000=396000	

Comparative value addition or net returns in lakhfrom various products of aonla per hectare

Sl.No.	Particulars	Total cost	Total returns	Returns from unprocessed Net		Ratio
1.	Candy	11,40,000	24,00,000	1,40,000	12.60	1:9.00
2.	Murabba 11,40,000	21,00,000	1,40,000	9.60	1:6.90	
3.	Powder 3,00,000	13,00,000	1,40,000	13.00	1:9.28	
4.	Juice	3,04,000	7,00,000	1,40,000	3.96	1:2.83

Ratio of returns from raw & processed aonla
Net is net returns

The highest net returns from value addition in aonla from one hectare are obtained through its processing into aonla powder which provides 9.28 times more returns than sale of aonla in raw form. The second highest net returns are obtained from preparation of aonl;a candy which provides nine times more returns than unprocessed aonla. Aonla juice gives lowest value addition from processing of aonla but still it is 2.8 times more profitable than unprocessed aonla. Thus value addition in any form is profitable than sale of aonla in its raw form.

A Simplified value chain for aonla

The sequence of Input Suppliers - Farmers - Traders - Processors - Exporters/ Importers - Retailers - Consumers outlines an agricultural value chain, serving as the economic unit of analysis for a specific commodity or group of commodities. This chain consists of interconnected economic activities, vertically linked through market relationships. It includes a network of organizations, institutions, resources, actors, and activities involved in input supply, production, processing, and distribution.

The emphasis is on the relationships among input suppliers, producers, traders, processors, and distributors, illustrating the addition of value as the product moves from input supply to consumption. Value chains also facilitate the flow of finance (revenues, credit, and working capital) from consumers to producers, the dissemination of technologies among producers, and the transmission of consumer demand preferences to producers and processors. In reality, value chains are more intricate than the example provided, as both input and output chains involve multiple channels and can serve multiple final markets.

A Complex Value Chain for Production and Value Addition in Aonla

Threats from ensuing agri-business and export

Under new economic policy, the agribusiness sector has emerged to be an important area for corporatization of agriculture particularly for agro-processing and export of agri-products. Diversification of cropping patterns, capitalistic farming, agro-processing, agri-exports and entry of corporate houses into agriculture are some of the features of agribusiness in the recent years. During the process there is a great need to protect the interest of agri-labourers as well as small and marginal farmers. The cropping patterns will have to be maintained more prudently to avoid shift from area of foodgrains as a result of diverfication towards export oriented crops posing problems of food security.

Opportunity for Food Processing Business in Odisha
- 10 agro climatic zones
- 08 nutrient rich soil types.
- 480 km long coastline (6.5% of India's coastline)
- Abundant water resources
- Wide range of raw material base
- Skilled manpower in Agri-allied sector
- Industrial parks for Food Processing units
- 83.61 lakh ha area under agriculture and horticulture crops

Leading Producer of Agri-commodities
- Largest producer of straw mushroom
- Largest producer of sweet potato
- Largest producer of Jackfruit
- 3rd largest producer of Cashew
- 4th largest producer of Shrimp

- 6th largest producer of Coconut
- 7th largest producer of Vegetables
- 4% of total spice production in India
- 3% of total flower production in India

Unique Offerings from Odisha

- Coffee production in Odisha during 2019-20 was 660MT
- Ginger grown in Koraput with unique taste
- Similipal forest is part of UNESCO world Network biosphere reserve and Wild Honey
- Paddy straw Mushrooms are grown commercially as a cottage industry.
- 8.73 lakh matric ton of total production and 3243 crore export value has huge scope for processing.
- High Curcumin content of Turmeric has got GI tag & production o ver 2.2 lakh MT
- Kuchinda Chilli has flavor and pungent as chilli powder

Index

9 798889 292033